FIRST SEAL

ROY BOEHM
and CHARLES W. SASSER

POCKET **STAR** BOOKS
New York London Toronto Sydney Tokyo Singapore

A Pocket Star Book Published by
POCKET BOOKS, a division of Simon & Schuster Inc.
1230 Avenue of the Americas, New York, NY 10020

Originally published in hardcover in 1997 by Pocket Books

ISBN: 0-671-53626-5

First Pocket Books paperback printing August 1998

10 9 8 7 6 5 4 3 2

Cover design and illustration by James Wang

Printed in the U.S.A.

This book is dedicated to all true men-of-war,
living or dead, past, present, or future

Acknowledgments

This project would not have been possible without the guidance of my lifelong friend and mentor, Adm. Edmond B. "Whitey" Taylor. I first met Whitey when he was captain of the USS *Duncan* (DD-485) and I was an 18-year-old seaman. I also had the honor of serving with him on the USS *Bennett* (DD-473) after the *Duncan* went down. Whitey gave my life purpose and rewarded my youthful wayward adventures with more correspondence courses than I can count.

Next, I would like to acknowledge Master Chief James H. "Hoot" Andrews. Hoot has been brother, friend, wise counsel, incorruptible adviser, and, occasionally, hanging judge. When people speak of the Old Navy, my beloved Rocks and Shoals Navy built of wooden ships and iron men, it is Hoot Andrews of whom I think.

I would also like to thank John Weisman, who encouraged, browbeat, corrected, cajoled, threatened, counseled, and forced me to stay the course while writing the first draft of this book. His patience and friendship never wavered.

Others I would like to thank include: my agent, Ethan Ellenberg, who believed in the project; senior editor Paul McCarthy, a gifted wordsmith; and my collaborator and co-author Chuck Sasser.

I should also like to thank my mother-in-law, Helen Gertrude Kelley, who somehow has found it possible to love both my tattoos and my profanity. Finally, I owe great thanks to my wife, Susan. It is Susan, if anyone, who kept me on course during the years the project took to complete. I am truly blessed by her presence.

—Roy Boehm

In addition to the above, I should like to return acknowledgment to the crusty, tough old man, Roy Boehm, whose friendship has become my rare privilege to enjoy. He has made my life richer for knowing him.

I should also like to acknowledge the encouragement I receive from my three sons, David, Michael, and Joshua Sasser, two of whom are presently serving in the U.S. armed forces; and, lastly, I owe my wife, Donna Sue, thanks. She has truly made better the lives of all who come into contact with her.

—Charles W. Sasser

Authors' Note

In this book we have endeavored to render the truth as accurately and vividly as possible. While this is my story, it is also the story of hundreds of others who played major or minor roles in the events narrated.

Dialogue and events are reported to the best of my recollection. While the content is accurate, naturally I cannot be certain every quote is entirely accurate word for word or that my interpretation of events will be exactly the same as someone else's. Much time has passed since many of these events occurred.

Most names in this book are the actual names of persons. Others, however, have been changed in instances where public exposure would serve no good purpose and may, in fact, prove dangerous to those persons involved. I have no desire to publicly embarrass individuals, no wish to needlessly harm anyone.

Occasionally in the narration, due to matters of national security, or for my own security, I cannot relate all details. I must be forgiven for these omissions if they are detected.

—Roy Boehm

Authors' Note

In this book, we have endeavored to [illegible] as accurately and vividly as possible. [illegible] the safety of innocent [illegible] others who played major or minor roles in the events depicted.

[illegible] While the [illegible] of events [illegible]

[illegible] in this book [illegible]

[illegible] national security [illegible]

CONTENTS

★ ★ ★ ★ ★

FIRST SEAL

INTRODUCTION
by
Richard Marcinko

Roy Boehm is not only the First SEAL; a consummate warrior; a friend; he is also one of my sea daddies. One of those key people in my life who made a great difference in my development both personally and professionally. As you read and begin to understand this cantankerous warrior, you will find that he always led from the front, and he always performed the mission first and doggedly looked out for the welfare of his men. His only standing order was that you pass on all you can to those who care to learn.

You will recognize familiar names from the *Rogue Warrior®* series within his story. Some of the same plank owners of SEAL TEAM TWO also helped me throughout the trials and tribulations of Vietnam, the formulation of SEAL TEAM SIX, and finally the frolicking escapades of *Red Cell*. The talented sailors who started the SEALs continued their dedicated service to their country with the same imagination and courage while serving with me. Roy chose the "pick of the litter" each time and molded them into his image—that of a true warrior, ready to fight the enemy or the system in order to accomplish the assigned mission. This story is packed with pride, commitment, and superior performance. It makes you proud to be an American and me especially proud to say that I was able to contribute to a cause he started. America will never have enough Roy Boehms to carry out the missions of life and meet tasks head-on. Those of us who know and love Roy know he still has so much more to say and he continues to give to those who want to carry the SEAL banner forward into destiny. As always, Roy: I SALUTE YOU!

INTRODUCTION
by
John Weisman

Roy Boehm's 30-year-long Navy career encompassed three wars, and more than his fair share of action.

- In the summer of 1942, as an 18-year-old enlisted man, he dove for bodies on the USS *Arizona.*
- Later that same year he was aboard the destroyer USS *Duncan* when it was hit by more than half a hundred shells and sunk during the largest single naval engagement of World War II, the Battle of Cape Esperance.
- In 1962, in the Caribbean, he assassinated a double agent at the behest of the CIA.
- Later that same year he infiltrated Cuba to verify the existence of Soviet nuclear missiles.
- In 1963 and 1964, in the Republic of Vietnam, he went one-on-one with Vietcong insurgents as a military adviser.

But the most dangerous, precarious, and risky battles Roy Boehm ever fought were with the United States Navy itself. In 1961, Boehm, a maverick mustang lieutenant who had gone through Underwater Demolition Team Replacement Training at the ripe age of 31, was selected to conceive, develop, select, train, and lead the newest component of what has since come to be known as unconventional warfare—the Navy's SEAL (for SEa, Air, and Land) teams. Roy Boehm is America's First SEAL.

By the time he'd completed his Presidential Priority One mission early in 1962, the crusty, gruff, often profane First

SEAL was facing *five* separate boards of inquiry pending courts-martial. With justification: He'd bullied, shocked, terrorized, even strong-armed the system in general and his superior officers in specific if he thought it was necessary to get the job done.

You want general? Impatient at the Navy's cumbersome procurement procedures, he cumshawed equipment the Navy told him he couldn't have. He was issued M-14s—great rifles at a thousand yards. But Boehm's SEALs were going to do most of their work up close and personal—at 150 yards and under. So he bought AR-15s without going through the system. And the Navy tried to hang him for it. At one point he shanghaied one of Admiral Hyman T. Rickover's top enlisted men, even though the formidable admiral had absolutely forbidden the transfer. He got his man—and Rickover's everlasting enmity.

You want specific? Well, there was the time the Navy, in the persona of a self-important dweeb of an engineer complete with plastic penholder in his shirt pocket, tried to foist a second-rate underwater breathing apparatus design on Roy's SEALs. The purchase had been preapproved. But Roy insisted on testing the device himself.

"It's not swimmable, and we're not gonna use it," said Roy, clambering out of the pool at the Navy test facility and tossing the worthless apparatus at the engineer's cap-toed feet.

"Yes it is," insisted the engineer. "It was designed to be swimmable."

"Well, it's not swimmable—it's like being in the water with a fucking refrigerator strapped to your chest," Roy said. "Have *you* swum with it?"

"Well, it so happens that I don't swim," said the engineer. "But that doesn't matter—it was designed ergonomically."

"Ergonomic, my Brooklyn ass," said Roy. "This thing's no better than a Mark I, Mod 0 Hypoduchenator rebreather."

The engineer scratched his head. "What's a Hypoduchenator rebreather?"

"It's a kind of closed-circuit rig. You clip a clothespin on your nose, then you take a piece of rubber hose, shove one end up your ass, stick the other end in your mouth, and breathe."

Now, Roy wasn't court-martialed for talking like that. But they did bring him up on charges after he half drowned the aforementioned dweeb engineer by tossing him into the swimming pool.

The Navy establishment considered Roy a rogue and a pariah because despite his lieutenant's "railroad tracks," he was always a boatswain's mate at heart—a feisty, pugnacious, brawling, ham-fisted, hard-drinking fleet sailor whose devotion to his shipmates superseded all other loyalties. That devotion, and the man-to-man unit integrity that went with it, was more important than rank, privilege—even family. "You can get yourselves another wife and have more kids," Roy told his men more than once, "but you can never get another Team."

Sounds cold, doesn't it? Well, that's Roy. The only course he knows is straight ahead, and the only speed he tolerates is flank. Besides, as you've already seen, Roy Boehm has never been one to mince words. Take the day he met President John F. Kennedy in 1962 to brief him on the progress of the Navy's SEALs.

The meeting took place in secret at Blair House. When the President walked into the room, Roy's first words to the leader of the free world were: "Sir, I didn't vote for you."

Before Kennedy could respond, Boehm continued: "But I'd die for you."

The President gave him a long and ultimately friendly look. "I wish there were more like you," he said.

Later that same year, Roy and a small group of his SEALs were assigned a precarious, clandestine reconnaissance mission in Cuban waters. They were to be delivered by submarine, then lock out, infiltrate, and chart the Cuban shoreline in advance of the amphibious invasion Kennedy planned during what has come to be known as the Cuban Missile Crisis.

Boehm and his SEALs made it in and out safely. But not

without problems. Problems, hell—not only did Mr. Murphy of Murphy's Law fame accompany Roy on the mission, Murphy brought his whole damn family with him. First, the propulsion devices (these were the days before SEALs had sophisticated SDVs, or Swimmer Delivery Vehicles) didn't work and they had to fight the currents as they infiltrated from and exfiltrated back to the submarine. And their rebreathers were faulty—dry rot had rendered them inoperable—and so the SEALs had to swim on the surface, making them more vulnerable to detection by Cuban patrol boats.

Some weeks later, a Navy commander from the staff of Adm. A. G. Ward, the COMPHIBLANT (COMmander, amPHIBious force, atLANTic), showed up at SEAL Team Two's quarterdeck, a series of ramshackle buildings on the far side of the Little Creek Amphibious Naval Base. He withdrew a notepad and pen from his briefcase and set them on Roy's desk.

"I am here," he announced to Roy, "to write commendations for you and your men. You are being recommended for a Silver Star; your men will get Bronze Stars."

"How come I get a Silver Star when my men only get Bronze?" Roy asked.

"You're the officer," the commander explained matter-of-factly.

"So what," Roy growled. "Listen, Commander, we swam in together—as a team. We all took the same damn risks—as a team. And if we'd been killed, it wouldn't have been as 'officer and men,' but as teammates. So either we all get Silver Stars, or we all get nothing."

"Sounds doable," said the commander. "Silver Stars for everyone—I think Admiral Ward'll go for that."

But Roy wasn't listening. He was pretty worked up by then over what he perceived as a slight to his teammates. In fact, when he describes the situation today, he says that "like so many times in my career, my bulldog mouth was about to overwhelm my Pekinese butt."

So instead of taking "yes" for an answer, he bored into the commander at flank speed. "Y'know, come to think of it, I'd rather that we didn't get any goddamn medals at all. First of all, we were only doing our jobs—we did what SEALs are supposed to do. And second, if you've got the power to get us all those goddamn medals so easy, what about using it to get us some fucking equipment that actually works?"

The commander sighed, replaced the notepad and pen in his briefcase, and returned to COMPHIBLANT. Neither medals nor equipment ever arrived for the SEALs.

But then, medals—or rank—were never important to Roy. His enlisted men, however, meant everything to him. As he once said about a general he liked, "I treated him with all the respect he would have deserved if he'd been a sergeant." He meant it, too.

I have spent scores of wonderful days listening to Roy's stories, learning from them, absorbing them (and recasting many in the *Rogue Warrior* novels). Roy has a true Warrior's heart: He respects his enemy even as he kills him. That is the essence of Warriordom. But perhaps more critical and significant, Roy has the Warrior's *soul.* He descends from the Warrior tradition of Joshua, Sun Tzu, and Musashi; in him resides the spirit of Nelson, and John Paul Jones; of Patton, Stillwell, and Bull Halsey.

That is because Roy comes from the Old Navy. And Roy's Old Navy was not like today's politically correct, zero-defect, Uniform Code of Military Justice Navy. It was a Rocks and Shoals Navy, where discipline in the ranks was administered by chiefs' fists and boots; where officers practiced tactics, not management. In Roy's Old Navy, the most respected title you could earn was not "admiral," but "Man o' Warsman."

Roy Boehm can never claim to be either politically correct or zero-defect—not that he would ever want to. But he was, he is, and he always will be a true Man o' Warsman.

PROLOGUE

★ ★ ★ ★ ★

Rear Adm. Whitey Taylor, U.S. Navy, telephoned me at the Little Creek Amphibious Base, Norfolk, Virginia. Through my office window I watched the rising sun, red behind a squad of newly formed Navy SEALs running by in formation, shouting cadence:

> I don't know but I been told—
> Eskimo pussy is mighty cold . . .

SEAL was an acronym for SEaAirLand. The Army had its Green Berets, its Special Forces. The Navy now had its SEALs. Go anywhere, anytime, by sea or by air or by land, and accomplish any goddamned thing our country demanded of us.

"Roy Boehm, do you own any civilian clothing?" Admiral Taylor asked.

"Sir, I got my new Sears and Rob-yer-buck suit and my hat with the feather in it."

"Don't wear the hat."

"Want me to pack some clothes?"

"No. It'll be a short trip."

"May I ask where we're going?"

"You may not."

"May I ask why we're going?"

"No."

A special jet flew us from Naval Air Station, Norfolk, to Dulles Field in Washington, D.C. A limousine drove us to Blair House. A *limousine.* We strode briskly through the front door of the historic mansion and across the foyer and turned right. Then we waited.

We were waiting, Admiral Taylor said, for President John F. Kennedy.

The *President of the United States* was meeting with Navy Lt. (jg) Roy Boehm. Only whaleshit and Annapolis ring knockers were lower than a jg. I must have really let my bulldog mouth overload my Pekinese ass this time.

Whitey Taylor said it was a miracle, a *goddamned miracle,* that I had only five courts-martial pending. But, damnit, the Navy assigned me a mission to launch U.S. sea power into unconventional warfare by forming and training the brightest, baddest, boldest bunch of motherfuckers on the face of the planet. So I took a few shortcuts along the way. Sit around waiting for the bureaucratic bean counters to get things done and you ended up with calluses on your ass and nothing else.

Fuck the bean counters. I had survived Japs and sunken ships, sharks and assassins. Castro hadn't laid a glove on me, yet, and now the Cold War offered Vietnam as a new kind of war requiring a new kind of warrior. *My* kind of warrior. The path I followed from the time I was 17 years old and tried on my first diver's hard hat had led inexorably to one point in time and to one goal—to the SEALs. Unconventional warriors for unconventional times.

Let the bu-shit-crats court-martial me. Getting the SEALs launched was worth *ten* courts-martial. I'd take it like a man with real balls, like a SEAL. Not even the President of the United States could take away the fact that as acting commander of SEAL Team Two, Lt. (jg) Roy Boehm had been the first SEAL.

The *First* SEAL. Goddamn.

PART I

Combat at Sea: Sharks and Frogmen (1941–1945)

"And as for war, my wars were global
from the start."
—Henry Reed

ONE

★ ★ ★ ★ ★

Skewered by a rattling scarlet ribbon of tracers, the Vietcong soldier with the flamethrower fell hard in the weeds outside the wire. Bursting flares hung in the night sky like miniature dying suns, illuminating with an eerie greenish light the grass flats surrounding Junk Force Base 33 on the banks of the Mekong River. A macabre scene, hazy and unreal in rapidly changing patterns of darkness and light. Peopled by flitting, menacing shadows. VC trying to crawl or dart to their fallen comrade to retrieve the flamethrower. Liquidlike fire dribbling from the weapon's thin snout, igniting grass round it.

The little bastards were trying to burn us out like a nest of water rats. Some of them were running and firing at us from within 50 yards outside the wire barriers.

Earlier against the attack I had placed a 30-caliber machine gun at the forward apex of the triangle-shaped compound with a gunner and ammo bearer from the little Vietnamese warriors I patterned and trained after my own U.S. Navy SEALs. I dropped to one knee behind the bags and released a burst from my carbine. My LDNN—*Lien Doc Nguoi Nhai,* "Soldiers Who Fight Under the Sea"—were putting up a fight of it.

Nearby, a couple of *Biet Hai,* river rats from the Vietnamese river assault junk force advised by U.S. Navy Comdr. Jerry Ashcroft, stood and giggled over a fallen comrade. The guy's intestines oozed out of his split belly like a pale blue-and-pink snake. Nervous giggling was how the Viets sometimes reacted to disaster; they didn't know what else to do.

I grabbed them and pointed to the downed enemy soldier with the flamethrower. Khe, my LDNN senior noncom, interpreted. Either he or Bode or Nguyen always ranged less than one step behind me.

"Don't let them get that flamethrower," I ordered, pointing.

A sudden cracking and flash of light. Mortar round. The earth shook and showered us with smoking dust. I shoved the *Biet Hai* into the interconnecting trench line that linked the defensive bunkers.

"The flamethrower!" I repeated, shouting above the din of battle. "Try to hit the flamethrower. They'll roast our nuts with the flamethrower if they get it."

"Numbah Ten! Numbah Ten!" the *Biet Hai* responded—and started laying down fire.

I motioned to Khe to follow me, then sprint-rushed along the breastworks, checking what remained of the base's defenses. The base was worse off than I expected. Commo had been cut off. Torn bodies lay scattered about like empty heaps of flesh. It was every man for himself. The Viets fought on merely because, with their backs to the river and surrounded by Minh's VC, they had no other choice.

Junk Force Base 33 at Vam Lang was only one of a network of junk fortresses established along Delta tributaries in efforts to pacify the countryside and cut off the trails used by VC for movement of their troops and supplies. They were annoying thorns in the enemy's side. Lieutenant Commander Ashcroft and I had been under way on a mission to the Rung Sat, the so-called Forest of Assassins, in three armed junks with 16 of my *Nguoi Nhai* and another 20 of his *Biet Hai* when Commander Minh and his 514th Vietcong Battalion attacked the base.

Ashcroft's radioman intercepted desperate transmissions between the junk base and Task Force headquarters at Vung Tau. Explosions and the rapid stutter of small arms fire lent urgent background to the Viet commander's radio plea for help. The base was under serious attack and not receiving mere H&I, harassment and interdiction fire.

Ashcroft gazed upriver through the night. Then he looked at me. "Boy-san, we have the only cavalry within the AO."

"My boys need a workout," I replied. "Let's give 'em a test."

The battle had already been raging for two hours by the time our relief force swept around a bend in the river within sight of the besieged fort. It was a triangle-shaped compound with its three corner bunkers anchoring 200-yard-long legs illuminated by bursting flares. The apex pointed across a grassland toward the jungle while its opposite leg stretched along the waterfront where several wooden piers rode on fixed pilings or floating drums. A zigzagging trench line connected smaller fighting bunkers and the defensive strong points, the corner bunkers. Outside the main wire that enclosed the compound were more barbed-wire entanglements, ditches, and deadly Claymore mines.

Most of the defensive homemade Claymores had already been blown. Sappers had blasted gaps in the wire entanglements. Fire within the outpost blazed among the dozen or so tin-roofed buildings with their walls sandbagged. Flares illuminated enemy soldiers closing in for the kill across the surrounding grasslands.

Ashcroft bellowed something like, "Give 'em hell!" and led the charge with his command boat, all guns blazing.

Biet Hai and my LDNN lay prone on the decks behind the low gunnels and opened automatic fire. I burst 30 rounds through my specially made 90-round banana clip as the junk swept in close and raced along next to shore. The boat's wake crashed against the mud banks.

Ashcroft's second and third junks spaced their intervals behind the command boat and made their own crackling runs. We circled on the river like a carnival ride, sweeping out to the center of the wide river, then nosing back toward shore at full throttle and on full automatic fire. Silver splashes in the moonlight resembled schools of leaping herring as enemy gunners ashore reached for our range. Machine gun tracers streaked in dazzling green arcs across our bows.

The wild river charges forced the VC to grant the base temporary respite. Charlie withdrew to jungle cover.

"Put us ashore," I requested of Ashcroft.

"You're stepping into a hornets' nest, Boy-san."

"We'll find out if my *Nguoi Nhai* can fight."

"They'd *better* fight."

LDNN and some of Ashcroft's *Biet Hai* scrambled from the boats with me onto the wooden docks during the lull in battle. The docks smelled of river and fish and darkness. The besieged base stank of burned cordite, wood-and-electrical smoke, fresh mortar-plowed earth, and fear. The Viet defenders' second-in-command met us at the docks. He explained through Khe that the commander had been shot through the head. Over half the defenders had become casualties—20 to 25 KIA. Bodies lay strewn everywhere. Garrison families crowded the compound with their pigs and chickens. They had beat a trail from their nearby waterfront village to the fort when the attack began. They huddled fearfully in bunkers and sandbagged buildings.

Clearly, while the enemy had retreated, he had not withdrawn. A VC 50-caliber machine gun off the apex of the base coughed heavy and rhythmic as it slowly raked the cantonment. An old woman's soul-keening wails, the squealing of pigs, and the crying of a child added counterpoint to the thudding of 50-caliber bullets seeking flesh in the rubble.

A rocket contrailed out of the jungle, wobbling in flight. It exploded in a blinding burst of light.

I calculated the enemy force to be about company strength, somewhere over 100 attackers. This was a major action in a war noted for quick raids, ambushes, tag-and-runs. The attack seemed well planned and organized, the mark of the elusive and deadly Minh and his 514th. Minh, it was whispered in the Delta, was always successful. Death to the invaders.

Minh had not yet tasted a SEAL's steel.

After dropping us off, Ashcroft's junks kicked in their engines and circled out into the river to provide support from that quarter. The Viet on-site second-in-command screamed like an old woman himself when he realized the boats weren't here to evacuate him. He dashed to the end of the dock. I thought he was going to jump into the river and swim after the departing boats.

"Come back!" he wailed in plaintive English. "Where they go?"

I grabbed him by his fighting harness. It was slimy from blood. Not his blood. The whites of his eyes flashed. I shook him hard. "Get it together, man."

"Tell boats come back! We all die. *We all die!*"

He began babbling in Vietnamese. Cowardly bastard. I shoved him aside and took charge.

The base took heavy incoming as the attack resumed. Stepping over the bodies of previous defenders, I stationed men with 30-caliber machine guns at all three points of the triangle. I spaced the others out along the two legs of the defensive line. It was a thin line. Damned thin. Too thin.

Had my American SEALs been with me—Lump-Lump and Hoot and the others, those whom I personally selected and trained back in the States at Little Creek, Virginia—I'd have taken on Minh and every VC from here to Saigon. And may God have had pity on their poor souls.

My LDNN, my Vietnamese SEAL/UDTs, however, were still largely an unknown equation in battle. But they knew one thing: I'd personally squeeze a slug into the skull of any chickenshit who tried to run from a fight.

I scurried up and down the lines and all over, directing and concentrating fire. Lack of leadership and communications had left the defenders in lonely and isolated pockets. Khe trailed behind me.

Firecracker-string explosions from enemy mortars rocked the base and flash-banged it with fractured light. B-40 rockets roared like freight trains, leaving contrails of white smoke. Green and red tracers crisscrossed like jet-powered fireflies in a frenzy. Minh had his attack well coordinated and orchestrated. His heavy 50-caliber machine guns sat back more than 400 yards, out of effective range of our own smaller 30-cals, and swept the apex of the triangle with devastating effect. Big chunks of flying lead from the 50 popped as they ate through the tin roofs of the dozen or so hootches and bunkers that housed the South Vietnam River Defense Forces.

You had to respect Minh, the magnificent bastard. His politics might be fucked up, but there was nothing wrong with his generalship. His 514th Vietcong irregulars—farmers and fishermen by day, fighters as soon as the sun went down—virtually controlled most of the canals and waterways of the Mekong Delta southwest of Saigon around the Rung Sat Forest. U.S. Army Special Forces with their Montagnards and Nungs had targeted Minh and his fellow chieftains, as had the first American SEALs and the ARVN (Army of the Republic of Vietnam) Rangers. So far, Minh had evaded ambushes, traps, and spies.

Even my LDNN inside the compound and Ashcroft's three junks out on the Mekong keeping the skies filled with flares and the flanks mowed with his 30-cals were not relieving the pressure. Weeds and jungles around the fort were infested with goddamned Indians. We were just barely covering our asses.

Minh, on the other hand, was in no hurry as he systematically reduced the river base to a pile of smoking dirt and debris, torn flesh and blood. At this rate, red dawn would rise over a mound of blood red Junk Force Base 33. Another sunrise for the First SEAL looked damned iffy.

"Dinky-dow, Boss-Frog!" Khe cried as we rushed about through the hail of death attempting to organize defenses. "You crazy, Lieutenant. Find cover!"

"Don't let them get to the flamethrower!" I kept shouting.

A *Biet Hai* fell kicking with a bullet in his chest. A thin spiral of smoke wriggled out of the bullet hole. The wound hissed with a hollowing, emptying sound of lungs deflating.

The old woman was screaming again.

Minh's probe almost reached the wire before it again fell apart. The VC gave up on trying to rescue their downed soldier with the flamethrower. They had another flamethrower anyhow. I saw it among the attackers. Fire dribbled from its long snout. It turned my blood cold. I fired at the soldier who had it, but he disappeared in the withdrawal. He'd be back. A flamethrower would turn the base into a cinder pile. Cook us all like slabs of steak over charcoal.

The fort could never withstand another concentrated attack. Minh had to know it too. I looked out across the field of dying at the dead VC and his flamethrower. It occurred to me suddenly that there was a wind and that it carried the swampy brown scent of the river. It was blowing off the river, across the compound, over the cleared grassland toward the jungle beyond.

That and the VC's flamethrower gave me the idea. Fire could work both ways.

"Khe!" I shouted. "Gasoline! Grab a couple of men and get together all the gasoline you can find!"

TWO

★ ★ ★ ★ ★

Thrusting my head toward Khe, shouting above the din of battle, I explained what I wanted. That he was to gather some men to help me fill jerry cans full of gasoline, then toss the cans over the wire onto the grass.

"Hurry!" I urged.

Minh was softening us up for another charge. Mortar shells showered cracking flashes of light. I used one of the hootches near the waterfront to distribute cans of gasoline. A *Biet Hai* died carrying out my orders to toss the full cans across the wire. Another fell wounded. His comrades dragged him to a supply hut turned aid station next to the piers.

After the cans had been distributed and tossed into the

breach between the attacking VC and our wire, I scurried along through the maze of trenches, shooting the containers with my .357 magnum revolver to let the fluid leak out onto the grass. If this didn't work . . . I had five rounds left in my carbine, one 30-round clip remaining in my magazine pouches, and three unfired bullets in my handgun. The *Nguoi Nhai* and the *Biet Hai* hadn't brought sufficient ammo for a sustained battle. The original defenders could not resupply them; some of them were down to less than a half-clip each for their carbines and M-14s.

By radio, I advised Ashcroft on the river of the critical situation.

"Roger that the little yellow motherfuckers are all around you," his radio voice replied calmly, "and that you're running out of potatoes to throw at them."

He came back a few minutes later with, "Frogfoot One, this is River Rat One. I've made contact with base. Can you hold out till dawn when we can get in resupply choppers?"

Dawn? Time has no meaning during battle. It stands still minute by minute—but then seems to race ahead in great chunks. I glanced anxiously toward the east. It wasn't my imagination. The sky was beginning to pale out. I could even make out Khe's grim features.

"River Rat One, do we have an alternative?" I radioed Ashcroft.

"You might pray, Boy-san."

"I'm a Buddhist."

"Then hum and chant and kiss the spirit asses of your ancestors."

"I'd kiss *your* ass, River Rat, for a couple of additional machine guns and a pallet of ammo."

"I'll remember you said that."

Khe's hand gripped my shoulder. He pointed. Crawling, scurrying shapes swarmed onto the clearest fields beneath the flickering greenish light of the flares Ashcroft's mortars kept hanging in the air like pale miniature suns. Minh's 50-cal out at the jungle's edge continued to spray grazing fire.

It was systematically chewing the compound down to ground level, like a scythe cutting through a wheat field.

I chose targets carefully and ordered my men to conserve ammo. *Wait until they almost reach the wire,* I directed. *Wait! Wait!*

So far, my LDNN had fought well. Not as well as American SEALs, of which there were no better warriors in the world, but well nonetheless. They had come to the mountain and were meeting the elephant.

The thigh-high grass in the field whispered dry and brittle after the ending of the monsoon rains. VC slithered through it like inky shadows. I scanned for the other flamethrower, but could not find it.

Some of the enemy reached the wire.

Now!

I lobbed a Willie Pete grenade from my trench. The white phosphorus combusted in the nearest pool of spilled gasoline with a gaseous whoosh. It was the signal. All around the perimeter, other WP grenades sailed over the wire to ignite spilled fuel. In an instant, a protective sheet of circling flames leaped 30 feet into the air, crackling and panting. It exposed the surprised enemy to bright searing light. Defenders opened fire on them as they leaped panic-stricken to their feet.

A VC human torch bolted madly, screeching across the field, spreading flames until he collapsed. Poor bastard.

Pushed by the river breeze, the wildfire raced through the grass nipping at the heels of the retreating enemy. It left the field in its wake charred and smoking. Lumps of burned flesh littered the field. Minh was paying a high price for his victory.

I held no illusion that we had won or that Minh would withdraw. Minh was set on having his victory. The 514th would return—and I was all out of tricks. And all but out of ammunition.

I faced the east, like a Muslim preparing for morning prayers.

"Come on, dawn," I breathed.

* * *

Later, when the war in Vietnam became known as the Helicopter War, choppers would carve out a lot of firsts for themselves—first night air assaults, first night extractions and resupply missions. In 1964, however, the U.S. Army's First Air Cav Division had not yet pioneered the way. Helicopters flew combat missions only during daylight hours. We bloodied and besieged defenders of Junk Base 33 waited and silently prayed for daybreak when the choppers could fly again.

The gasoline fire on the perimeter had singed Minh's feathers, but it had not deterred him. Smoke eddied from the field around the fortress and pockets of flame still flared here and there. The base resembled a municipal landfill dump outside Pittsburgh or Atlanta. The old woman wailed occasionally, hiccuping as she wailed, sounding hoarse like her vocal cords were about to go, thank God. A rooster crowed out of the rubble where the civilians hid and pigs grunted inquiringly.

What kind of fucking war was this?

To our rear the river stretched brown and over a half-mile wide, with jungle on both banks lapping at it. Ashcroft's junks rode low in the water, bristling with armaments as the sky continued to lighten. They rode out the lull in the battle by circling warily beyond small arms range. Ashcroft radioed that he had summoned more junks and that Vung Tau would launch an ammo resupply Huey within the hour.

Could we last the hour? My ass was dragging. Exhausted defenders nodded asleep over their weapons. I found sufficient energy to check the perimeter for holes, then returned to the triangle apex where I could best exert command and control. I lay back in the trench behind sandbags and closed my eyes. Just for a minute.

I suddenly felt old for a war like this. Hell, I *was* old. Nearly 40. I had been going to war in one place or another for over two decades, beginning with World War II. Guadalcanal. Guam. Tinian. China. Korea. Cuba. The Dominican Republic. Vietnam. Sometimes people referred to me as a *pioneer* in Special Ops, in Special Warfare. Father of the

U.S. Navy SEALs. All that happy horseshit that meant you were getting old.

Sometimes I thought I had already done it all, volunteering for every goddamned hazardous mission to come down the pike and accomplishing them all. I had fought on the sea, underneath the sea, and around the sea. Gone down with a ship, swam in seas so thick with corpses you could have walked on them like floating logs. Slipped into Castro's Cuba on preinvasion planning, conducted spy missions, performed an assassination.

The profession of arms, I believed, was an honorable one in defense of and in support of your country. Patriotism would never go out of fashion for Navy Lieutenant Roy Boehm, mustang officer who rose through the ranks the hard way. I had offered my life in sacrifice for my country many times over the years.

Now, on this dawn in a shitbag country no one cared about, it looked like a Vietcong commander no one outside the Mekong Delta had ever heard of would finally accept my sacrifice.

Khe shook me. I must have dozed off. I blinked, unsure of where I was.

"VC come," Khe said.

I scrambled to my feet in the trench and checked my weapons. Only one clip remaining for the carbine.

The VC were coming all right. Scurrying across the field through the haze of smoke and mist, with the huge red sun behind them rising above the forest. From both flanks across the burned field still smoldering, looking like a swarm of cockroaches in their short black pajamas and cone hats. Minh's 50-cal opened up again, along with B-40 rockets and mortars. The ground trembled. Everything seemed prepared for Roy Boehm's last act.

I knew how Custer must have felt at the Little Big Horn.

I shouted into my radio mike: "River Rat One . . . River Rat . . . ?"

"I see them, Frogfoot."

"It's after dawn. Where the fuck is that helicopter?"

"Hold on, Boy-san. You've got to hold out."

Ashcroft once again joined in the defense, revving his engines and stepping up his junks on the water. He buzzed back and forth near the muddy shore, raking the burned field with his rattling 30-cals. My own *Nguoi Nhai*-manned machine guns sang until they ran out of ammo. I picked targets carefully, using my last magazine. I selected the little attackers one by one in my iron sights and squeezed the trigger. Exhilaration booted me to a high every time one went down.

It was too late to save the base by the time a lone Huey chopper flew in low and fast off the river, like a giant angry mosquito. There were no U.S. gunships in 1964, but the Huey had a gunner leaning out the door over his machine gun, tethered in place by an umbilical cord. He left little puffs of smoke in the air over the battlefield. I marked the general location of Minh's heavy machine gun with a round from an M-79 grenade launcher. The chopper worked out on the VC gun nest until heavy small arms ground fire drove it off.

The base proved too hot for air resupply. The helicopter hovered over Ashcroft's command junk in the middle of the river and lowered crates of ammo onto the deck. I raised River Rat on the radio.

"The natives are hostile, Papa-san. This is one tough bunch. We've been outgeneraled, outfought, and the little sonsofbitches are on their final assault. Bring in every junk you got. We need a ticket out of here with no passenger delays. Get us the fuck out of here. *Di di mau!*"

Gradually, bloody foot by foot, we defenders were driven back from the wire and compressed toward the waterfront. Men abandoned their posts to help their families transfer kids, ducks, pigs, chickens, and whatever else they could carry to the piers. Refugees howled, pleading at the tops of their collective voices for rescue each time Ashcroft's junks screamed past, guns banging at the encircling VC. The Vietcong would execute every man, woman, and child if they captured us, then eat the livestock.

LDNN and some of the *Biet Hai* fought a delaying action as Ashcroft brought his junks and two others that had joined him in fast to piers so crowded they threatened to sink into the mud. Charlie was already inside the wire and fighting in the trenches. Among the cacophony of barnyard sounds, the wailing and screaming on the piers. *Biet Hai* fought off terrified refugees with sticks and rifle butts to prevent their all piling onto one single boat and sinking it.

We had lost both the fight and Base 33. We ran like curs driven off spoiled meat. I found more cans of gasoline and sloshed the contents against the few standing hootches as we withdrew, still fighting yard by yard to provide Ashcroft time for evacuation.

"Give me a count!" I demanded of Khe as we retreated.

The *Nguoi Nhai* were up, not even one wounded seriously. Three *Biet Hai* were dead, left behind in the rubble. Another was being carried out in a poncho. I heard the gurgling in his chest. Four were patched up but still walking. The bodies of 30 or so original base defenders remained behind. There was no time to bring out the dead with us.

In a final act of defiance, I hurled a WP grenade at the gasoline-soaked hootches before loading with my men onto the last junk out of town. The base exploded in flames.

"Fuck you, Minh!" I yelled.

Looking back from the middle of the river, back past the inferno the junk base had become, I watched groups of VC moving in from both sides. They walked slowly, upright, no longer firing. Minh had won this one. He could have what we left of the fort.

THREE

★ ★ ★ ★ ★

My *Nguoi Nhai* fought bravely and well at Junk Base 33, had finally gone to the mountain and met the elephant, but Commander Minh still beat us like beating a village cur. The defeat stuck hard and thorny in my craw. What little satisfaction I derived from our withdrawal lay in the fact that Khe, Nguyen, Bode, and I doused the camp buildings with gasoline and torched them before we fled. Minh inherited little beyond a pile of ashes in materiel, although the victory gave him tons in propaganda value. He now controlled much of the Mekong Delta northwest of Vung Tau.

Flames played against the dawn sky as Minh's victorious 514th swarmed across the scorched earth into one end of the base while at the other end survivors of the defense, their families, and a smelly assortment of livestock loaded into the boats as though picked up hurriedly by giant scoops and dumped aboard. Engines labored as the junks clawed their way into the middle of the river, out of small arms range.

Saigon sent word to off-load the remaining junk base soldiers on a spit of land downstream and on the other side of the river from the original installation. The chosen site was a malaria-looking mud-and-sand beach backed by old clearings and trails through the jungle. Nearby was an ancient cemetery where vines crept around molded and cracked tombstones and crawled up the giant face of a neglected stone Buddha with its nose broken off.

The Viets weren't too happy about being kicked ashore with their ducks and potbellied pigs and whatever other supplies they managed to salvage in their stampede to escape their old homes. Their shrill voices clamored as they gesticulated and pointed at the cemetery.

"Tell them their leaders have selected this specific spot for a new Junk Base 33," Ashcroft instructed Khe. "They'll have to get off the boats."

"They afraid of this place," Khe explained.

Neither Ashcroft nor I gave a rat's fuck about them at the moment or what they did or did not want. If they had set up proper defenses, we would never have lost the base to Minh in the first place.

Several days later, a little Buddhist monk named Thay Wu whom I had befriended in Vung Tau delivered news that most of the Vietnamese survivors had abandoned the new junk base. The monk knew virtually everything that occurred along the river. Many of the unhappy Viets had made their way to Saigon, while others disappeared into the jungle and went over to the enemy's National Liberation Front.

"Most Vietnamese people as well as the mountain people believe in religion of animism," Thay Wu explained. "They believe in ghosts and spirits of the dead. They are most afraid of the spirits called *Pratas.*"

The Orient offered endless fascination. "It was the graveyard," I said.

"Yes. It is the kind of burial grounds where Pratas rise. Pratas are unattended and uncared-for spirits who have died violently through accident or war or who, in the case of women, have died without fulfilling their mission of bearing children. They are angry, greedy, deceptive, unpredictable spirits—just like mankind. They are hostile to individuals, to families, and to communities. That is why the people fled."

I submitted my After Action Report to Captain Drachnik, head of the Navy Section, Military Assistance Advisory Group (MAAG). I included the part about Pratas.

Drachnik scoffed, demanding, "Do you *believe* this load of water buffalo crap?"

"If the people believe it, then it's true as far as they're concerned."

"*Mister* Boehm, you're trying my patience again. The French came to this country before World War II. It is a civilized country. There are no such things as spirits and ghosts and, for God's sake, *Pratas.* Take mention of it out of your reports. I'm not submitting *that* to Washington."

I stared.

"Another thing, *Mister* Boehm. Omit the part about the flamethrower. Our Intelligence units report that the VC do not have sophisticated weapons like flamethrowers."

"It looked like a flamethrower. It shot fire 30 or 40 yards."

"Obviously, you were mistaken."

"Obviously. It could have been a Bic cigarette lighter. Maybe a trained dragon."

"You're overstepping your boundaries, mister. Your report should also include the declaration that we moved Junk Base 33 across the river to provide South Vietnamese troops with accessibility and a superior vantage point."

"Aye, aye, sir. We claim a stunning victory on paper and everyone's happy in Washington. Progress is indeed our most important product."

"*Mister* Boehm . . ."

Fortunately, Commander Jerry Ashcroft, former submariner and now senior American naval adviser to the South Vietnamese junk force, was a fighter-leader, not a Drachnik-type manager. He was a man built like a square oaken block, all angles and tough grains, two or three years older than I and maybe an inch or so shorter than my five nine. He had a broad grin and a habit of brushing straight sandy hair off his forehead. He offered me a bourbon at his apartment in the Majestic Hotel in downtown Saigon. The hotel was left over from the French days—Asia-colonist decor out of a Humphrey Bogart movie, a cozy bar on the roof, and slowly turning ceiling fans in the rooms.

"Boy-san," Ashcroft began, "I've gone over your reports.

You're about to stir up some shit. It looks like you're capable of agitating God."

Ashcroft and I were rehashing the battle over bourbon and water. Ashcroft's maid hovered within earshot. She was gorgeous in that dainty, petite way reserved for Asian women with a strain of French somewhere in their genetic background. She looked pretty enough to stand up on a mantel to be admired. Ashcroft caught my look and laughed.

"Co-Van is VC down to her ornery round-eyed-hating ass and looks forward to the day she will kill me," he explained. "But relax. She won't kill either of us as long as she thinks she is getting information to pass on to Commander Minh and the other VC. We have no secrets anyhow in this country as long as we're conducting joint ops with the South Vietnamese."

Co-Van's eyes swept coldly over both of us. Unusual maid Ashcroft had there. Nice ass.

"Boy-san, put your eyeballs back in," Ashcroft chided. "You put the truth in your reports, rest assured you'll not be loved for it. Take my advice. Play the proper game and then go out and fight the war. They're two separate and different things."

Ashcroft and I had combined our forces—the LDNN and his river rat *Biet Hai*—to run down the elusive Minh and the other warlords and exterminate them. Ash helped me with the proper, *progressive* paperwork to satisfy MAAG while we concealed how "advising" could be stretched around the edges to include much more.

We continued our rehashing of the battle, ignoring Co-Van. She went about her duties with one ear presumably cocked to our conversation while pretending not to understand. I confided in Ashcroft how I could not help but admire Commander Minh's generalship: the strategic placement of his 50-cal machine gun; attack orchestrated to place maximum force at our weakest points; his ability to remain fluid and versatile, making corrections quickly during the ebb and flow of battle. He suffered casualties, true, but the prize of winning control of that part of the river in a morale-busting defeat of his enemy more than made up for his losses.

"If the NLF had many battalions like the 514th," I said, "we'd either have to pack up and go home or send in the U.S. Marines. Minh's troops can *fight.* He was brilliant. We could learn from him. I'd like to at least meet that genius of a warrior and shake his hand."

The next afternoon I stopped for a drink in the French-decor bar on the second floor of the Tax Building where I lived with Doc Shultz and Lt. Ted Reilman whenever I was in Saigon. Sipping a bourbon and listening to American rock 'n' roll on the jukebox, I noticed a kid scamper into the darkened bar and whisper something to the mama-san. She nodded and looked in my direction. She made her way among the tables toward me.

"Roy-san, someone at door wishes speak with you."

I glanced toward the door. There was no one there.

"Outside," she said.

American military wore civvies while in Saigon to avoid conspicuousness. I wore slacks and an open-necked shirt loose enough to conceal the .38 revolver snugged into my waistband. Aware that the VC had a bounty on my head, I readjusted the Colt for fast access and slipped out a side entrance, intending to come up behind whoever waited for me at the front door of the Tax Building. I thought I was pretty slick.

I cut down a side street and flattened myself to the wall to peep around the corner and check out my mysterious caller. A voice directly behind me raised the cold hackles in my neck.

"I understand you wanted to meet me?"

Excellent English, clipped and precise.

"Have I fucked up or what?" I murmured, kicking myself mentally. I turned slowly, careful to keep my hands in sight, and confronted a tall Vietnamese of about 35 with a broad forehead and a thin nose and mouth. Intelligence brooded from large brown eyes. They were not black and sharp and slanted like those of most natives. I suspected their owner claimed European ancestry somewhere in his background. Probably French.

"Have we met before?" I asked.

"You are *Ohmja Nguoi Nhai?"*

I chuckled. "I am the *Old Frog,"* I admitted.

"You befriended my family on one of the weekend medical visits you and your kindly Dr. Shultz make to the villages. I have heard much talk about you in Vung Tau."

"And you are?" I asked.

"My name is Minh."

I gave him a sharp look. "Minh is a name like Smith or Jones in America. Men use such names to check into motel rooms with women who are not their wives."

It was his turn to chuckle. *"Commander* Minh. When not driving cab, I command one of the local People's Battalions. Would you like to have something to eat and a drink with an enemy commander?"

I pondered. He wore loose black peasant trousers and an even looser white smock. I noticed a faint outline in his pocket and a slight bulge at his waist.

I shrugged. "What the hell. You could have already taken me out with the miniature 9mm you're carrying in your belt or the stiletto in your pocket if you had wanted to."

"I see that you are also heeled, Mr. Boehm."

He studied me a moment with his intense brown eyes. His eyes were solemn, inquiring, purposeful. Thay Wu had spoken of the warlord's intensity, of how he looked like a man who has combat burned into his soul. Instinctively, oddly, I trusted this man. He also seemed to make up his mind about me.

"You wouldn't want my Prata riding your ass if you killed me like this," I decided.

"Yours is undoubtedly a badass spirit, judging from what I have seen and heard. The *Nguoi Nhai* you have trained fight well, as do you. I have also heard good things about you as a man. Shall we go? A truce for the evening?"

"A truce," I acknowledged.

A dented, ancient version of a New York Yellow Cab sat

parked at the curb. Minh climbed behind the wheel and motioned me into the front seat with him.

"Cholon?" he asked.

Cholon was the Chinese section of Saigon and off-limits to Americans after dark. It was sheer foolhardiness for me to accompany a VC warlord into a forbidden zone owned by the enemy as soon as the sun went down.

"Cholon," I agreed. Minh smiled approval.

The dented cab ricocheted through narrow dark streets, Minh skillfully parting the throngs with the generous use of his horn.

"Would you feel more at ease if I gave you my weapon?" he asked.

"Probably. But it would be less than dignified not to play this game out once it's started."

He laughed softly. "Neither of us will go down," he said, "unless it is honorably in battle."

He parked the cab in front of a small storefront restaurant. I noticed his smooth, oiled, catlike movements as we exited the car. He walked on the balls of his feet like he was constantly prepared to spring. Although he was smaller than I in stature and weight, I wasn't sure I could take him in a hand-to-hand fight. Not too many men of whatever size impressed me like that.

My presence caused something of a stir inside the crowded café. Americans were a rarity here. Minh requested a table against the far wall.

"Are you right-handed or left?" he inquired.

"Right."

"You sit on my right, I'll sit on your left."

That left my gun hand free. We sat with our backs to the wall.

"If you would live long and healthy, my friend," he said, "you must learn to eat what we eat, not only for the body but for the soul as well. We Vietnamese know what is good for your inner health. For example, dark fish is better for you than white."

And that was the way it began, the unusual friendship

between a communist warlord and an American SEAL adviser. It came to birth out of mutual respect, professional courtesy, and simply human liking one for the other. By the time the evening was over, I learned that Minh had three children and a wife who lived in Saigon. The scion of a once wealthy plantation owner, he had been well educated in both France and England. He fought against the French while still a teenager, then took up the cause against the Americans. He burned, he said, for a North and a South Vietnam unified and free of *all* foreign influence and control.

In the coming months, we would have long and intense discussions about communism, nationalism, and the right of South Vietnam to choose her own destiny. For the moment, however, we steered clear of most sensitive issues. Our conversation centered on topics of interest two regular men might have in common as they became friends. I began enjoying his company.

"Our meeting was not only because you expressed a desire to meet me," he admitted presently. "I wanted to see what kind of a man it was who sometimes lives at Madam Vinh's in Vung Tau and who befriends a Buddhist monk. I am not disappointed. There is a code of honor among men like us. You and your *Nguoi Nhai* fight fiercely—but, of course, I shall have to defeat you. I suspect we shall meet again in combat."

"I shall return."

"Spoken truly like your General MacArthur."

The First SEAL had come a long hard way in becoming the First SEAL. If I had proved one thing along the way, it was that I would not be stopped.

FOUR

★ ★ ★ ★ ★

Had I any regrets, I sometimes wondered, about the way I had lived my life in the pursuit of arms? But, then, why should I have regrets? I had done life my way. What else could a guy like me, rough around the edges, expect out of life except to raise hell and live life his way?

"You're just like your father," Mom used to say back in Long Island. "You're a real hell-raiser. You'll either grow up to be a hero—or you'll end up dead or in prison. There is no middle way for the Boehm men."

Dad and a friend used to fly an old Stinson airplane out to sea. They flew it upside down with the blue-green and the spindrifts below their heads.

"Who put the goddamned ocean so near the shore?" Dad always demanded.

I grew up wondering that too. Who put the goddamned ocean so near the shore? As a boy I sometimes stood with hands thrust in the pockets of baggy trousers and gazed longingly out toward the open sea. Wondering what lay over that watery horizon and then over the next horizon and then beyond that one. Some men were destined to be born, to grow up, to live, and to be buried almost within sight of their birthplaces. Other men were destined to be wanderers.

I remembered the date—19 November 1939—that determined which sort of man I'd be. I was 15 years old. Dad was a short man, and stocky, with hands as big and leathery as boxing gloves. He dropped one of the boxing gloves onto my shoulders.

"You're going with me to the Yard today," he announced.

He was a carpenter at the Brooklyn Navy Shipyard. "Today is a day you will never forget."

At the Yard I stood between Dad and big Mike Sullivan. Mike, who had been in the Navy during WWI, kept me supplied with sailor hats, navy blue woolen jumpers, bellbottom trousers, and daring tales of war and warships. Mike stood with his awkward big hands hanging and tears streaking his thorny cheeks during the launching ceremonies for the battlewagon USS *North Carolina.* The ship was the size of a New York skyscraper turned on its side, only larger and so magnificent that merely looking at her put a knot in my throat.

I waited through the interminable speeches and the smashing of champagne bottles for that moment when the great battleship slid into the East River and was born. Finally, the moment arrived. She glided down the launching ramp, slowly at first, then picked up speed. Her stern went first. It smashed the water and tore up a frothed tidal wave that bounced the tugs as they scrambled to catch up with her. Horns and sirens charged the air. Crowds cheered. A band played "Anchors Aweigh" and fire boats shot streams of water that caught sparks from the sun. I tasted salt in the air from the spray kicked up by the wonderful ship.

Aboard a warship like that, there would never be a need to ask who put the ocean so near the shore. She could sail *forever.* The launching of the *North Carolina* launched my imagination upon a course for the sea and the adventures the sea and war promised. It was only a matter of time. I knew from that moment that I could never be happy tethered to a single point on dry earth.

War already loomed red and inflamed over the horizon. The rattling of arms in Europe clawed black headlines across the front pages of the *New York Times.* Each day began with the unfolding of great events. I read names like *Hitler* and *Churchill* and *Mussolini.* People's expectant voices filled the air with excitement whenever they spoke of the prospect of war in Europe.

Most people were unabashedly patriotic in those more

innocent times. Our Great Country from sea to shining sea. My country right or wrong. That sort of thing. I memorized the preamble to the Constitution. I devoured books on naval tradition and on American history and America's wars. I was afraid the war would begin and end before I was old enough to participate.

In January 1941, during a raging snowstorm, my parents announced they were getting divorced. I wouldn't be 17 for three more months. The revelation shattered my life. Divorce was a scandal only rarely whispered about in my circle of friends and relatives.

"Which one of us do you want to live with?" my parents asked. I was their only child.

"I'm enlisting in the Navy," I informed them. "Just as soon as I can. I don't want to miss the war."

Roy Boehm hadn't missed a war since then. I had the scars to prove it.

FIVE

★ ★ ★ ★ ★

I always figured I was cut out for something special. An attitude like that was bound to make a guy cocky. In July 1941, fresh out of Navy boot camp, Seaman Second Class Roy Boehm, complete with a five-dollar bill stuck in my shoe and an accordion in a box tucked underneath my arm, reported for his first seagoing duty aboard the USS *Griffin*, a submarine tender undergoing repairs at Robbins Ship Yard in New York. I looked damned strac in my white bell-bottoms. I saluted the colors and then the officer of the deck.

"What's in the box, sailor?" the OOD asked.

I was a wiseass. "My lunch, sir."

The ship's bos'n standing nearby cocked a disapproving eye. Bos'n Mate Second Class Michaud was the Navy's light heavyweight boxing champ, an old salt with a jaw saw-edged into angles and a nose crushed so many times it seemed to flatten into his face. He promptly put the smartass to work scrubbing the quarterdeck.

The proper way to swab a deck is to push and feather. I worked the lubberly way, swinging the swab back and forth as I backed down. Suddenly, the swab struck something. I froze. My gaze slid across the deck to a pair of perfectly pressed bellbottoms. The tendrils from my swab clutched Bos'n Michaud's spit-shined shoes like the tentacles of an octopus, confirming my greatest terror.

"Lad," he drawled, "that ain't the way to swab."

Then he punched me. The punch loosened two of my teeth, one of which I eventually lost. There was no UCMJ, Uniform Code of Military Justice, before World War II. The Navy operated under the stern tenets of the old "Rocks and Shoals." A ship's captain was God. Bos'ns were tough taskmasters only slightly less than God. I lay on the deck and looked up at Michaud.

"Get some sand and canvas to scrub the deck," he said. "I don't want to see any blood on it when I come back."

The lesson seemed clear. My teeth's survival depended upon learning marlin spike seamanship. I threw myself into mastering the splicing of wire and line, the intricacies of working ground tackle and rigging, the principles of sailing warships. Most skills and knowledge during the prewar traveled from mouth to ear, a carryover from when few sailors could either read or write. I memorized dozens of rhymes used as teaching aids.

On your starboard tack with your sheets braced tight,
See that your green and red are bright.
For green to green and red to red
Is perfect safe to go ahead.

While Bos'n Michaud started me on my career with a hard punch to the mouth, Swede Johnson took over with less physical emphasis. In September for reasons known only to bean counters and yeomen, I was transferred to the USS *Alcor*, a destroyer tender. Swede was the petty officer-in-charge of the ship's hard-hat divers. It didn't take long to see that divers considered themselves a special breed and that other sailors concurred.

Growing up next to the sea, I had always been intrigued by it. *Underneath* the sea—now, that seemed a real challenge. The U.S. Navy in that period before the war had little underwater capability except for hard-hat divers wearing canvas suits, clumsy weighted shoes, and cumbersome copper helmets connected to the surface by lifelines and air hoses. The diving Navy confined itself to underwater repair and salvage. It shunned amphibious operations or innovations involving divers as warriors.

I saw myself as special. I marched to the Swede's diving locker.

"I want to be a diver," I proclaimed.

"It is hard work, lad, being a diver," Swede responded. "It is not a natural thing."

I began hanging around the locker. I was a 17-year-old kid asking questions and trying to pick up a little knowledge about my newfound passion. I often worked through the night splicing wire straps or whatever the ship's bos'n had me doing in order to have the day free to work with Swede. I would be waiting for him, leaning on the rail outside his dive locker, gazing across the flat gray water of Chesapeake Bay as though trying to penetrate the surface to see what lay underneath.

Swede was a big, solemn man with short gray hair at the top of a face as long and sad-looking as that of a stable rent-a-horse. The Navy had been his home for over 20 years. He seldom smiled. He said he was too old for smiling and had seen too much and what he saw was nothing to smile about. Fortunately, he had patience and I lost no more teeth. He gradually accepted me and my ardor for diving. Neither of us realized, of course, where my interest might eventually lead me.

I always had a dozen questions waiting for him. He looked at me in that solemn way of his.

"You'll work for it, lad," he said with his thick accent. "And you'll likely pay for it as well. My blues need washing, my shoes need shining, and coffee needs making. After you do that, I'll tell you what you want to know."

Fair enough.

Swede taught me how to take a hard-hat helmet apart, right down to the copper, and put it back together again. I learned about hand pumps and air lines and water pressure and how it affected the human body. I memorized Boyle's law on how underwater pressure changes the volume of gases in your lungs, and Charles's law on how gas volume varies directly according to temperature.

Swede suggested books on diving, which I devoured, enchanted. It amazed me to learn that man had been exploring beneath the sea for at least a thousand years. Would-be underwater explorers had experimented with leather hoods connected to the surface by leather tubes, with breathing bags made from the bladders of sheep. Upright diving barrels with one end closed and one end opened led to the use of diving bells. A Hindustani painting from the late 1500s depicted Alexander the Great descending into the Mediterranean in a kind of barrel.

In 1819, a former German artillery officer named Augustus Siebe devised a miniature diving bell with a window. The helmet fitted over a man's head and was held on his shoulders with weights. Air was pumped to the helmet from the surface through a hose.

Siebe's logical next step was to seal the helmet to a rubber watertight suit that could be inflated to balance water pressure. This outfit became the prototype of hard-hat rigs used by the U.S. Navy and others.

Already fascinated as I was by diving, the historical use of divers and swimmers for warfare totally captured my imagination. Persian King Xerxes I employed combat divers

400 years before the birth of Christ on his seagoing campaigns to sabotage enemy shipping. Athenian underwater soldiers destroyed enemy coastal defenses at Syracuse. Military divers hacked through enemy anchor cables at Byzantium. As recently as WWI, military divers experimented with free-diving closed-circuit breathing systems for rescuing trapped submariners and for clandestine operations against enemy shipping.

The seed was planted. Nurtured by the Swede, the idea grew in my mind. *Undersea warriors.* They could be used in a variety of ways to revolutionize warfare, *if* they could be freed from the air lines that tethered them to the surface. I envisioned battalions of troops rising out of dark waters in surprise attacks against an enemy. Swimmers invisible from enemy guns until they suddenly surfaced with weapons blazing.

"Divers will be used in the next war," Swede predicted.

Swede and his divers frequently loaded the *Alcor*'s 50-foot motor launch with hard-hat suits and hand air pumps and chugged out onto Chesapeake Bay for practice dives. I went along to power the hand pump.

"When will I dive?" I implored.

"You must have patience, Boehm."

In November, my solemn mentor's eyes twinkled unexpectedly as he loaded the launch for a day's diving. I hovered nearby. Once the diving began, I occupied my usual place at the air pump.

"Would you like a picture of yourself in a diving rig to send to the folks back home?" Swede asked casually. "You won't tell them you're a full-fledged diver, will you?"

My eyes went wide. "Oh, no. Not until I really am one," I promised.

I had seldom seen the Swede laugh. "Dress the kid," he said.

I sat in the diving suit with the helmet balanced on my knee and posed for a photo.

"That kid is so damned ugly," Swede said. "Put the helmet on the lad and send him down so I don't have to look at him."

It didn't matter that visibility in the murky water was so poor I could barely see my own shadowy hands and feet. I bounced down to 90 feet and walked around kicking up silt from the bottom of the ocean floor. I felt like I had just stepped onto the moon for the first time. I bubbled with the excitement of it when Swede pulled me up and announced that I was now officially a qualified second-class diver.

Qualification meant I still did all the menial diving tasks—cleaning and repairing the ship's hull, that sort of thing. Swede assigned me to tending other divers. He sometimes used me as an example to a diver who failed to meet his expectations, sending me to the bottom to find a flange or other such small item he dropped overboard.

"If your tender can find the flange and you can't," he would say to the diver, "then perhaps you need some more time tending."

Although there was little adventure and glamour in it, in the back of my mind lurked that indelible vision of the day when diving broke its umbilical cord and special undersea warriors were called upon to conduct special hazardous missions in defense of their country. I intended to be among them.

SIX

★ ★ ★ ★ ★

On that fateful Sunday morning, 7 December 1941, when the Japanese struck Pearl Harbor, 94 U.S. naval vessels rode densely clustered at anchor in an area not three miles square, with but one channel to the open sea. Seven towering gray vessels, the battleships *California, Maryland, Oklahoma, Tennessee, West Virginia, Arizona,* and *Nevada,* were lined up like dominoes on "Battleship Row" on the eastern edge of Ford Island in the center of the harbor. Only *Maryland* and *Nevada* escaped the surprise attack relatively undamaged.

Booming and crackling, struck by both torpedoes and bombs, *Arizona* sank so fast that 80 percent of her crew, more than 1,000 sailors, went to their deaths with her. Of the 2,403 fatal casualties inflicted upon the United States at Pearl Harbor, nearly half died trapped inside the sinking *Arizona*'s compartments.

Back in New York, my mother's excited voice summoned me to the radio. I had drawn Christmas leave from 5 December to 17 December. President Roosevelt was about to deliver his famous "Day of Infamy" speech. The Japanese had attacked Pearl Harbor. The United States was at war. All military personnel on pass, liberty, or leave were ordered to report immediately back to their ships or stations.

I was elated to find myself reassigned to the destroyer USS *Duncan,* a newly commissioned Livermore-class man-of-war. She entered the wreckage of Pearl Harbor for last-minute repairs and refitting before proceeding to the ocean war in the South Pacific. Qualified divers on all vessels entering Pearl Harbor were temporarily assigned to the base to assist in salvage of sunken ships.

I found myself peering down into the murky harbor water to the shadowy outline of where the battlewagon *Arizona* lay some 30 feet or so beneath the bay's surface. The oily-restless water lent the tomb a ghostly, otherworldly air. All corpses easy to reach had already been removed and sent stateside for burial. At barely 18 years old, I was about to be introduced to the human detritus of war.

The boat cox'n handed me some net bags and a line. "If you find a full corpse down there," he instructed, "tie the line to it and we'll pull it up. Put heads and arms and loose stuff in the bags. Graves Registration can sort it all out later."

I had never seen a dead person outside a casket, but macho was the order of the day. I figured I could outmacho any hairy-legged swinging dick aboard the *Duncan.* I had already won a pending court-martial because of a raucous night of liberty in Panama on the cruise through to the Pacific. Women and booze marked the true man-of-warsman.

The ship's commander, Lt. Comdr. Edmond B. "Whitey" Taylor, who became and remained my mentor and "sea daddy" for most of my career in the Navy, had shaken his head. "Boehm, you seem to be a damned good sailor as long as we keep you at sea," he said.

"It's women and booze, sir," I apologized. "I can't resist 'em, sir."

"Boehm, you're going to have to learn to keep quiet sometimes."

"It's a failing of mine, sir. I have a bulldog mouth."

"Don't let it override your Pekinese ass," he scolded mildly.

My dive partner and I donned "Jack Brown" outfits to dive on the *Arizona.* The Jack Brown was a light outfit consisting of a full face mask with an air adjustment valve, a leather belt with lead weights, and about 300 feet of two-inch oxygen hose. Air was pumped down from the surface.

Arizona lay majestically intact on the sand. She lay at an angle on her port side with a gaping hole down through the center of her decks. Clouds of feeding fish swarmed the ship, fading out of our path in gentle waves, like wind through a ripe wheat field. Debris of all sorts scabbed the ship—drifting lines, snags of canvas, netting, and tackle. It sloughed off the vessel like I imagined skin sloughed off waterlogged corpses.

Sucking air, my dive mate and I slipped into the ship's dark bowels through her terrible wound. Underwater torches illuminated watertight hatches, most of which hung ajar, and gangways where more wreckage floated eerily in the yellow-white liquid light. Shadows seemed to breathe and undulate.

I loosened a closed hatch by undogging the locks, braced my sneakered feet against the bulkhead, and pulled. I thrust my torch out ahead and cautiously led the way through into the compartment beyond. Our entry stirred the water and disturbed the haunted rest of several corpses. They moved about in a kind of weird slow-motion dance. Hair, skin, and minute particles of flesh misted into the water, attracting a feeding frenzy of tiny fish.

I flashed my light back and forth between the cadavers, as though covering myself against a surprise attack. A large crack in the bulkhead had admitted the sea's tiny scavengers. Light beams picked out black cavities where fish had sucked out eyeballs, gleamed on teeth exposed by lips having been gnawed away. Dead arms slowly beckoned, as though attempting to draw us with them into their watery graves. Silent anguished screams filled the compartment, deafening me.

I backswam. Striking my head on the edge of the steel hatch stunned me momentarily. I shot out of the macabre tomb like a squid, my partner directly behind me, while my stomach deposited its contents into my mask. I no longer felt so damned macho, what with my poor young heart pounding like bombs exploding and the vomit in my mask choking and blinding me and burning my eyes and nose with stomach acid. I thought I was drowning in my own breakfast.

I finally recovered sufficient presence of mind to hold my breath and wash out the mask, clearing it. Tiny fish swarmed like mosquitos to dine on fresh scraps. I shot for the surface, gagging and retching and panting to reach air.

"That's a graveyard down there!" I gasped upon surfacing.

Young men caught up in the glory and excitement of war are seldom prepared for its reality. My faith in an impartial God suffered during the following days. Living with the inhuman human debris of war, especially like that underwater, tested my faith and found it lacking. God must suspend his presence on earth when men went to war with each other.

Hatred grew in me like some parasitic undersea creature feeding on my intestines. I hated the Japanese *personally* as I probed below the *Arizona*'s decks. I never expected diving to be like this. I never expected the sea to contain such horrors. Swede was right; I was paying for my underwater knowledge.

I never thought I would feel relieved to get out of the water. Lt. Cdr. Taylor canceled all shore liberty and assembled ship's company on the *Duncan*'s fantail. Something big was coming down. A huge weight lifted from my spirits.

"Men, the USS *Duncan* has received orders," the skipper announced. "We shall leave port within the day. We have a job to do."

That was all he said. "God and country" speeches came from those who sent cannon fodder to war, not from those who went to war themselves.

A lusty cheer erupted from the throats of 260 destroyer sailors. I silently vowed never again to dive into an American graveyard.

SEVEN

★ ★ ★ ★ ★

During the months after *Duncan* departed Pearl Harbor, it seemed we were always on the periphery of action. Always the bridesmaid but never the bride. We had been operating around Guadalcanal for the past two months. The island appeared at first glance to have little value. It was roughly oblong-shaped and covered about 2,500 square miles with jungle, mountain wilderness, and, in the clearings, grass taller than a man. The nugget, the prize for which every man was killed, every ship sunk, and every plane shot down, was the airfield. The side that controlled the airfield gained an important advantage for supremacy in the South Pacific.

The Japanese were first to occupy Guadalcanal at the end of June 1942. They started building the airstrip. American Marines landed a month later in the first American ground action of the Pacific war. They drove the Japanese into the jungles and held them off while Seabees completed the work the enemy had started on the airstrip now known as Henderson Field.

Neither side anticipated the struggle to be as long and severe as it became. Ground, sea, and air forces all hurled themselves at each other. U.S. naval ships hammered Japanese artillery positions and supply dumps. U.S. Army heavy bombers flew long-range over-water recon missions in the contest for the sea approaches to the island. During the day, U.S. aircraft sank enemy ships and strafed enemy beaches. By night, Japanese naval gunfire caught the planes on the ground while their infantry hidden in the jungle surrounding the airfield attacked weary defenders.

Supply lines for both sides depended upon the sea approaches to Guadalcanal, where submarines and aircraft from both sides struck without warning and turned the approaches into a no-man's-land. The Japanese used destroyers, cruisers, and sometimes submarines as transports, making use of high speed and the cover of darkness to land reinforcements and supplies. This nighttime movement of Japanese bringing support for their ground forces and punishment for Henderson Field was called the *Tokyo Express.*

No single participant in something this big ever saw much of the war outside his immediate area. The lower a man's rank, the less he saw and the more he depended upon rumor to know what was going on. Aboard the *Duncan,* I helped deliver cargoes of gasoline from New Caledonia on Saint Maria de Santos to Maggot Beach at Henderson Field. U.S. aircraft suffered from chronic shortages of fuel.

A sunken Japanese freighter lay beached with only her stacks and upper superstructure visible above the surface of the water. The beach then rose gently into scarcely a square mile of cleared land containing the muddy airstrip where planes sometimes got stuck trying to take off after a downpour. Bomb craters from overnight Japanese navy bombardment had to be repaired every morning. Barracks for air crews and service personnel were nonexistent; everyone had a sandbagged foxhole. The Marines who came down to Maggot Beach to help unload supplies were gaunt; they had been limited to two meals a day for most of the time since their landing.

Until we ourselves ran short of food, we threw food to them like rich men feeding beggar kids.

"Poor fucking Joes," Dubiel murmured. Dubiel was a member of my gun crew. "At least we got a warm rack to sleep in and three hot squares a day. That's luxury penthouse living in this war."

He thought about it a minute.

"But they ain't gonna get their island sunk out from under them," he added.

Small Japanese subs roamed the water like sharks. That

was the way to attack an enemy, I thought. Hide beneath the waves, sneak in on your enemy, slash at his guts, and then get the hell out of the way of his death throes.

On 14 September, Naval Task Force 61 landed the 7th Marine Regiment to reinforce Guadalcanal. Destroyers *Duncan, Lansdowne,* and *Lardner* ran plane guard and submarine screen for the transports and aircraft carriers *Wasp* and *Hornet.* The day was typical of those latitudes—sunny bright, blue skies dotted with soft puffs of cloud. Swarms of planes launched from the carriers reminded me of sparrows seen while I lay underneath a shade tree in Central Park.

Two U.S. scout planes chased a Japanese bomber into sight, rattling at it with their nose guns. A thin wisp of smoke trailed after the yawing bomber. It lost altitude, then crashed into the sea beyond the horizon. Sailors aboard the *Duncan* cheered.

By early afternoon, the action had moved elsewhere. I lounged on watch in the starboard hatchway of gun #2's powder room, scuttlebutting with Shurney, the black shell man. The *Wasp* sailed about a half-mile out to *Duncan*'s port. Even at that distance she seemed to tower above us, like a great block of sea gray steel, like the Chrysler Building floating on its side.

Suddenly, the unseen enemy struck again from beneath the sea. The *Wasp* shuddered convulsively as smoke, dust, and water spewed. It didn't seem possible that a vessel that awesome could have her throat ripped by an enemy who failed to show himself.

GQ sounded. I darted for my gun mount, spreading the alarm: "*Submarines!* They've hit the *Wasp!*"

Wasp listed slightly and slowly veered to port as she went dead in the water. Black smoke poured from her forward hangar deck. It pumped high and boiling to smudge and mar the tropical sky. Tongues of flame flickered. They lapped at the first oil spilled on the ocean. I watched horrified as sailors leaped and tumbled from the wounded lady, out of the smoke and into the blaze. Their distant screams rent the afternoon. *This* was what Dante had in mind when he wrote his *Inferno.*

Duncan changed course. Men heaved life jackets, wooden crates, and whatever else would float overboard to survivors bobbing in the waves. One young blond sailor's eyes widened and his mouth hollowed as he realized the *Duncan* could not stop for even one survivor. She could not risk giving the enemy a stationary target.

Duncan launched her whaleboats. I ripped the canopy off the captain's gig and had it lowered. I disconnected the boat's bow painter, knotted hand grips into the line, and then, line trailing behind, raced across the burning ocean at full speed.

"Grab the line!" I shouted as I entered the flames.

Fire seared my hair and eyebrows and blistered exposed skin as the gig slowly pulled survivors clear of the burning cauldron. Burned skin peeled off the arms of some of the *Wasp* sailors as my crew pulled them into the boat. They writhed in agony.

Duncan rescued 778 shipwrecked sailors from the *Wasp* before the day ended. It seemed *Duncan* herself might sink under the added weight. Half the fantail was underwater, water sloshed over the main deck aft of the after deckhouse. We emptied our lockers to provide dry clothing for the survivors and gave the wounded and injured our bunks. They lay in them two to a bed. Other men sprawled everywhere—on the decks, inside the gun mounts, even on the bridge. Many of them were retching from having swallowed oil and salt water.

The tropical night settled over a scene of devastation. Fires from the *Wasp* lit up the sea for hundreds of yards around. Deep rumblings and poppings from her bowels accompanied bombs and torpedoes exploding in her armories and handling rooms. Destroyer *Lansdowne* finally gave the carrier the merciful *coup de grâce* by squeezing two torpedoes into her undefended hull.

Flames belched. The great ship pitched to starboard. Monstrous secondary explosions obliterated her after flight deck and blew holes in her sides and bottom. With a final groan as agonizing and heart-wrenching as the death rattle from some great stricken beast, the *Wasp* rolled over and let the sea claim her.

"Rest in peace, ol' girl," someone intoned reverently.

Exhausted and with nowhere else to go to rest since wounded sailors occupied my bunk, I poked around until I found a tarp on the deck next to the aft deckhouse. It was warm underneath the tarp because it lay over the engine room. Two other guys were already sleeping there. I crawled in between them.

Hours later, I awoke gagging and wheezing from a terrible stench. It even burned my eyes. I flung off the tarp. To my horror, my sleeping partners weren't sleeping. Two dead *Wasp* sailors had been placed underneath the tarp for safekeeping. The warm deck above the engine room was starting to cook them.

EIGHT

★ ★ ★ ★ ★

Three weeks after the sinking of the *Wasp,* destroyer *Duncan* was on course to become the bride. A premonition that the *Duncan* might not return had swept over the ship like dysentery as night spilled ink over the South Pacific. Virtually every man aboard had showered before sunset, for cleanliness in case of wounds, and donned his best dungarees for the impending battle. I found the preparations macabre. I had clambered topside to my battle station at gun mount #2 and sat there in the peace of the dying sun's rays. Sunsets in the Pacific tropics are redder and more violent and more of *everything* than anywhere else in the world. I watched the ocean, the sunset, the low furry outline of distant Guadalcanal Island, whiffed the gardenia-scented air that drifted seaward from dry land.

As Task Group 64.2 steamed north to engage the Japanese fleet, Rabbit, the #2 gun captain, joined me at the five-inch gun. We quietly smoked cigarettes. Each man handled impending action in his own way.

Dubiel walked up. He was about 21, a couple of years older than I, a few pounds heavier, and a couple of inches taller. His accent marked him as Joisey or somewhere in the Northeast.

"The showers ain't so crowded now, Boehm," he said. "You still got time, man."

"What the fuck for?"

Most seamen harbored a strange abiding fear of the sea. They almost panicked at the thought of losing a ship and being dipped into the brine. I laughed. I was a diver. I had seen what lay beneath the surface. I pretended that even the human cadavers in the *Arizona* had not put me off.

"The sea is your friend," I quipped with more bravado than conviction.

Word had started spreading as early as 1500 hours that American B-17s had come across a convoy of eight Japanese ships scurrying through a point in the Slot between Kolambangara and Choiseul islands, steering for Guadalcanal. Six destroyers enclosed two cruisers in a screening oval on the blue surface of the water. Over the ships buzzed a protective flight of Zeros.

We expected our Task Group composed of five destroyers—*Farenholt, McCalla, Buchanan, Laffey,* and *Duncan*—and four cruisers—*San Francisco, Salt Lake City, Helena,* and *Boise*—to intercept the Japanese convoy around 2300 hours, certainly no later than midnight, on the sea passage between the northern tip of Guadalcanal and tiny Savo Island. Tonight's Tokyo Express had to be stopped.

Shortly after sunset, Task Group Commander Rear Adm. Norman Scott in his flagship *San Francisco* sounded GQ,

General Quarters, and sent all hands to battle stations. It was Sunday evening, 11 October 1942. The nine ships of Task Group 64.2 squatted slightly with bows up and sterns down, a certain indicator of high speed, as they raced north off the western flank of Guadalcanal. The destroyers fanned into an antisubmarine screen ahead of and off the bows of the cruisers. Wakes trailed in narrow contrails of white foam on the sea's gentle surface. The horizon lay like a huge crystal dome of fading colors, empty except for a massive thunderhead towering to the east.

I gazed out through the aiming slot of gun mount #2, across the flat black sea toward Guadalcanal. We were closing on the enemy fast. Word spread that the Japanese ships were only 110 miles away. I felt vicious little animals with teeth and claws writhing inside my guts.

Would I react in a manner that would bring honor to those who depended upon me? Would I die as a man if necessary? Would I do my duty?

I needed to present myself as a competent professional fighting man. I *needed* it.

The #2 gun mount was the first five-inch gun forward of *Duncan*'s bridge. Nine men were required to operate the gun mount in battle—gun captain, pointer, fuse setter, trainer, sight setter, shell man, powder man, spade man, and hot shell man. As pointer, I operated the weapon's elevation-and-depression mechanism and controlled the trigger for firing. The trainer managed the horizontal controls. Working together, the two of us brought the crosshairs onto the enemy while the rest of the crew praised God and passed the ammo, emptied the spent casings from the gun, and reloaded. We called ourselves the fastest gun west of San Diego.

Control lights bathed the inside of the enclosed mount in a dim red wash. Dubiel's broad face looked surreal in the dim light, fixed and unchanging like that of a painting in the dark. I saw he wore his shined liberty shoes and his best set of dungarees.

Slowly growing louder, from the after deckhouse rose the

plaintive voice of someone singing. His voice was as clear as the tones of a church bell. And it was beautiful. Dubiel behind and below me, sitting on the deck with his legs draped through the open hatch of the handling room, froze to listen. So did Rabbit, the gun captain. A hush deeper than before fell over *Duncan.* The ship went into reverent suspended animation for the length of time it took one young and frightened sailor 3,000 miles from home to sing an old country hymn.

Amazing Grace, how sweet the sound
That saved a soul like me-e-e-e-e-e-

NINE

★ ★ ★ ★ ★

The last stanzas of "Amazing Grace" faded thinly into our wake. The ship's crew still seemed to hold its collective breath. Men whispered as tension mounted thicker and darker than the moonless night.

"See anything yet?" Dubiel asked nervously as he paced outside the mount and then back inside.

"Yes."

He hesitated. "What do you see, Boehm?"

"The dark."

"Boehm, I don't want any of your bullshit tonight."

As with many battles, a series of minor blunders led Task Group 64.2 into contact with the Japanese Tokyo Express. Since a man sees only his small part of a battle, it was not until much later that I discovered the "Big Picture" of what occurred during the Battle of Cape Esperance.

At 2225 hours, Guadalcanal's Cape Esperance lay abeam.

Admiral Scott, the Group Commander, formed his nine-vessel task force for battle and changed track, heading directly for Savo Island, visible only as a tiny ink blot on the horizon. Destroyers *Farenholt, Duncan,* and *Laffey* led the battle column in that order while *Buchanan* and *McCalla* sailed drag behind the four cruisers. The column bristled with a total of 19 eight-inch guns, 30 six-inchers, 56 five-inchers, 25 torpedo tubes, and 6,000 men.

At 2330 hours, Savo Island lay four and a half miles abeam of *Farenholt.* Admiral Scott ordered a reverse course, intent on patrolling the southern "gateway" between Savo and Cape Esperance and forcing the Japanese to come to him on his own terms. Somehow, his orders were misunderstood. While lead ships *Farenholt, Duncan,* and *Laffey* executed the tactical turn in simple column, like a string of railroad cars following the leader, cruiser *San Francisco* and the rest of the column reversed simultaneously, like reversing the slats of a Venetian blind, cutting the three lead destroyers out of the formation.

The Japanese formation blundered into the American ships during the confusion of the turn. Having circled wider than the other ships, *Duncan* found herself alone on a heading directly into the pathway of the advancing enemy warships. One moment, I saw nothing but darkness and the faint sheen of starlight on calm seas. The next moment, ghostly forms took shape. Ships seemed to suddenly leap out of the darkness.

The first ship, less than 2,000 yards away, carried the swept-back stacks of a Japanese heavy cruiser. Behind it sailed a file of vessels appearing one by one out of distant darkness. Not counting the sunken freighter at Maggot Beach, I had never seen enemy ships at such close range. They were heading directly for us. Had no one else spotted them? Adrenaline pumped my heart into double time.

I called out to Rabbit: "Enemy ships—visible to the naked eye!"

My voice quivered with fear and excitement.

Other stations on other ships were also ringing the alarm.

Duncan's engines immediately kicked up to full speed. The steel deck vibrated as she veered toward the Japanese vessels. Like us, they appeared to be in a long column, about to cross our *T. Duncan*'s bow swept across the enemy cruiser's bow at a 45-degree angle.

Mesmerized, I watched as a *Duncan* torpedo inscribed a phosphorescent wake in a slightly curving line across the black surface of the ocean. Its wake grew smaller and smaller as it streaked toward the cruiser.

The night erupted before our torpedo struck its target. American warships opened up with everything in a gigantic continuing explosion of bright flashes and flaming meteors. It was like being in the heart of a violent electrical storm. Star clusters bursting high aloft bathed the desperately maneuvering mixture of friendly and enemy ships with eerie shadows and reflections. Streaks of flame belched from every big gun.

In the middle of the storm, cut off from the American column, *Duncan* found herself occupying a precarious no-man's-land between the guns of the enemy and the guns of her own ships.

Rabbit's shrill exhortation: "Fire! Goddamnit, *fire!*"

I had the Japanese cruiser in my sights. I closed the trigger. Kept it closed. My finger froze on it. The five-incher fired as rapidly as the loading crew could pass up armor-piercing projectiles from the ammunition room and load them. I squeezed the trigger on the elevation-and-depression wheel so tightly I must have left indentations in it. After the initial thunder, I no longer heard the noise. I locked my feet around the base of the high seat and fired and kept firing while I rode out the ship's recoil.

I aimed at the cruiser's bridge. The target was so near that tracers hardly arced. Shells trailing red flame streaked straight across the water and ate at the enemy vessel.

I was in combat and, by God, I was doing all right!

Duncan's torpedo finally struck in a heavy explosion that grabbed the Japanese man-of-war and rode her out of the water on a red ball of flame. I continued pumping armor-piercing rounds into her deckhouse. They blossomed into blazing orchids.

The cruiser refused to die easily; her guns blazed back at us. *Duncan* maintained pursuit, intent on dogging her to her grave.

By this time, the joined battle had turned into a game of blindman's bluff in which it was difficult to tell friend from foe among the bursting of shells and the burning of ships and oil on the water. Shooting stars streaked in level flight across the sea, detonating into great glowing flowers. Violent shallow-arced rainbows formed and reformed as the American cruisers fired tracers of distinctive colors.

Alone and trapped between friendly and enemy guns, *Duncan* became a lightning rod attracting fire from both sides. Riding her felt like a great wolf was attacking and shaking her to break her back. There were blinding flashes as explosions rippled along her sides where she was being torn.

Suddenly, I found myself thrown into the middle of intense heat and light. The five-inch gun tilted on the warped deck. Blood hot on my face, blinding me. Searing pain from my right leg trapped underneath the crumpled gun mount. I fought to free myself, to ward off panic.

Miraculously, as the *Duncan* took more hits, the deck warped in the *other* direction. I broke free.

I spotted Dubiel lying unconscious on the mount deck, his legs draped into the open hatchway to the powder room. Fire glowed below. Shurney looked trapped against the bulkhead. His eyes reflected flames against his dark face. My eyes must have been as wide and white as his.

"They're all dead!" Shurney shouted. He looked around in shock. "It got them all, Boehm."

The wolf had settled in to shaking and tearing the *Duncan.* I felt my bladder loosen. Warm piss ran down my leg. Scared the piss right out of me. But I wasn't through fighting. Yet. I wasn't going down without a fight. Goddamnit, I *wasn't.*

"Shurney!"

The black shell man looked at me. I thought he and I were the only survivors of mount #2.

"Let's give the fuckers hell back, Shurney."

Shurney shook himself out of shock. "The handling room's burning," he yelled. "There ain't no more ammo."

Two shells were always secured to the side of the gun mount, a star cluster and a white phosphorus. "Do we have any powder?" I asked.

"Damn you, Boehm. There's one powder in the shuttle and one in the tray. That's all."

"Get the star shell."

I clambered back into my high seat at the trigger. The gun mount seemed bent and askew. Maybe it was the ship that was askew. Still under steam, the *Duncan* circled slowly to port. I glimpsed flames hissing from our bridge. Beyond, the Japanese cruiser was also ablaze.

An enemy destroyer glided like a shadow between my gun and the burning cruiser. A perfect silhouette. Like an eclipse. If we went down, we'd go down with guns blazing like in an Old West gunfight.

I squeezed the trigger.

Nothing. The destroyer kept on gliding.

I kept her in my sights for another try. The gun's firing mechanism was all fucked up. There was a kicking mechanism at the base of the gun that allowed it to be fired that way. I stomped the kicking lever. It worked. The star meteored into the destroyer's bridge and splashed fire.

"Boehm, the powder room's about to explode!" Shurney warned.

"One more shot. Load it."

I fired. The Willie Pete splashed aft of the destroyer's bridge.

"That's it!" Shurney bellowed to be heard above the bedlam. "The powder room's going. Get the hell out of here!"

He lurched through the mount's hatchway and disappeared just as the *Duncan*'s death throes tossed me from my seat. The ship shook so violently I couldn't regain my feet. I crawled on hands and knees toward the hatch. The heat on the steel deck from the fire below blistered my hands. Flames shooting from the open powder room engulfed Dubiel's dangling legs and feet.

Dubiel moaned. He wasn't dead after all. I reached for him. I was past the point of rational thinking. I simply reacted. I dragged his leaden body toward the hot shell port where expended casings were tossed out onto the deck. Alone, I'd never be able to get him through the hatchway.

Duncan was taking hits from our own *Boise*'s six-inch guns on one side and the Japanese cruiser's eight-inch guns on the other. I learned later she absorbed 56 shells, half of them striking between gun mount #2 and the #1 stack. She was literally being blown apart, like a chip of wood thrown onto a pond for target practice.

Impact jarred me over Dubiel's unconscious body, slamming my head against the mount's steel bulkhead. When I regained consciousness, flames were shooting into the mount from every crack, fissure, and loose fitting. Even more desperately now, I dragged Dubiel onto the open deck through the hot shell port. I couldn't have done it without the pump of adrenaline. *Duncan*'s #1 stack had been blown off. The bridge had been replaced by flames and black smoke.

A thin crying sound came from the starboard 20mm antiaircraft gun mount. It sounded like a trapped kitten. I dragged Dubiel away from the #2 mount and left him on deck while I checked on the antiaircraft guy.

Dark blood gushed from the guy's open mouth when I tried to lift him. He died with a deep rattle in his chest. I removed his life jacket and put it on Dubiel. We had a shortage of life jackets because of our having rescued *Wasp* survivors.

Dubiel screamed. His legs were charred black; I didn't know what other wounds he might have suffered. I dragged him screaming to the port-side main deck and left him where I could easily find him. Thankfully, he went unconscious again.

It occurred to me in my half-addled state that others might need help. I didn't realize it then, but I had shrapnel stuck in both legs and in my skull. I wandered about the burning ship as secondary explosions jolted her bowels, letting in seawater. Ammunition cooked off. Surreal scenes flitted before my eyes: screaming, shouting seamen running madly about like hell's denizens; fiery debris exploding in the air; flames hissing and coiling out of burning ammo magazines like great serpents; men jumping over the sides into the dark, oily waters.

Fleeting snatches of events. Grotesque images. Seamen sitting on a side rail staring down into the sea as into eternity. Faces reflecting red from the fire and their legs flapping as they tried to balance themselves before taking the plunge.

Below decks. Flames filled the ammo handling room for gun mount #2. Rizzi in the blaze melting like a wax doll. I knew it was Rizzi in the fire because he always stenciled his name in large letters on the back of his dungaree shirt. I saw his name in the fire. *RIZZI. RIZZI. RIZZI.* Then the name was gone and so was he. Consumed.

John J. Puzines, the Navy's wrestling champ, standing in the hatchway of the mess hall, frozen, blocking it.

"Puzines, let me out," I said.

I pushed him. He felt as cold and hard as Michelangelo's marble *David.* I slugged him to bring him out of it. He seemed neither to feel the blow nor see the man who delivered it. I managed to squeeze past him between his leg and arm. I left him standing there as though he were Samson single-handedly attempting to hold the ship together.

Into the chiefs' quarters, topside to the foc'sle. A keening, wailing, pleading voice: "Lord, I have sinned . . . I have sinned . . . *I have sinned . . .*"

Chief Boatswain's Mate Davenport and some people from gun mount #1 attempting to organize the evacuation. The chief grabbed me. "Boehm, where are you going?"

I stared at him. Blood and sweat stung my eyes, half blinded me. I pointed. "I left Puzines below deck."

"Go get him," the chief ordered.

That gave me purpose. I had a mission.

Puzines remained standing in the mess hall hatchway. I

still couldn't budge him. As far as I know he perished with the ship.

"Cut me some hose," Chief Davenport instructed when I returned.

I sliced off a long length of fire hose with my sheath knife. Davenport tied off the hose and threw the bitter end over the side. Climbing down the makeshift line was safer than taking a chance of hitting floating debris by jumping or diving.

"Good-bye," I said to Chief Davenport and walked off. I had to return to Dubiel.

The ship was like a giant flamethrower shooting fire out from either side with frightful hisses. I found Dubiel where I'd left him on the main deck next to the railing. He was unconscious but still breathing. I checked his kapok life jacket and then, struggling, dragged him to the edge and hurled him overboard. He hit the water with a flat splash.

"Good luck, buddy."

I looked around a last time. The *Duncan* with her beautiful polished battleship decks and sleek Livermore lines was about to go to her watery grave. Like the *Arizona.* I stood momentarily on the thin Mercator between blazing chaos aboard ship and the calm black of the ocean below and beyond. I would take my chances with the sea.

I made a racing dive over the side of the ship, trusting momentum to carry me through the licking flames. The sea was about to teach me another valuable lesson about surprise and terror.

TEN

★ ★ ★ ★ ★

The plunge overboard drove me deep into dark warm waters. I fought to hold on to my senses. If I passed out, I would just keep sinking. I wore no kapok. I experienced an instant vision of the silt at the murky bottom of Chesapeake Bay.

I floundered to the surface, the shock of the water having cleared my head of some of the smoke and confusion. Flames from burning ships along with flares and gunfire lanterned the ocean for miles around. Flotsam littered the surface of the sea. Something banged against me. I grabbed it. A wooden spar the size of a telephone pole. From a Japanese ship, since American warships were built entirely of metal. Spluttering water, I bellied onto the spar.

A bedraggled figure clinging to the other end of the spar cried out in alarm and threat. I reached cautiously for my sheath knife as the Japanese sailor and I eyed each other through the haze of night and battle. I figured he'd come for me. He must have figured I'd go for him. We remained frozen with indecision for a long moment.

Then, I eased off the spar on my end; he eased off on his end. We swam away as fast as we could in opposite directions. Both of us had had all the fight we wanted.

Looking back over my shoulder as I stroked, I half expected to see the Japanese chasing me. What I saw was even more horrifying. The *Duncan* was chasing me. Still steaming wild in a tight circle, blazing like a Viking's funeral pyre, she bore straight down upon me, growing larger as she approached, spewing fire and smoke from every opening.

I dug my strokes deep into the ocean. I wished I could run on water.

As luck would have it, I splashed into someone else floating faceup in a kapok jacket. Dubiel was raving, out of his mind with pain. *"Look out! Look out! . . . God! God. I wanna go home . . ."*

I almost resented his getting in my way. *Duncan*'s blazing prow loomed above us. I grabbed the ranting sailor by the nape of his life jacket. Confusion swept over me about which way to flee. I started one way, then backstroked quickly.

The stricken destroyer's prow wake glistened white as the ship rushed by so near I thought I could reach out and grab her. I held on to Dubiel and his life jacket with a drowning man's grip as the wake caught us and drove us tumbling underwater. Once again I felt the queer sinking sensation of pending unconsciousness.

When we surfaced, after what seemed hours, the world had grown quiet and warm and peaceful. I thought I must have died. It wasn't so bad. Then I spotted the *Duncan* flaming away across the sea in the distance. I must have passed out for a minute or two.

The battle appeared to have abruptly ended. The oppressive weight of the tropical night seemed to have flattened the sea. The only vessel within view was the pinprick of match flame that marked *Duncan*'s departure. I heard nothing. Were Dubiel and I the only survivors?

"Home . . . ," Dubiel pleaded. *"Home . . ."*

The presence of another human being in that vast, dark expanse of water, even though he was injured and only semiconscious, provided a great immediate comfort. His life jacket also kept us both afloat.

"Dubiel?" I said, hoping. "Dubiel, can you hear me?"

His head bobbed next to mine. "Who . . . ? Who . . . ?"

"Roy Boehm. How's the pain?"

"My legs . . . I can't feel them anymore. . . . Boehm, I want to go home. . . . We're not going to make it, are we?"

As the swell of water lifted us, I glimpsed an ink blot far against the stars on the horizon. I lost sight of it in the shallow trough, but caught it again on the upswell. It had to be Savo Island.

"We'll make it, buddy," I said.

I began swimming toward the ink blot, towing Dubiel with one hand.

"Home . . . ," he said. "Mom . . . ? *Mom, are you there?"*

Dubiel drifted in and out of coma throughout the long night while I towed him. We made better time when he passed out and stopped babbling and struggling. The sun rose so fiercely directly above that at first, dazed and exhausted as I was, I thought it must be a fire or an explosion. I treaded water. Dubiel's scream shrieked into my guts.

"Look out! Look out!"

I was tempted to drown his ass just to make him shut up. Salt water had swollen my face. My eyes felt like they were dipped in acid. My vision was blurred. My tongue felt like a dry sea cucumber stuffed down my throat. I feared it would block my windpipe. Periodically throughout the long night I had stopped swimming to change hands on Dubiel, retch out the seawater in my stomach, and rest, bobbing on the surface.

I calculated we had gone into the drink about midnight. Now it was daylight. I had been swimming for hours, towing Dubiel, gauging direction mainly by instinct. Hoping we were still on course toward Savo. I felt drained, verging on the point of total exhaustion. I'd start babbling like Dubiel if this kept on for many hours more.

I couldn't give up. I had to keep going. *Keep going* played itself over and over in my brain, like a stuck record. A needle wearing a groove directly through the center of my gray matter. *Keep going.*

Although I felt lost and alone with Dubiel on the vast sea, the truth was something entirely different. Wreckage, human dead, and surviving seamen filled the gateway between Savo and Guadalcanal. The 30-minute sea battle had ended with the sinking of four Japanese destroyers, one cruiser, and one transport. The American cruisers *Boise* and

Salt Lake City and the destroyer *Farenholt* were badly damaged, but damage control parties managed to extinguish the fires and save them. Only *Duncan* was lost.

The Battle of Cape Esperance claimed the lives of 107 Americans. More than 200 seamen from *Duncan* took to the water to escape the floating inferno. While rescue attempts began immediately, many battle survivors remained in the ocean until late the following day. Commingled American and Japanese blood acted as bait chum in the water. Sharks sliced toward the battle site, intent on feasting upon helpless prey. I would later reflect upon the sharks and upon the terror caused by the approach of unseen enemies, but for the moment I had tunnel vision focused upon that most elemental of human wants and needs—survival.

At some point I shed my shoes and dungaree shirt and knifed off the legs of my trousers to make swimming easier. My entire body felt numb. During moments of temporarily cleared vision, I thought I must be gaining on Savo Island, that it looked nearer than it had an hour or so before. Maybe I was merely hallucinating.

I heard my own breath rasping hollow deep inside my throat and lungs. I didn't care if Savo was occupied by friendly or enemy forces. It simply did not matter. Savo was the only hope for Dubiel and me.

As the sun inched upward into a hard blue sky, I somehow became aware that Dubiel and I were no longer alone in the bright sea. I felt *other* presence. I treaded water, blinking my eyes rapidly to clear them. I saw . . .

Fins. Cutting the surface like the blades of knives.

Until then, I thought I had passed the point of feeling anything. But I had never experienced such utter fear, such near-mindless horror, not even when the gun mount exploded the night before. Merely sighting a shark was enough to strike panic into the bravest heart. But to be in the water *with* them!

Four or five fins circled. How long had they been nearby without my noticing? Swimming nearer and nearer, getting bolder. I reached for my knife. It was gone, lost during the night's long swim.

I had but one choice—continue swimming. I had heard that showing panic immediately induced an attack. Thank God Dubiel was blissfully unconscious. I prayed he wouldn't come to and start thrashing about. I steeled myself to crawl slowly through the water, attempting to avoid the appearance of being a potential victim.

The sharks closed in.

The casual, detached way they approached set my heart pounding and ignited every nerve ending. Black dorsals slicing the water, snake eyes glinting, drooping teeth-filled jaws. Looking us over as impersonally as a trout about to take a live grasshopper.

One of the fish, larger and bolder than the others, darted in for a bite. A scratching, tingling sensation in my foot. I shouted, struck at the fish. Drove it off.

My foot was bleeding. Not ten feet away glistened the dark back of the giant predator.

It circled.

I drove it off again and again. The smaller sharks retreated, leaving the field to the large one. My head ratcheted on my neck as I attempted to keep an eye on the fish and anticipate its next approach. Exhaustion, wounds, and now debilitating fright were taking their toll. It required every ounce of strength and resolve I possessed simply to remain afloat and hold on to the unconscious Dubiel.

There was something to say for unconsciousness; Dubiel didn't know we were about to become some creature's main course.

The shark's fin disappeared beneath the sea. *Not* seeing the shark proved more terrifying than seeing it. I spun in the water like a top, searching, darting eyes peering into the clear green waters, wincing from the reflected brightness of the sun. I felt like a deer surrounded by wolves.

A dark shape deep, deep below. Rapidly growing larger. *Larger.* Like looking through a zoom lens and zooming suddenly to maximum close-up. Screams welled into my throat, blocking it.

Big and powerful, the fish brushed sandpaper-rough against my bare legs.

I screamed then, all control lost.

Dubiel screamed too. He must have had some awareness at the last instant as his body exploded out of the water. He twisted violently in the white froth and then he was gone in the attack, wrenched from my grip, scream broken off to linger forever in my nightmares.

It was all over that fast. A smear of red stained the sea, trailing down into the depths. I lost all control. I beat the water frantically with arms and legs as I swam with renewed desperation, knowing deep down I could never outswim sharks but determined to make them work for their supper.

For some curious reason, the sharks kept their distance after snatching Dubiel. I was all but delirious when a rescue boat of U.S. Marines plucked me out of the brine. Voices. I thought I was hallucinating. Cracking up. A boat loomed directly beside me. I gave a start. Someone thrust out a boat hook for me to grab. I struggled weakly to climb into the boat. I fell back exhausted into the water.

"Here, Boats. Give us your hand."

I wore a bos'n whistle around my neck. That was how they knew.

"I can make it myself," I said, brushing off helping hands. I was a stubborn little bastard. Always had been, always would be.

"Yeah, Boats. You made it this far, we're sure you can make it the rest of the way."

ELEVEN

★ ★ ★ ★ ★

Survivors of the *Duncan* were a ragged bunch clad in whatever surplus clothing we could find. I wore cutoff dungaree trousers and a jacket with no sleeves. Cpt. Whitey Taylor had had a broken arm when he finally abandoned command of the *Duncan* and went into the drink. He was swimming with his one good arm when he came upon a wounded seaman.

"Save yourself, Skipper," the kid said.

Captain Taylor gave the kid his broken arm and said, "Here, hang on to this." He pulled the kid all night long with the seaman hanging on to his broken arm.

I admired Whitey Taylor tremendously. Serving in the *Duncan* with him began a career for me that would parallel his for years. Much of what I later became in the Navy world of Special Operations I owed to him. It was he who saw whatever potential I possessed and forced me to develop it through correspondence courses. I could never have become a commissioned officer if he had court-martialed me all the times I deserved it.

"You're lucky, Boehm," he said to me, "that your court-martial papers for your wild night in Panama went down with the *Duncan.*"

Prior to our being awarded survivors' leave stateside, Captain Taylor assembled the remaining crew of the *Duncan* on the fantail of the cruiser *Salt Lake City*. Adm. "Bull" Halsey personally read off a list of names of men who demonstrated particular valor during the Battle of Cape Esperance. Somehow my name was on the list.

"Boehm, front and center. What's your rate, Boehm?"

I wore my tattered dungaree shorts and the ripped-up jersey. "Uh, cox'n, sir."

"You're now advanced to Second Class," he said.

"Thank you, sir." I stepped smartly back into ranks. The guy behind me whispered, "Boehm, you stupid sonofabitch. If you had told him you were First Class, you'd be a Chief now."

Admiral Halsey overheard. He came back. "He's right," he said to me. "You would have been Chief."

Almost getting munched by the shark had scared the hell out of me. I was 18 years old and I had already been shown my own mortality. The nightmares started while I was on survivor's leave back in New York—always that big badass fish snatching Dubiel from my grasp. It tormented me that the dreams might continue for the rest of my life. I wondered if the piece of shrapnel lodged inside my skull, so close to the brain that the docs were afraid to remove it, had anything to do with the nightmares. I often had severe headaches along with the bad dreams.

Otherwise, as a wounded combat veteran, I was treated like a returning hero. My godparents, the McPhersons, took me to Radio City Music Hall to see the ballet. I had about as much culture as a mule. Dress up a mule like a racehorse, he's still a mule. Mom McPherson smiled.

"We want you to meet someone," she said. "She's gorgeous. She's heard all about your heroics in the war."

We found seats in the darkened theater and the production began. The curtain opened to reveal a beautiful field of flowers. The blossoms opened one by one to display a lovely girl. Mom McPherson pointed. "That's her. That's Tawny."

My breath stuck in my throat. I stared. Elizabeth Marie Morris—"Tawny"—was about five feet tall with honey blond hair and sparkling wide green eyes that lit up the theater. She walked on the most gorgeous pair of gams I had ever seen. I didn't know such legs existed. By comparison, she turned every other flower in the production into stinkweed.

When Mom McPherson introduced us afterwards, my feet kept growing until they stretched out the door of the theater and I kept stumbling over them.

"Gee whiz, I *love* you," I finally blurted. "I'm gonna kill every Jap there is so the war'll be over and I can get back to New York."

By the time I returned to the war, Tawny and I were engaged to be married. Whirlwind romances during those hectic times blossomed like the flower Tawny played onstage. I reported back to the South Pacific nicknamed "Seasick the Sailor," because that was the title of one of Tawny's favorite books when she was a little girl. I vowed to dedicate myself to the single goal of surviving the war, getting out of the Navy, and marrying my beautiful little Elizabeth.

Even as early in the war as late 1942, I had heard about and made inquiries into a special swimmers unit training in Florida and Hawaii. From what intelligence I collected piecemeal, I learned the unit, whose members would soon be known as *Frogmen,* was going to be used in secret water operations against the Japanese during America's island-hopping campaign toward Japan. The Swede had instilled in me the idea of warrior divers. If anything, my encounter with the shark fed that idea. The thought of sea commandos rising out of the depths like sharks to strike terror into the hearts of the enemy fascinated me. I hated the Japanese personally, not only for Pearl Harbor and the *Arizona* but now also for the *Duncan.*

My inquiries about the swimmers fell flat, the unit was still so secret. Friends advised me to count myself fortunate to have escaped one close underwater encounter and to strive to stay on the surface of the water from now on. Besides, I now had Tawny and our impending marriage to think about. I still felt I was destined for something *special,* but it didn't have to be in the Navy.

"Tawny, my life is yours," I wrote. "The war can't take it, because it belongs to you. I'll love you forever. Seasick the Sailor."

I opted to stay with destroyers. A personnel yeoman tried to send me to the destroyer *Schubert* instead of to Cpt. Whitey Taylor's new command, the destroyer USS *Floyd Bennett,* DD-473, the "Battlin' B," a flush-deck destroyer of the Fletcher class. Many survivors from the *Duncan* and from the *O'Brien,* hit and eventually sunk while trying to make port the same day the *Wasp* went down, made up the *Bennett*'s crew. When Captain Taylor walked into the personnel office, I had the recalcitrant yeoman on the deck with a wastepaper basket over his head and was beating on the basket with my fists.

The yeoman wailed, "Sir, this . . . this petty officer said he was going to kill me if I didn't change his orders from *Schubert* to *Bennett.*"

Captain Taylor looked at me, then at the pale-faced yeoman. "Well, then," he drawled, "if I were you I'd change his orders."

Aside, he said to me, "Boehm, I have this new correspondence course I want you to take."

Correspondence courses were the skipper's way of punishing me. I was working on five courses at the same time when the *Duncan* perished.

"Sir, I'm already working on three others . . . ," I tried to protest. I would be one of only a few ever in the Navy to complete Navigation Part I and Navigation Part II at the same time.

Captain Taylor's eyes narrowed.

"Yes, sir," I surrendered.

"See you aboard *Bennett,* Boats."

Captain Taylor's executive officer aboard the *Bennett* was Lt. Comdr. Phillip H. Hauck, former gunnery officer aboard *Duncan.* The crew called him "Uncle Phil." Roy Henry Boehm, 19 years old, frocked Bos'n Second Class by Adm. Bull Halsey personally, became petty officer-in-charge of First Division, which included the ship's anchors, and was made captain of #2 gun mount.

On 31 July 1943, Taylor advanced to become commander of DESRON-45, Destroyer Squadron 45, of which *Bennett* was a part. Lieutenant Commander Hauck became *Bennett*'s skipper. The new captain continued two traditions in my career and upbringing initiated by Captain Taylor. I was a good man at sea, Whitey Taylor always said, but a lousy damned risk in port. Hauck made sure I had plenty of correspondence courses to keep me busy.

"Boats," he said dryly, "I don't see any reason to change a winning combination, do you? You keep getting in trouble, we'll keep getting you educated. The Navy'll have to make you an officer someday."

The second tradition began over a "coffeepot" I made from a five-inch gunpowder can mounted above a "hot plate." I kept the coffeepot and a food locker in the boatswains' compartment for use on long night watches at sea. Captain Taylor stopped by one night, saying, "Buy me a sandwich and a cup of coffee, Boats?"

While I built a sandwich of CPO dogs, Vienna sausage, and raw onions, he took a sip from my coffee cup. It was laced with 90-proof torpedo juice. I held my breath. No liquor was allowed aboard ship. I was about to explain that torpedo juice eased the splitting headaches I suffered from shrapnel when he took another sip, without change of expression.

I promptly laced *his* coffee with a little torpedo juice. We sat there together, sipping and snacking and listening to Tokyo Rose play Glenn Miller and warn the Americans that we were losing the war. When he got up to leave, he said, "I'm going to have to do this more often."

"Uncle Phil" Hauck paid a complimentary visit to the boatswain's compartment as soon as he relieved Captain Taylor. "Boehm," he said, "I understand from Captain Taylor that you make a pretty good sandwich and one hell of a cup of coffee."

Once back in the South Pacific, I placed Tawny's photo in the #2 gun mount where I could look up and see it. I didn't need the photo to see her. Whenever I closed my eyes, I looked into those amazing green eyes of hers and admired those lovely long legs. I was smitten. Tawny and her romantic barrage of letters kept me going through the fury and gore of the war to end all wars. Kamikaze attacks, wolf pack raids. Saipan, Tinian, Guam, Okinawa. I wanted this goddamned war to end. I wanted out of the Navy.

I wanted to go *home* to my girl.

TWELVE

★ ★ ★ ★ ★

Seizing island bases held by the Japanese in America's island-hopping drive across the Pacific not only impeded free movement of Japan's navy, it also provided the United States a springboard from which, in time, air attacks could be launched against Tokyo itself. The Battlin' B fought through the Pacific campaigns one by one—convoy and patrol duties; antishipping raids; sub screening; cover for assaults; preinvasion shelling of Guam, Saipan, and Tinian; battle line screening for carriers during the so-called Turkey Shoot against Japanese shipping; firing on counterattacking enemy troops; close fire support for land-based marines; antiaircraft duty . . .

Speeches by FDR and Winston Churchill rebroadcast through the destroyer's intercommunications system helped me understand that "the war to end all wars" was perhaps the single most important event of my lifetime, indeed of the century. During 27 months at sea, I kept a journal to chronicle the war for the benefit and education of the children and grandchildren Tawny and I would begin having as soon as the war ended. Funny how love of a woman changed a man's perspective.

> *23 September 1943:* Damn near got torpedoed laying at anchor off Maggot Beach. A year ago I lost

my ship in the same place I am at this very minute. . . .

10 December 1943: Sixth trip to Bougainville. USS *Denver* got hit by Jap planes. I've got some good friends on her . . . Gen and Don, they are okay, but Ace O'Brien got hit. I guess he never knew what hit him. . . .

8 May 1944: General quarters. Six thousand yards from beach of "Shortland Islands." Jap-held territory. We were going to knock a couple of Japs off a lookout tower. Their six-inch shore battery from the beach opened up on us. . . . A shell went between our stacks. Shells fell off our bow and straddled us amidship. All around us. We returned fire. Have no idea how much damage we done to them. The Japs were still firing at us at 21,000 yards. After it was over, we picked shrapnel off the deck. No one got hurt. The Japanese has six six-inch guns against our five five-inch. Our bombers are going over now to see what they can do. . . . The USS *Hollford,* the other can with us, took a beating and we both made a hasty retreat. . . .

21 May 1944: Things in the division are running fairly smooth and that gives me time to check the division books. No room for complaints, but despite the smoothness there is an air of tension, ill feeling among the crew. I've seen it happen before—the calm before the storm. . . . They are fed up with the continuous on the go. We have only had six days of rest since we have left the States, and the crew stayed drunk all six. Instead of relaxing the tension, it added to it. . . .

I guess what's behind it all is I'm tired of the beautiful Pacific and terribly in love with Tawny and want to see her and hold her. The whole damn crew have their own reasons—wives, sweethearts, loved ones, kids, dogs, cats, and one guy says he misses his pet bear. I understand the next invasion is going to be one hell of a tough one. Sure would be nice to go home after it, for a little while. . . .

11 June 1944: We are now proceeding to our destination on Jap-held Saipan. The veterans are acting natural enough, but there is a funny assortment of reactions among the new men who have yet to see action. Some are loud and boisterous and some are like scared kittens.

13 June 1944: Before dawn we approached our objective of Saipan from the south. Started bombardment at dawn. Other force is letting them have it from the north. . . .

USS *California* received a hit in her radar and main battery detector, but is still in the fight. . . .

Four men from the demolition squad went into the coral reef to take soundings. Japs opened up on them with everything they had. Four men swam back out. Brought a pilot back with them who was shot down the day before and took refuge on the reef. . . .

Saipan is burning nicely from two or three ammo dumps and a few fuel dumps. . . .

At night, ships took turns in illuminating the beach and then dropping shells on it. This went on all night while the demolition squad worked clearing a channel through the coral. . . .

18 June 1944: 150 miles from Saipan and Guam, waiting for the Japs. Received word that our boys on Saipan have suffered 2200 casualties, 1500 of them are dead. . . . This is the hardest part of the war for me—our boys being killed and all we can do is sit here and wait for the Jap fleet to get up enough nerve to come out and fight, the yellow bastards. . . .

19 June 1944: We were attacked by Japanese dive bombers. . . .

Today was a tough one, but well worth it. The score as it stands is 205 Jap planes shot down and only one bomb hit in our formation. . . .

Flags were flown at half mast for the men that were killed. . . .

Marines on Saipan have advanced clear across the island. Our forces have sunk seven Jap evacuation barges filled to the gunnels with the yellow rats trying to clear out of Saipan. . . .

13 July 1944: Entered Saipan to refuel. The water is littered with dead bloated Jap bodies floating by the side of the ship. . . . Among the dead Japs are dead livestock—horses, cows, goats and dogs. . . .

15 August 1944: Received a letter from my girl today. Sounds like she has something on her mind she wants to tell me. . . .

Listened to Tokyo Rose. She don't say much anymore. Maybe we should send her some fan letters. . . .

THIRTEEN

★ ★ ★ ★ ★

I kept hearing about these *Frogmen.* Combat divers who blew up coral reefs and other obstructions in order to open water passages for troop landings. It wasn't until the invasion of Saipan, however, that I actually encountered them. *Bennett* briefly took aboard some of these divers when their TNT-loaded APB collided with the USS *Pennsylvania* and took on water. They were kept isolated from the destroyer's crew until another landing craft came for them. I couldn't help being intrigued.

There was no comparison between my diving and theirs. I might as well have been diving in a swimming pool. Chiseled, hard-muscled young specimens, they carried themselves with a reckless, *special* air. Each man was flagged with blue-green paint as camouflage and then marked with black stripes from toes to chin and down each arm in order to use their bodies to measure the depth of water near shore.

Their gear consisted of: helmet; dive masks; cork gloves to protect their hands from coral; swim fins, which they obviously knew how to use; swim trunks; knee pads; knives and life belts; first aid packets; pencils that wrote underwater; and small Plexiglas slate tablets. Although SCUBA (Self Contained Underwater Breathing Apparatus) wouldn't be introduced to the U.S. military until after the war, the divers were equipped with a pair of rigs each consisting of a portable oxygen bottle encased in flotation gear with a long air hose leading from it to a Jack Brown dive mask. Rather than depending on a boat-based compressor, the blue men with the black stripes took their air with them in a bottle. I thought it a great idea.

The swimmers were members of a special unit called UDT—*Underwater Demolition Team.* It was said a man had to be "half fish and half nuts" in order to join up.

"Look at them, Boats," one of my gunners chided. "Ain't they what you been talkin' about—commandos in the sea? Why don't you go with them? Get your ass shot off. I'll take care of your girlfriend for you."

I scowled. I intended getting out of the Navy and marrying Tawny of the wonderful eyes and legs. Didn't I?

Nonetheless, I nosed around to see what I could learn about UDT. It wasn't exactly what I had in mind when it came to undersea warriors, but it was a start.

UDT was known by various designations in the beginning. Its sole purpose was to aid in amphibious assaults against enemy beaches. The first such U.S. assault was against Guadalcanal on 7 August 1942, but it went unopposed. Invasion forces preparing to land in French North Africa at the mouth of the Wadi Sefou River near Casablanca in French Morocco faced a different situation.

Vichy French had constructed a massive boom and net arrangement across the river just inside the jetties that flanked the river mouth. Beyond, a large stone fortress bristling with 155mm and 75mm guns guarded the river entrance. Planners recruited a demolitions expert, Navy Lt. Mark Starkweather, and 16 other men to clear the mouth of the Wadi Sefou. Their official designation was CDU—Combat Demolition Unit. Starkweather was the predecessor of America's undersea commandos. He was the *first.*

CDU began training for its mission in September 1942. On 8 November, it failed in its first attempt against the river obstructions when Nazi defenders in the stone fort spotted the team on rough seas and opened fire, driving the boat back out to sea. Three days later, CDU tried again and this time succeeded in blowing up the obstructions and clearing the way for a landing. This was the first action utilizing underwater demolitions men.

In June 1943, Navy Lt. Comdr. Draper L. Kauffman, a bomb disposal expert, was given the job of organizing the first Naval Clearance Diving Unit (NCDU) at Fort Pierce, Florida. The unit was so secret that virtually no one in the Navy knew what it was. First volunteers learned hydrographic reconnaissance and mapping as well as demolitions. They operated out of small boats and wore full combat fatigues with life belts and combat boots to protect their feet from coral reefs. Hooked to safety lines, they were not expected to do any swimming.

The tragic invasion of Tarawa in November 1943 awakened the Navy to its need for underwater surveillance. More than 1,000 Marines were killed and 2,500 wounded because they could not get over the island's reef. Demolition swimmers had not been used to clear the way. They *were* used during all subsequent landings. The aftermath of Tarawa also opened the way for UDT.

At Kwajalein, the cox'n of the landing craft taking NCDU men toward shore grew nervous because of the large numbers of coral heads. Ensign Lewis F. Luehrs and Seabee Chief Bill Acheson stripped down to swim trunks worn underneath their fatigues. They spent 45 minutes in the water measuring its depth and checking for obstructions. In addition to coral heads in the water that would prevent the effective use of landing craft, the men discovered hidden gun emplacements and log barricades ashore. They recommended amtracs, amphibious tractors, be used instead of landing craft for the invasion.

Adm. Richmond Kelly Turner, amphibious commander, was impressed with the concept of NCDU men being swimmers as well as demolitioneers. With Turner's encouragement, Lt. Comdr. Kauffman at Fort Pierce designed a tough new program for the soon-to-be-designated UDTs to toughen *special* men for demanding duty. He felt a UDT man should be capable of ten times the physical effort he thought he was.

Lt. Comdr. John T. Koehler, commander of UDT-2, took the concept a step farther. Realizing that the future of UDT operations lay with swimmers, he abandoned conventional ties to watercraft, took to the sea, and began studying the use of fins and dive masks, compasses, and mine-detecting devices.

Kauffman's organizational setup became the pattern for all UDTs—each team consisting of one headquarters division and four operational platoons of three officers and 16 men each, for a total team strength of 100 men. Two NCDUs went to the Mediterranean, where they participated in the invasion of southern France. One went to England. Two UDTs were sent to Guadalcanal and three were assigned for use by Admiral Turner out of Hawaii.

By the time *Bennett* took Frogmen aboard off Saipan and I received my first astonished look at these blue-green camouflage-painted men with the black stripes, their operations as swimmers were becoming stabilized. They were being trained for close prelanding reconnaissance of reefs and beaches. Dropped from rubber boats, they swam and waded ashore where they planted and detonated underwater explosives to knock out man-made obstacles and mapped enemy minefields by swimming among the mines and counting them. They cut underwater cables to let enemy mines bob to the surface or blew the devices in place.

All this was accomplished under fierce Japanese shore defenses' fire while armed only with knives, carrying explosive packs, and wearing no more than sneakers, fins, swim trunks, and dive masks. Frogmen—a term coined by noncombatants because of the UDTs' blue-green camouflage paint—porpoised over the surface of the water, grabbing a breath of air as they could between mortar rounds and machine gun fire. Aspirants for service in UDT had to be in top physical condition, capable of swimming two miles at a stretch, and immune to sudden loud noises.

Frogmen caused a stir wherever they appeared. Deep chuckles of amused appreciation greeted the story of how Kauffman was called by the landing beach master for a consultation on the Saipan beachhead. He and a UDT lieutenant hailed a passing amtrac and rode it in. They were dressed in swimming trunks and sneakers, and still had stripes painted around their bodies.

A Marine looked out of his foxhole. "Christ, I've seen everything," he cracked. "We ain't even got the beach yet and the tourists are here already."

In preparation for the invasion of Guam, 200 UDT men worked around the clock blowing obstructions. A hand-painted sign greeted the first Marines of the invasion force to wade ashore: *Welcome, U.S. Marines. U.S.O. Two Blocks. Signed UDT Team #4.*

Although encountering Frogmen at Saipan and learning something about their legendary exploits had more impact on me than I first supposed, as time would tell, at the moment I was war-weary and wanted only to go home. Diving had lost much of its allure, to the point that I all but abandoned my idea of sea commandos. I associated diving and the underseas world with *death.* It started with the corpses in the *Arizona.* Then there was the shark and Dubiel. I couldn't help but look around for sharks every time I went over the side to clear the ship's screws or props or hull.

At Saipan after the invasion, sloppy line handling resulted in knotted lines in our screw. I had to dive into all that floating death in the harbor—bloated Jap cadavers bobbing mixed with dead cows, donkeys, goats, and dogs.

A thin film of hair, skin, and body fats slicked the surface of the water between the *Bennett* and an LST onto which we had been transferring ammunition when the lines fouled. Inland three or four miles, the muted thunder of the battle continued.

"Get some hooks and try to keep all this dead shit cleared away," I ordered my deck crew as I hooked an air line to the ship's air compressor and slipped overboard.

It took two hours to clear the screw. Above me and around me buoyed the grotesque swollen things that had once been human beings.

Too much death and dying, so much of it associated with the sea. Plus, the shrapnel lodged in my skull continued to give me problems. Big guns pounding at Saipan or Tinian or Guam pounded in my head at the same time. Sometimes the pain drove me to my knees.

Week after week, month after month, American forces marched toward Japan, island by island. Each time we thought the Japs had shot their wad, they dug in and kept fighting on the next beachhead. The weeks dragged on with deadly monotony.

As gun captain of the *Bennett*'s #2 five-inch gun, I drilled my gunners until their arms were six inches longer than normal from handling heavy shells and their legs were three inches shorter. Or so they complained. *Drill,* I preached, was the essence of success in battle—and survival. Although I seldom threatened my people, preferring to lead by example instead, short tempers all around, my own accelerated by headaches, meant I had to be ready to quell rebellion.

"See these?" I declared, displaying bos'n fists hardened from handling line and tackle in salt water. "My Navy ain't no goddamned democracy. I'm here to keep you fuckers alive and fighting."

Captain Hauck stopped by the boatswain's compartment for a cup of coffee and something from the food locker. I had taken the test for bos'n first class, but turned down the promotion.

"Roy, I'll guarantee you chief petty officer if you'll stay aboard the *Bennett,*" the skipper began.

"Cap'n, it doesn't make any difference now whether I'm first class, chief, or whatever," I replied. "I'm not staying. I'm not proud of the way I've been acting lately. I'm not myself. I lose patience easily trying to train these new kids coming aboard. These damned headaches. I'm not sure if I'm losing my mind or turning yellow. I'm not fit to train anyone anymore."

Uncle Phil nodded. "Boats, you're rough and you're loud, but you never shirk duty. I can count on you always being in the middle of a fight—whether it's with the Japs or a fistfight at a club when we're in port. You're the kind of guy America needs when there's a war going on. I'm not sure how you'll fit into the peacetime Navy, but right now we need you."

"I appreciate what you're saying, sir. But as soon as we kill these goddamned Japs and the lights go on all over the world again, I'm out of here. I'm going to marry my girl and live a *normal* life."

FOURTEEN

★ ★ ★ ★ ★

Victory over Japan. I was in Leyte Gulf on V-J Day. Warships shot off fireworks and filled the sky with ordnance in celebration. I gripped my aching head with both hands and tried to crush out the demons. I staggered to the railing as strength drained from my body. We were going home.

The only thing on my mind when I hit stateside after 27 months at sea and at war was Elizabeth, my Tawny. I donned dress blues and hailed a cab from the Brooklyn docks to the Morrises' big house on Long Island. Tawny's mother, whom I adored, met me at the door with a cry of pleased surprise and a warm hug. The look on her face, however, carried a warning. She looked away.

"Elizabeth's upstairs," she said. "I'm going to the store."

Foreboding leadened my feet as I climbed the stairs to Tawny's room. She hugged me, tentatively, and then began silently crying as we stood looking at each other for a long time, both of us filled with questions and answers neither seemed prepared to face.

I took her in my arms again and held her round and soft. I closed my eyes and willed back the tears. Mr. Macho, crying in a woman's arms.

She took me gently by the hand and led me to a crib where a baby girl was sleeping. The baby was about four months old. I stared. Seasick the Sailor was about to be sick.

I finally managed the question. "Yours?"

After a moment, she nodded. Then she explained that the father was the owner of the Casino Real for whom she began dancing after her gig ended at Radio City Music Hall.

She hadn't wanted to tell me about the baby while the war was still on. I was thankful to her for that at least.

She gave me back my engagement ring and I left. I needed a good drunk and a fight. The Navy *was* my home after all. It sure as hell wasn't in New York City with Elizabeth Marie "Tawny" Morris.

PART II

UDT: Underwater Warriors (1945–1960)

"In war, he mounts the
warrior's steed."
—Sir Walter Scott

FIFTEEN

★ ★ ★ ★ ★

Caught between the end of the war and an impending peacetime military, I rode out another few months on the aircraft carrier USS *Roosevelt.* Waiting before I made a decision about my future. I had to answer questions troubling many returning veterans. Had WWII and nearly four years of combat action turned me into an adrenaline junkie? Had I reached the point, in fact, where I preferred war over boredom?

What was so goddamned *special* about a nine-to-five civilian job, a little ticky-tacky house in the suburbs, grandchildren eventually, and Social Security? Roy Henry Boehm, something *special,* hanging around the VFW hall with all the other old coots telling war stories. Was that the only reason I survived the sinking of the *Duncan* and the shark—to end up at the VFW talking about what *could* have been?

Events seemed to make the decisions for me. *Roosevelt* pulled back into New York after a short cruise to the Mediterranean. Friends fixed me up with a date.

"You have to get out and meet a *nice* girl, Boehm."

"I don't want a *nice* girl."

Eleanor Wasson, my date, wasn't particularly good-looking, although she was attractive in a home-and-kitchen sort of way. She had mouse-colored hair pulled back into a severe bun, preached against makeup and dancing, but wore skirts so tight a ship's master-at-arms could have bounced a quarter off her ass. She had a tendency to be a bit squat and would probably turn matronly with age. She was honest, however, and dependable. A Seventh-Day Adventist, she had social skills that might prompt her to try to convert sinners at a cocktail party. From the beginning, she was bound and determined to save Roy Boehm's soul from the flaming bowels of hell.

The war was over. All my shipmates were getting married. I donned my dress blues with the bos'n second class crow on the sleeve, stood up like I had real balls, and said, "I do?"

I still had my headaches. Sometimes I felt like a bos'n had heated a marlin spike and driven it into my brain. The Navy finally had to do something about the headaches after what happened when Charley Ball, in charge of the ship's galley division, went on two weeks' leave and I volunteered to run his seven mess halls for him as well as my own deck division.

The noon meal one day pushed beef stew, not a favorite with the crew. Garbage cans consumed more than the men. I noticed when I made my rounds that three garbage cans in one of the mess halls were about to overflow. I pointed them out to one of the mess cooks, a stocky well-built kid from New York.

"Sailor, take those garbage cans out to the pier and empty them before they leak stew all over the place."

"Aye, aye, Boats. No problem."

I finished making my rounds and returned. Garbage cans had flooded the deck. Sailors were slipping and sliding.

"Hey," I hailed the New York mess cook. "I thought I told you to empty those cans."

"Keep your shirt on, Boats. I'll get around to it."

It was one of my headache days. I slugged the mess cook with a short right hook that splattered blood and teeth. Then I jerked him off the deck and shoved him ass down into one of the full garbage cans of stew. His head between his upthrust legs offered an excellent target. I did a little speed bag work on it until the garbage can with him in it fell over. I glared.

"When I tell you to do something, asshole, you do it."

The UCMJ had replaced the era of instant justice prevalent under the old Rocks and Shoals. The Navy was now a more sensitive, caring Navy. Which meant I probably faced a court-martial. The military no longer needed cannon fodder. Unauthorized *sneezing* could get you kicked out with few rights or benefits.

I marched directly from the mess hall to sick bay where I told the corpsman, "You gotta do something about these headaches. I just blacked out and hit a guy. Didn't even realize I was doing it."

I was sent to the "nuts and nerves" ward at Portsmouth Naval Hospital for evaluation. There was no such thing, those days, as post-traumatic delayed stress syndrome and not being able to "cope." X rays revealed the piece of shrapnel from the sinking of the *Duncan* had encapsulated and as it grew put pressure on my brain, causing severe headaches and, presumably, my bad temper.

It was dangerous surgery, what with the shrapnel so near the brain, but doctors said they had no other choice but to remove it. I was too damned tough to die after all I'd endured. During convalescence, the Navy gave me the option of immediately accepting a medical discharge or taking expiration of enlistment leave and applying for medical disability benefits once I was formally discharged. As I intended getting out anyhow, I applied for the latter. I left the USS *Roosevelt* and my Navy. I looked back at the aircraft carrier tied at the pier.

"Come on, honey," Ellie encouraged. "You'll like having a *real* life."

What had the last five years been?

Ellie soon gave birth to a baby son and I landed a job with the New York Aetna Elevator Company. I commuted to Brooklyn in a 1929 Chevy with bad brakes and lived on Long Island in a boardinghouse my mother-in-law owned. Mother-in-law didn't even display my picture. Ellie cleaned rooms during the day and I played bouncer-landlord at night.

I sucked in my discontent like a good trooper and did the best I could in a world of alien *civilians.* The more I saw of *civilians,* the more distasteful they became. It was a *boring* fucking life. Ups and downs in the elevator business were never the same as ups and downs diving in the ocean for the Navy. Somewhere deep in my brain, past the shrapnel scars, lurked still the feeling that I was destined for something *special.* I occasionally dreamed about daring undersea commando warriors.

I took off work and went down to the ocean and gazed out to the blue-gray horizon. It seemed appropriate that Dad should have always complained, "Who put the goddamned ocean so near the shore?"

On the 87th day of my exile, three days short of the maximum 90 within which I could still reenlist, I said to my wife, "Ellie, you can either stay here and be a civilian, or you can go with me. I'm going home."

I charged down to Church Street and reenlisted in the United States Navy with my old rate of boatswain's mate second class. I no longer had the headaches. That was probably due as much to my escaping civilian life as to the surgery on my cranium. I had a destiny again. I was bound for China.

SIXTEEN

★ ★ ★ ★ ★

Angry seas off Okinawa battered the USS *Furse,* DDR-882, radar picket destroyer, for three days as she steamed toward China and my first Far East cruise since the end of the war. Twin five-inch guns and a giant tripod mast to support sophisticated radar made the ship a bit top-heavy, especially in heavy weather. She loped along like an awkward foal, hanging out too long in a heavy roll, taking off from the crest of one roller to crash into the next with a shock that jarred her framework and rattled the crew's teeth in their skulls. Squall winds howled and moaned through the lines and riggings. Green water splashed and drummed washing over the decks. Seams parted. The hull cracked and the destroyer took on water in her fuel tanks and lower compartments.

Okinawan waters either made a seaman or broke him.

I repaired the gripes that secured a whaleboat and made my way through the stinging spray toward the bridge. A gunner's mate at the helm shouted down to me above the keening of the wind. "Rough enough for you, Boats?"

"Hell, no!" I shouted back. "Bet you can't roll her over."

The ship's captain choked on his coffee and spilled it trying to maintain balance on the rolling deck.

"Since you can evidently walk better than I, Boats," he said, "how about getting me another cup of tar?"

"No problem for a *sailor.*"

I laughed a roaring laugh in the face of the fledgling typhoon. God, it felt good to be *home.* To be back at sea to meet my destiny.

"Teach me how to speak Chinese," I requested of the ship's torpedo man, whose Chinese parents lived in San Francisco's Chinatown.

"Chinese is a race, not a language," he muttered. "We have a number of dialects."

"Teach me a dialect."

"Boats, I only know a few words."

"You ought to be ashamed not to speak your parents' language."

"Then you teach me German."

I saw his point.

"Why do you want to learn Chinese?" he asked.

"It'll be fun to go into a bar and order in Chinese."

He taught me a phrase that sounded something like: *Dow yaow ego pee-jo melee.* I could hardly wait to try it out. I was the only one aboard prepared to bridge the language gap when we reached China.

Furse pulled into Tsingtao, currently held by Nationalist President Chiang Kai-shek in his struggle against the communist Mao Tse-tung. The U.S. backed Chiang. Sailors on liberty poured off the ship and bellbottomed uptown. I bellied up to the bar and winked at my shipmates as a barmaid hustled toward us with a friendly professional smile and a working knowledge of waterfront English.

"Welcome aboard, Joe. Name you poison."

Everyone ordered in English. I winked again when it came my turn and blurted, *"Dow yaow ego pee-jo melee."*

The barmaid looked at me. She shrugged. "Have it you way, Joe."

The others finished their drinks and started another round.

"Hey, what happened to mine?" I protested.

"It coming. Keep you shirt on, Joe."

Presently, she set a glass containing a milky-looking substance in front of me.

"What the hell is *this?"*

"It what you order, Joe. Goat milk."

During the recent war, the Japanese remained faceless enemies to either kill or be killed by. In China, however, starting with my ordering goat milk, I experienced the beginning of a slow awakening to foreign cultural experiences that would serve me well as the United States drifted toward the concept and practice of unconventional warfare. Although I might not have realized it at the time, each such step I took led me inexorably toward a destiny I must have started carving out for myself the first time Swede placed a helmet over my head and sent me underwater. With time, Roy Henry Boehm was to become more and more unconventional, whereas the Navy remained only a little unconventional.

In Tsingtao, I became involved for the first time with more-or-less irregular troops as Chiang Kai-shek fought to keep Mao's forces from conquering the city. Fighting erupted on the city outskirts each evening as soon as night fell. Junks and sampans and foreign shipping filled the harbor, creating a city of slums on the water where life and commerce continued beneath the sounds of war. I stood on the deck of the *Furse* in the purple nightfall to listen to distant gunfire. Come morning, deck crews swept spent bullets off the weather decks.

As I had acquired some background in demolitions and weapons, I was assigned to train a platoon of Chiang's Nationalist troops. I caught a rickshaw at the piers and rode it to where a truck transported me to a long mud building cordoned off by wire and sandbags on the city's outskirts. A young, skinny lieutenant with a sad face, the platoon commander, presented me to his ragtag outfit. The men wore makeshift cotton uniforms and sandals and carried WWI Springfields and U.S.-surplus .45 pistols. The lieutenant gave me a swagger stick that concealed the blade of a bayonet.

"With which to discipline the troops," he explained in precise English. "To touch the troops with bare hands to discipline them is poor form."

I began by teaching the Nationalist soldiers how to field-strip, maintain, and fire their weapons. Eventually, I directed them into defensive and offensive tactics and acquired for training plastic explosives and some dynamite so old and unstable that nitro seeped through the wrappings. I never used the lieutenant's swagger stick.

While I worked with the troops in their compound, I made my first fascinating forays into the Oriental mind and the unique way Asians viewed life and war. The lieutenant platoon commander lived with the general population outside the compound. Next door to him in another mud hut lived a holy man, a very quiet, peaceful old man with a wispy gray beard hanging long from his chin like mist rising from a primordial sea. Li wore a dirty black robe over his birdlike body and a black cap that could have been either a beret or a yarmulke.

Soon, I was spending three hours with wise old Li for every one I worked with the Nationalists. I always entered his hut with a bow and folded prayer hands. He returned the formality. Then we sat cross-legged on rugs facing each other while women in the background served hot tea in tiny porcelain cups.

Li was a Confucianist. Confucius was known in the Western world chiefly as a wise man, a teacher speaking in moral maxims. To the Oriental mind, he was a discipline. Virtue through ritual, good manners, and a sense of propriety. A sense of honor through self-respect and respect for others. Emphasis on ritual and music created a moral harmony that at its highest political level made government unnecessary.

"You are a communist!" I exclaimed.

"Think about that," Li commanded in his excellent English. "Do you believe the communists have moral harmony when they bring about compliance through the use of force?"

I thought about it.

"Confucianism has won victory over a host of philosophies in the Orient," he said. "It will modify communism in Asia and China. The doctrines of Karl Marx and Confucius have no common meeting ground."

He smiled slightly. "How do you ensure compliance to society in America?" he asked.

"Well. We . . . we *punish* those who break the law."

"What is the goal of your society in regards to punishment?"

"Not to be punished. That is obvious."

"Regulation of your people is achieved through threats of punishment and the desire to avoid punishment?"

He had a way of trapping me.

"To regulate the people through threat of punishment," he said, "is to compel the people to comply by seeking to avoid jail rather than complying out of a sense of honor or shame. Is that not so?"

He applied the same logic to topic after topic.

"True manhood describes a state of mind, a state one searches for, attains, feels at peace in, departs from, and dwells in as he dwells in a house."

I visited Li for the last time the day before *Furse* pulled out of port. The United States was withdrawing from China to permit Mao and the Nationalists to work out China's destiny between them. At least we were leaving the country with both its dignity and our own dignity intact.

"You are a warrior," Li said to me in farewell, "who has a mind willing to learn. As a warrior, you will be involved in much and have many things upon which to think. Guerrilla wars, both nationalist and revolutionary, will by their very nature flare up in many countries. Outbreaks may be initiated on many grounds, but all will be supported by communism and all will be anti-Western."

Leaving the old man left a void somewhere inside. I couldn't help thinking about his comments on guerrilla warfare. In the Philippines, I had witnessed smaller unconventional forces overwhelming Japanese conventional forces. It appeared I could not avoid my youthful idea of sea commandos.

Still, I had to face facts. Although unconventional warfare had been practiced in America by Indians, frontiersmen, "Leathershirts," Roger's Rangers, and other patriots during the Revolutionary War, by guerrilla bands such as Quantrill's Raiders during the Civil War, and even by Yank outfits like Merrill's Marauders in WWII, current prospects of the United States participating in guerrilla warfare along the teachings of Mao were as alien to the American military mind as the teachings of Confucius. The Navy especially was not yet ready for "new" concepts. The Navy remained steeped in the doctrines of large-scale global conflict.

I began studying Mao and Sun Tzu, picking up everything I could find on unconventional doctrine, tactics, and strategy. I became immersed in it, fascinated. Would there, I wondered, ever be room in the U.S. Navy for the Mao in me?

SEVENTEEN

★ ★ ★ ★ ★

In San Diego, I wired a tin cup to the manifold of a 1937 Pontiac coupe, loaded up Ellie and baby Roy, and set out cross-country for the U.S. Navy Mine Countermeasures Station in Panama City, Florida. The tin cup on the manifold was for warming bottles and baby food. I had requested a diving assignment and received it. It was my first in which diving was my principal duty.

Panama City gave me more experience in deep-sea diving than I had acquired since back when the Swede let me hang around his dive locker. Much of the work was experimental and secret. We secured hydrophones and magnetic recording devices to the ocean floor, then ran different kinds of vessels across the surface to test the equipment's ability to take magnetic signatures and identify the type of craft. Without being specifically aware of it, I was in training for greater challenges looming in the not-too-distant future.

Diving to 75 feet, another diver named Young and I guided concrete posts being lowered by a floating crane. Using underwater-to-surface radios, we directed the posts to positions in the bottom mud about 30 feet apart. Then huge cement crossbeams were lowered and attached to the posts to support the hydrophones.

Movement underseas was in slow motion. The water at depth was murky, filled with plankton and other microbiology. In his heavy suit and with his great caged head, Young reminded me of a Jules Verne character, shadowy and a bit unreal as he performed his slow ballet of guiding the opposite end of my long crossbeam to its post. The beam seemed to float on the cable that secured it in the center to the crane above on its barge.

Suddenly, the cable snapped. Its frayed end recoiled and whipped through the sea like a frenzied eel. The heavy concrete beam fell with amazing swiftness, entangling and trapping our air hoses and safety lines underneath it.

I was jerked off my feet, dusting up a cloud of blinding silt. I struggled frantically to keep my feet lower than my helmet. Even the best hard-hat suits leaked a little and filled the feet of the suit with water. A diver could drown in his own suit if he got turned upside down.

I gagged on salt water as I kicked and pushed, struggling for balance. Unable to see through the silt. Afraid the beam might still be settling. I scrambled to my feet and took two steps before my lines jerked me down again. Like a dog on a short leash.

On my feet again. I took deep breaths while I reconsolidated. At least the beam hadn't pinched off my air supply. I forced jangled nerves to settle in the same slow way that silt settled. When I could see again, I found the heavy beam trapping my lines underneath it. Young signaled from the opposite end of the beam that he was in a similar predicament. My intercom still worked.

"This is an emergency," I radioed, trying not to sound like a hysterical woman. "Our lines are trapped. We need replacements."

Replacing one set of lines with a fresh set seemed a simple procedure. Except for certain details that made it as hairy as smacking a grizzly in the ass with a switch. The air hose had to be disconnected from the helmet. Normally, a nonreturn valve prevented air venting from the helmet and suit. A damaged or malfunctioning air connector could prevent reattachment of a fresh air line, causing the diver to gradually suffocate. Even worse, surrounding sea pressure could squeeze a diver right up into his helmet should a damaged nonreturn valve permit venting from the suit, creating a partial vacuum. I had heard horror stories of dive suits returned to the surface containing little but a basketful or so of blood, shit, brains, and guts.

"Hold on," came the reply from the surface ship. "We've sent for Squires."

No one was better at undersea rescue than Walter Squires. Back in 1939, he passed out while working to salvage the sunken submarine *Squallis* and blew to the surface. He was hauled in and taken back down to 165 feet in the decompression chamber. Doctors and medics worked over him in the chamber before finally pronouncing him dead and throwing a sheet over his face.

As the medics were leaving, the sheet slid off Squires. He pushed himself up to one elbow, his heart apparently restarted by the gases in his body, and asked, "Where the hell is everybody going?"

Now, nine years later, Squires sank next to me and pressed his full face mask to my eye window. Communications were difficult since he was not in a hard hat. He grinned at me and mouthed, "I know what I'm doing."

"Get my ass up and I'll believe you," I mouthed back.

He replaced my telephone and lifelines first. Then came the all-critical air line. He wrenched the trapped air hose loose from my helmet. Some bubbling. There wasn't supposed to be. My eyes widened.

Squires gave me a blast of air, then exhausted my suit to equalize pressure. He quickly tightened the fresh hose to my helmet. I was free.

I breathed deeply. I found I had been holding my breath. Squires gave me a thumbs up: *Go to the surface.* I hesitated momentarily as he moved off toward Young to release him. He gave me another signal: *It's under control.* I started up.

The sea, I thought, never failed to surprise and shock with its endless perils. It never let you forget that it was an alien environment, as unpredictable and dangerous as the shark that took Dubiel and left me. Still, I had survived it again. Roy Boehm had a destiny.

"Roy, I know this is how you want to live and I know no one can change you," Ellie cried. "But you must start thinking about your family. We have one son and another child on the way."

A wife and *two* kids. Not particularly unconventional for a sailor who still had unconventional on the brain.

EIGHTEEN

The end of WWII had looked like the end for American Frogmen. In 1945, there were 34 UDTs consisting of about 3,500 men. By 1946, most of the UDTs had been disbanded and their equipment sold as surplus. In 1948, all that remained was a skeleton crew of seven officers and 45 enlisted men.

Draper Kauffman's foresight may have created the Underwater Demolition Teams, but it was the insight of Francis Douglas Fane that prevented their extinction. While other officers with stars in their eyes moved on to "the real Navy," Commander Fane, better known as "Red Dog" until after his hair turned white, took charge of what remained of the dying UDTs on the East Coast.

Although Fane could not swim when the war began, was in fact afraid of the water, he volunteered for the secret UDTs. All he knew about them was that the duty was especially hazardous and involved the use of explosives. While on leave in Chicago, he took a crash course in swimming that prepared him well enough to qualify for UDT training. He became commanding officer of UDT-13.

He saw a great advantage in UDT swimmers being able to remain underwater for as long as possible. He began experimenting with breath-holding and hyperventilating. Soon, all his men could remain underwater for three or four minutes. One of his Frogs could hold his breath and swim three lengths of a swimming pool without surfacing. Several held their breath long enough to dive 100 feet and swim underneath a submerged submarine from one side to the other, and then surface.

Toward the end of the war, Fane and six other Frogmen engaged in an operation that led UDTs closer to the concept of guerrilla warfare. They swam to the Japanese island of Kiuschu where they accepted the surrender of a huge Japanese ammunition depot. The nearby mountains were honeycombed with gun revetments, which would have made a landing very bloody had the Japanese chosen to resist.

After the war, Fane struggled to retain UDTs and expand upon their capabilities.

"I realized," he explained to higher commanders, "that if we were going to come in, in future wars, we would have to be better prepared than just swimming on the surface as we did. So I thought of the idea of working underwater all the way. Working with submersibles out of submarines. Coming in surreptitiously at night. Of being dropped by helicopter into the water. I envisioned this whole system."

More than just envisioning a system, he researched, designed, and implemented it. The postwar role of UDT Frogmen stopped shrinking after 1948 as he worked with scientists around the world in designing open-circuit and closed-circuit underwater breathing apparatus. He developed new missions for his sea warriors. With the help of an underwater photographer named Eldridge Fennimore Johnson, he documented his work with swimmers and submersibles and showed the film to Adm. Gerald Wright, Chief of Naval Operations.

"My God!" the CNO exclaimed. "How long has this been going on?"

"About two years, sir."

"If you have any problems," Admiral Wright declared, "come and see me."

By the time the Korean War began, UDT training had been modified to include land operations, small unit tactics, and weapons. By action if not by name, UDT had come a long way toward becoming the underseas unconventional warriors I had long envisioned. Yet, I had paid little attention to them since the end of the war, assuming they were dead fish and that any movement to breed sea warriors would have to come from a new angle.

On 27 July 1950, the light cruiser USS *Worcester,* the *Wooster,* the *Big Woo,* pulled out of Greece with orders to join the Seventh Fleet off Korea. Having been transferred back to sea duty, I was bos'n mate first class in charge of the ship's Third Division, which included nearly half the *Wooster*'s gun mounts. Boats Boehm back to war. I had long ago come to terms with the idea that peace is boring, war is a challenge.

In Ceylon, I returned to ship with a shoe box under my arm. I saluted the OOD.

"What's in the shoe box, Boats?"

Most of the crew knew I still hauled around my old accordion, which I sometimes played. This was neither it nor my lunch.

"Shoes, sir," I said. Booze was still prohibited aboard ship.

"Let me see them," the officer said.

I tossed the box over the side with, "Hell, they didn't fit anyhow."

The OOD lifted his eyebrows at the sound of glass shattering when the box struck the "camel" that kept the ship from rubbing against the pier. "Must have been glass slippers," he commented drily. "You planned on going to a ball?"

"Yessir. In Korea."

The *Big Woo* joined the 77th Carrier Group in shelling the Korean coastline. For the Navy, Korea was a war primarily of support and not direct combat participation. Sound and fury. Big guns roaring and little offense from the enemy other than mines in the harbors. *Wooster* lay offshore in the Yellow Sea and fired her five- and six-inch batteries.

We covered the withdrawal of the U.S. Marines from the Frozen Chos'n and delivered fire missions on request. During the Inchon landing, the cruiser and her sister ships rode offshore as near the breakers as possible and belched continuous flame, the fury of our attacks shuddering the great warships and making ripples in the sea.

Perhaps, I thought, the era of the great naval sea battles like the one at Cape Esperance was over, never to be experienced again. I felt some reluctant nostalgia for the Tokyo Express and the crazy kamikazes. For the Navy, at least, the Cold War that followed the end of WWII produced a different, more boring war in which I felt a mere spectator.

My ancient Chinese friend Li in Tsingtao had convinced me that Cold War conflicts were apt to be uprisings of the "people" against their oppressors. Guerrilla warfare. If I expected unconventionality, Korea proved anything but. I chafed at my nonparticipation and bided my time. One day, I predicted, the brushfire wars would be over and the world would settle down to cloak-and-dagger behind-the-headlines *unconventional* warfare, per Mao Tse-tung. The Orient, I predicted, would lead the way in that style of war. Li believed the East would use unconventionality to one day rule the world.

Orientals had the work ethic, they were disciplined, they revered honor and respect, and they could be ruthless. They also had patience. If something was not accomplished in this lifetime, there was always the next lifetime.

Americans, on the other hand, I thought, were losing their qualities of greatness. Signs of decay already showed their roots. Korea was a war that tried America's faith, as would Vietnam a little more than a decade later.

"When a people lose faith in those appointed over them," said Confucius, 600 years before Christ, "then a government of the people is an impossibility."

Although I was largely unaware of it, seeing only my small part of the war, Korea proved to be the turning point for the teams. The Navy, grudgingly perhaps, was growing more amphibious in meeting Cold War realities. Almost under my nose, without my awareness, the UDTs were emerging ready and tailor-made for guerrilla warfare with a tremendous surge of unconventional activity.

In addition to maritime operations, UDTs conducted inland raids behind enemy lines. They cut off enemy supply lines by demolitioning railroad bridges and tunnels. They disrupted enemy food supplies by destroying North Korean fishing nets. They infiltrated and exfiltrated guerrilla soldiers inside enemy-held territory. Fighting both undersea and on the beaches. Shark under the water and tiger on land.

In the meantime, I looked to diving—but not necessarily to the little-known UDTs—as the pathway to eventual sea commandos. My journey to unconventional operations continued its circuitous route when I applied for admission to the Navy's First Class Diving School. I had been diving for 10 years, but this was my first formal diving school. Roy Boehm wanted to be ready to be at least a *participant* in any new venture to kick ass *unconventionally.*

NINETEEN

★ ★ ★ ★ ★

Although I had been diving for a decade, learning mostly by trial and error, formal training revealed how little I actually knew about it and how much farther I had to go. I stashed Ellie and the sons, Roy and Robert, in a 35-foot Anderson trailer near the U.S. Naval Gun Factory in Washington, D.C., and reported to the school. For the next few weeks I saw so little of my family Ellie made me show my ID before she would let me in the door.

A familiar voice hailed me the moment I showed up for training, as though its owner had been waiting. "Hey, Charlie!"

No one but Harry Richard "Lump-Lump" Williams called everybody "Charlie" so he wouldn't have to remember names. He loped up and enveloped my hand in a paw twice the size of an ordinary man's. He was only an inch or two taller than my five nine, but his shoulders were the width of a door. Short-cropped brown hair bristled. He and I had met off Korea when he was stationed aboard a sister ship to the *Big Woo.* We had gotten ourselves volunteered for the smokers—boxing matches—and ended up bashing each other around. He had the quickest reflexes of any man I had ever known. I would wind up for a right cross and he'd hook me with three lefts before I blinked.

"Hey, Lump! Built like Tarzan, hung like Mickey Mouse," I responded with a standing joke. "What the hell are you doing here?"

"Like this, Charlie. This gal says to me, 'Hey, baby?' Naturally, I says, 'Hey, baby' back. She wants to play house, but I tells her, 'All I want to do is drive your big car and play with your big tits.' It turns out she's the post commander's daughter. I had to haul anchor real fast. So, I heard you were going to diving school and here I am."

I had the feeling that friendship with Harry Dick the Lump was not going to be career enhancing.

Chief Warrant Bos'n Walter Dommagalla ran the school, along with his assistant, Bos'n Tom Moss. Both were respected in the experimental diving Navy. They and their instructors were perfectionists.

"While you are here," Bos'n Dommagalla greeted the students, "we will require your presence at all times. There will be no excuses such as, 'My wife, she . . .' or 'My car, it . . .' Both come under the category of 'Not now, dear.' If that's not understood, report immediately to the office with your seabag packed to pick up your orders to return to the fleet."

I hit the books. While Swede had taught me the application of the diving laws, such as Boyle's law and Charles's, I had never completely understood the physics of it all.

"Here, considering your low mentality," the instructors said, "we will walk you through diving physics a simple step at a time."

I learned that air is composed roughly of 78 percent N_2 (nitrogen) and 20.94 percent O_2 (oxygen). The remaining 1.06 percent is rare gases—carbon dioxide, hydrogen, neon, helium, krypton, and xenon. Nitrogen is the dangerous gas. Not only does it make a diver drunk at great depths, a condition known as "rapture of the deep" or "nitrogen narcosis," it also penetrates blood vessels under pressure and lodges in fatty tissues. A slow ascent from a deep dive allows gases to escape from tissues properly, a process known as *decompression,* while surfacing too rapidly might cause painful and possibly lethal decompression sickness, or *bends.*

Instructor Snake Dennison explained it with a rough example. "Bubbles lodging in a diver's joints is what causes *bends* or *caisson disease.* It works this way. An inverted coffee cup on the surface is full of air. Submerge the cup to a depth of one atmosphere—33⅓ feet—and approximately one-third of the cup would be full of water. The deeper you dive, the smaller grows the bubble of air until eventually it would be so small you could hardly see it. Small enough to seep through your blood vessels into tissue and bone joints.

"Reverse the process now. Place the almost-invisible bubble of air into a small balloon and start to the surface with it. The bubble expands to fill the balloon. By the time you reach the surface, you have a cupful of air again. But say you are at depth and fill the balloon with a cupful of *compressed* air and start to the surface. The balloon would pop. That's the same thing that happens to your lungs if you fill them at depth and start up too quickly. They'd rupture and give you an air embolism. It could kill you unless you recompress immediately.

"Recompression can be accomplished by taking you back down to depth in either the sea itself or a decompression chamber to recompress the bubbles and ease them back off slowly."

I learned to mix gases as a breathing medium, how to

extract CO_2 from recycled air, and how to use decompression tables. I became more proficient in hard-hat diving while practicing underwater welding, cutting, construction, and salvage. SCUBA remained in the experimental stages. Still thinking of my commandos, I ached to experiment with self-contained breathing. The only way sea warriors could ever be used effectively was to free them from their telltale air hoses, lifelines, and surface support crews.

"Leave tank diving to the Frogmen," I was advised. "SCUBA will never be as effective as hard hats. You'll never be able to get the depth."

"Do you believe *this* is as far as the Navy will go in using divers in war?" I asked Petty Officer Fogwell, one of the instructors.

Foggy was a wiry little man who had lost one eye in a diving accident. He often stopped by the 8th Street Bar with Lump-Lump and me after hours. He would drop his glass eye into his beer to watch it when he had to go to the head. A story went around that he inadvertently drank his own eye once. He recovered it, but the experience left him with a shitty outlook on life.

"What else could you use divers for?" Foggy grumbled.

"Undersea commandos," I blurted.

He looked at me like I had lost my mind. "I have to drain my bilges," he said. "Watch my beer for me. On second thought," he added, taking out his eye, "I'll watch it myself."

I went through diving school with a broad grin and an attitude. I felt so natural underwater, I boasted to Lump-Lump, that even the sharks wouldn't tangle with me anymore.

"I wouldn't eat you either, Charlie," Lump conceded. "You're so nasty and tough you'd give a shark terminal diarrhea."

During neutral buoyancy exams, divers in full hard-hat gear were dunked into a diving tank filled with 10 feet of water. We had to manipulate the air in the suit to float neutral for a minimum of four minutes without either surfacing or sinking.

I balanced for seven minutes. Snake Dennison watched

through the little window in the side of the tank. "Okay, red diver," he said, finally. "Prepare to surface."

"What kind of mark did you give me?" I asked with a smug grin.

He didn't look up. "Three point seven five."

"That was a *perfect* balancing dive!" I cried, outraged.

"Look, Boehm. I'm a three point eight five diver myself. You sure as hell ain't any better than I am."

I laughed. "Damned if you don't learn something new every day."

Lump-Lump and I were scheduled to report to USS *Penguin,* ASR-12, a submarine rescue vessel out of Key West, Florida, following the end of the school. The two warrant officers, Bos'ns Dommagalla and Moss, were also going to the *Penguin.* Somehow, my orders were changed, assigning me to the USS *Skylark* instead.

"How did that happen?" I asked the school's senior officer.

He laughed. "I can't understand it."

By this time, my old friend, sea daddy, ex-commander, and fellow survivor of the *Duncan,* Cpt. Whitey Taylor, was a senior captain in the Bureau of the Navy in Washington. His secretary stopped me in the outer office.

"I'd like to see Cap'n Taylor," I said.

"Do you have an appointment?"

"You know damned well I don't."

A voice suddenly boomed from behind the inner door. "Does that ugly, gravel-voiced sailor out there happen to be named Boehm?" Captain Taylor roared. "Send him on in before he kicks the door down."

I winked at the secretary.

"Damn," the captain said, "it's good to see a real blue-water swabbie in this brass-heavy political circus they call D.C."

We kicked around old times. Then I said, "Sir, I'm not here under false colors. I need a favor."

"Then we don't have to work up to the problem delicately, do we?"

"Hell no, sir."

Even after my meeting, I was still scheduled for the *Skylark* up to the last day. I figured Captain Taylor couldn't help me. Seabag in hand, I was checking out of the school when a personnel yeoman dashed in.

"Hey, Boehm. Hold on. We have a change of orders for you. You're going to *Penguin* instead."

I presented the amended orders to the officer who had changed them in the first place.

"How in hell did that happen?" he asked.

It was my turn to laugh. "I can't understand it."

It was neither the first time nor the last that Cpt. Whitey Taylor appeared in my corner. His changing my orders turned into an unforeseen and comical set of circumstances launching me directly into unconventional warfare.

TWENTY

★ ★ ★ ★ ★

It was almost like it was planned by some higher fate that I be thrown aboard the *Penguin* with the grandest assortment of characters and scalawags ever to sail the high seas. There was Lump-Lump, of course, who could always be counted on for an inappropriate laugh. Then there was the cook, a boozer named Paevie who started predicting the end of the world, along with two mischievous Heckle-and-Jeckle deck apes named Clements and Holloran. Chief Warrants Moss and Dommagalla from the diving school were always coming up with new diving experiments requiring a sacrificial diver as guinea pig.

"Anytime you need an animal for your experiments," Lump-Lump volunteered, "you can call on Boehm. I ain't figured out what *kind* of an animal he is, but he's definitely an animal."

After Lump and I reported aboard the *Penguin* in Key West, Chief Bos'n Dommagalla ordered us to take a crew and stow a load of line, chain, fair lead blocks, and other gear in forward stowage. The added weight brought the bow down and the stern up.

"That'll never do," the chief bos'n declared. "Move it aft."

That brought the bow up and the stern down.

Lump and I were catching a breather when we heard voices. The captain and Chief Bos'n Dommagalla.

"We are down in the stern," the skipper said. "We had better move about half of this cordage forward to trim ship."

"You're right, sir," the chief bos'n agreed. "I'll have them get started on it right away."

Harry Dick the Lump straightened up wearily and looked at the bos'n. "Hey, Bos'n," he said, true to form, "this shit ain't like an erection. You don't move it with a thought."

Bos'n Dommagalla had his own sense of humor. During a fleet inspection, a visiting officer asked him, "How do you work these guys so hard and have them still look so happy?"

"Dog biscuits," Dommagalla replied, deadpan. He took a Milk Bone out of his pocket and munched on it. Almost everyone carried dog biscuits for the ship's mascot, a boxer named Bowser. "They're good for your teeth too. Sure you won't have one?"

Penguin was responsible for taking care of the 12 submarines in her Key West squadron. The primary purpose of an ASR was to rescue crews from stricken submarines. The rescue diving bell for extracting sunken sailors was seven feet in circumference and large enough to accommodate five men at a time. It was lowered into the sea by winch. Either a diver or an operator inside the bell, depending upon the depth of the water, mated the lower hatch of the bell to the submarine's topside hatch to permit shipwrecked seamen to escape from the disabled boat into the bell, which was then resealed and winched to the surface.

It was a hairy operation fraught with the possibility of mishap. The bell could always be jerked or swept off its mating with the sub to flood the submarine with high-pressure seawater. An Event 1000, a practice rescue, was performed annually by each submarine in the squadron.

Chief Warrant Tom Moss nonetheless had plenty of time to continue his underwater experiments. His adventures usually involved Lump-Lump and me, since we had been his students at the diving school in D.C. Some of his first ventures had to do with SCUBA and with experimental Aqua-Lungs. UDTs were starting to use three-bottle open-circuit tanks and breathing apparatus. The rest of the diving fleet, including submarine rescue, went to two-bottle units, much like those in modern use except they were larger and heavier.

I was ecstatic over the implications of having finally cut the umbilical air line and therefore a willing subject for Bos'n Moss's undertakings. SCUBA advanced to *probable* the possibility of highly mobile undersea unconventional warriors.

The newly established Underwater Swim School at Key West had an N_2–O_2 mixed-gas rig, strictly experimental. The idea behind the closed-circuit rig was to eliminate telltale bubbles and permit divers to go deeper and stay longer with greater mobility and less decompression. Used air was expelled into a tube that filtered it through a rebreather containing mostly lime. The rebreather extracted CO_2, replaced oxygen, and restarted the cycle.

The thing had been tested in diver tanks, where rescue was only seconds away or eight feet up in the event of failure—but it had never been taken on an open-water dive. Moss and the Swim School needed an animal to test it.

I shrugged into the heavy webbing harness that contained the two heavy tanks and the lime filter and cast an anxious glance across the bay from the pier to the quay wall. Seawater broke in white mares' tails over the distant wall of stones, about two miles away. I knew the average depth of the harbor to be about 50 feet.

Moss patted me on the shoulder and grinned. "I'll be following you in the boat," he assured me.

"There are no bubbles. How will you know where I am?"

"Just stay on course. If it's any comfort, the system has not failed even once in the test tank." He paused. "Well, there was that one time when—"

"I don't want to hear it, Bos'n."

I slipped into the warm water, diving. The heavy tanks slid me along the mud-sand directly to the bottom. I crawled along like a crippled crab. A school of yellowtails flashed by, as though mocking my clumsy progress. A nurse shark stared. It was harmless, but I hated fucking sharks. I waved it away and continued pulling myself along the bottom. The tanks felt like two boulders on my back. If underseas commandos were ever going to use them, Moss and his fish brains would have to come up with something lighter than a submarine on your back.

I thought that since I couldn't get off the bottom I would have to crawl up on the quay wall like a salamander when I reached it. Instead, the tanks became buoys as I used air, leaving semivacuums. I had to fight to stay underwater. By the time I reached the quay wall, my ass and the tanks were bobbing on the surface like fishing corks. I kept my head thrust underwater in order to legitimately claim I made the entire swim submerged.

Bos'n Moss in the motor whaleboat was all grins. "We can fix it," he said. "You left no bubbles. We had no idea where you were until your big ass started bobbing up."

UDT reentered the picture in a roundabout way through the loss of one of the *Penguin*'s three cooks, Paevie, who worked for my deck division, and his subsequent replacement by Clements and Holloran.

Paevie had two obvious vices, both of which were obsessive and interlinked. One was booze, the other religion. Whenever he got drunk, he started predicting the end of the world and shouting, "Repent! Sinners, repent!" He would stagger-march to the jail in downtown Key West and stand outside with his guitar, singing "Bringing in the Sheaves."

One afternoon while the *Penguin* sat in the shipyard for

yard repairs, Lump and I found Paevie huddled in a corner of the galley, mumbling, "It's in the book. It's in the book," while the crew threatened to keelhaul him for having the effrontery to serve creamed sardines on toast for lunch. Lump and I felt he needed some divine guidance.

"I'm inspired to think of Samson," I said. "You know. The guy who took the jawbone and beat the ass off 10,000 Philadelphians. I don't know what Samson did to piss off them Philadelphians, but it couldn't have been anything as bad as serving creamed sardines on toast."

Paevie stared through confused, bloodshot eyes. "It's in the book," he murmured.

The next morning he was gone. AWOL. Lump and I blew the cast-iron lids off his stove trying to prepare breakfast. The watch stuck his head into the smoke-filled galley.

"What the hell happened in here?"

Lump shrugged innocently. "We lost the keys to the refrigerator and had to blow the door open with plastics," he said.

The Florida Highway Patrol picked up Paevie roller-skating north on Highway 1 with a bottle of booze underneath one arm and his Bible underneath the other.

"It's in the book," he mumbled.

"*What's* in the book?"

"It's in the book."

Psychiatrists must have leaped for joy when the authorities presented to them fresh material for their Medical Shrinks Journal. Paevie never returned to the *Penguin.* I figured, years later, it might have been Paevie underneath all that Tammy Bakker makeup.

Heckle and Jeckle in the form of Clements and Holloran showed up to take Paevie's place. I couldn't let them play with fire in the galley, so someone else moved up to cook and the disaster twins went out on deck. They had already been booted out of the Arlington National Cemetery Honor Guard.

It appeared their career change occurred because of an all-night rain prior to a burial. The officer-in-charge of the

Honor Guard led the solemn procession through the cemetery on a morning still dull and dreary and dripping water. He slipped and fell into an open grave and couldn't climb the slippery red clay walls. The Guard had been trained to accept any catastrophe and continue marching. However, the sight of the officer in the grave, white dress cap jarred over one ear, white gloves clawing at red clay, sent Heckle and Jeckle into peals of laughter. The entire Honor Guard broke up.

The Navy promptly settled the matter of the Honor Guard that could not contain itself. *Hide the bastards.* Clements and Holloran ended up aboard the *Penguin* at the southernmost point of the United States, where their antics and wry humor kept them on the edge of disaster with the skipper.

The captain finally had enough of them following an afternoon during which I assigned the pair to swabbing the forward decks. Eaten up with the rifle drills they learned while in the Honor Guard, the duo marched in perfect step across the deck, swabs dripping dirty water at right shoulder arms. Just as they were executing the Queen Anne Salute in perfect precision, the skipper and Bos'n Dommagalla emerged on deck from the officers' mess. Spinning their swabs, Heckle and Jeckle each dropped to one knee, left hand across the chest, palm down, while the shafts of their swabs snapped smartly into position against their right arms. Filthy water sprayed the shoes and neatly starched khaki uniforms of both the skipper and the chief bos'n.

"That's the final straw," the captain decreed. "Boats, you do something about those two—or else."

A notice had arrived with the morning reports soliciting volunteers for Underwater Demolition Training. I summoned the pranksters to the personnel office.

"This is a good deal," I assured them. "You should volunteer while you're still able."

"How come you're not going yourself, Boats, if it's such a good deal?" Holloran demanded.

"I've already signed up," I lied.

Lump-Lump Williams happened to overhear the exchange as he charged down the ladder. He lifted one eyebrow. "You're going to UDT, Roy?"

"Lump, we're all going to be *Frogmen!*" Clements cheered.

Harry Dick hesitated perhaps one second. Then he pointed a thick finger at the personnel clerk. "Charlie, put me down for that Frogman stuff too."

UDT orders came in for my troublemakers and for Lump-Lump a few weeks later.

"I got my orders, Roysi," Lump said. "Did you get yours?"

"Jesus, Lump. I thought you knew. I was just trying to get rid of Clem and Holloran."

TWENTY-ONE

★ ★ ★ ★ ★

Damned if I didn't miss Two Lump when he shipped out for UDT with Heckle and Jeckle. I considered volunteering also, to fulfill my longtime dream about underwater warriors, but I reminded myself that I was 31 years old and slowing down. *Young* men had difficulty surviving UDT. I continued to procrastinate, arguing with myself the pros and cons of pursuing an old fantasy. Didn't I have to face reality?

In July, *Penguin* steamed south to Saint Thomas in the Virgin Islands to support submarine operations with UDT advanced underwater training. There, in the warm Caribbean, it was easy to slip into the slower, easier life of the islands and accept that while Boehm might once have had amazing dreams, in fact still nurtured them, he was rapidly approaching middle age. Christ, I was halfway to retirement.

Tom Moss and I dived at every opportunity in waters as clear as air. We speared grouper and snared lobster for the ship's crew. Fresh seafood. No more creamed sardines *à la Paevie.*

Moss, another diver named Campion, and I were spear-fishing out of a whaleboat in 40 feet of water between Saint Thomas and Saint Johns when I spotted a shark basking on the bottom. It was a blacktip about eight feet long, one of the so-called man-eaters. A chill trickled along my spine as I flashbacked to Cape Esperance and the shark's snatching Dubiel. I had carried around inside me for a dozen years the nightmare of the shark and Dubiel and Dubiel's blood trailing off into the deep.

Rarely did you encounter a shark not in perpetual motion. Suddenly, it occurred to me that I had never extracted revenge for that long-ago day of terror. On an irresistible impulse and with a flick of my fins, I dove straight toward the unsuspecting fish. I ripped my combat knife from its sheath at my belt. Air bubbles trailed off behind me in a thin stream. Campion treaded water in surprise, posed like a question mark.

I wanted to kill this shark more than I had ever wanted anything. Killing it had to be up close and personal. *Mano a mano.* I had to prove to myself that my greatest enemy was not invincible. Subconsciously at least, I must have realized that Dubiel's shark had bruised something vital inside me that prevented my further underwater advancement. I had to get rid of that mental block if I hoped ever to move on.

I became the predator. I flew swiftly through the clear seawater, coming down on top of the fish from slightly behind. He sensed my approach, but it was too late. As it had been too late for Dubiel.

Sharks are not slick and slimy like most fish. Their skin is as rough as a wood rasp. I grabbed the shark's left fin close to its body, knife poised for a death blow to the creature's rudimentary brain stem.

The knife flashed. Blood spurted.

I missed the brain stem. The big fish *exploded.* The ride was on. With my legs and one arm wrapped around the fish, I stuck to its sandpaper hide like wool to a rasp. We thrashed across the bottom, boiling up sand and silt and blood. I kept stabbing the fish with my knife, polluting the water with an oily stream of blood and a constant flush of unspoken invective.

I stabbed the sonofabitch and I stabbed it. It twisted like a catfish on a line with me riding it. Around and twisting like a bolt of gunmetal gray lightning.

Its hide rasped skin from my cheeks and hands and legs and belly.

I sank teeth into my breathing mouthpiece to keep it from being ripped from my mouth and drowning me. Water filled my mask; it stung my eyes, half blinding me.

I wouldn't let go. I *couldn't* let go.

The wounded shark darted for an underwater cave I had explored earlier. It was shallow and dead-ended. I released the fish at the cave's entrance. The confined space would have torn the air tanks from my back.

The fish crashed blindly into the dead end.

Sonofabitch. Now it knew the terror I had known.

It switched ends as quickly as a cat and charged me. I glimpsed its sleek steel gray body through the stinging salt water in my mask. Black lifeless eyes like chips of anthracite coal. Rows of vicious teeth.

Sonofabitch.

I mounted it again as it tried to ram past me in the narrow opening.

Stabbing. Stabbing. Filling the water with a pink cloud. Knife point biting into the animal. Twenty times. Thirty. Forty.

I felt its muscled body begin twitching. Then, slowly, in its death throes, with me still attached to it, the blacktip sank to the sandy bottom. I cleared water from my mask in time to greet Tom Moss diving toward me. He jabbed his finger into the sea.

"You crazy bastard," he mouthed around his air piece.

The struggle and the blood in the water would attract other predators. I later learned that Tom had spotted a number of surface fins slicing in our direction. I pointed at my dying fish. I wasn't going to leave without it.

Moss circled, hurrying me on. I grasped the slender part next to the shark's tail fin and started to the surface. Moss was waving frantically. *Shark! Shark!*

Fuck 'em. I had slain the monster's mystique and destroyed the power it held over me. Sharks were *not* the ultimate predators of the sea. Man was the ultimate predator. On sea, on land, and in the air, it was *man.*

I lashed the conquered fish to the side of our whaleboat, like Hemingway's hero had done with his great fish in *The Old Man and the Sea.* I had been scraped and torn raw from the fierce battle, but I grinned happily. Hell, I wasn't too old for UDT. I wasn't too old for *anything.* I'd never be too old.

I looked at Bos'n Moss. I was still grinning. "Will you approve my transfer chit to UDT school?" I asked suddenly.

"Agewise, you're on the borderline, Roy."

I slapped the dead shark. "You call me *old,* after this?"

"Tell you what, Roy. I'll sign your UDT chit if you can swim the two and a half miles back to the ship in less than two hours."

"You're on," I called back over my shoulder as I dove overboard.

TWENTY-TWO

★ ★ ★ ★ ★

Psychiatrists and psychologists have had field days over the years trying to figure out what kind of man it takes to succeed in Special Warfare units such as UDT, SEALs, and Army Special Forces. Trying to predict who might endure the torture of pain, fatigue, humiliation, mental and physical exhaustion, cold, and heat to complete the training phases of these special schools. The profile of the ideal candidate calls for a man drug free, morally acceptable (within certain reasonable limits), capable of passing a security check, intelligent, and naturally phlegmatic under pressure. He must have endurance, physical strength, a high threshold for pain and discomfort, and a sense of humor in order to endure immense stress without falling apart.

If there is a common physical type in Special Warfare, it is a guy of average build, medium height and weight *who simply will not quit,* no matter what. You can always give a man training, but you're wasting your time if he doesn't have heart.

"Who comes first, me or the Navy?" demanded Ellie, long-suffering and pregnant with our third child, after I was accepted for UDT.

"I sure wish you'd quit asking me that," I responded. "Hell, there is only *one* Navy."

Ellie proceeded to Long Island with our two sons to stay with her folks and prepare for the launching of our newest arrival while I reported to NAVPHIBSCOL, Navy Amphibious School, at Little Creek, Virginia, for UDTR. When daughter Kathy was born, she was the only one of the three offspring to inherit her old man's abrasive and adventurous spirit.

"If one of them *had* to be like you," Ellie wailed, "why did it have to be our daughter?"

Over a decade had passed since my brief introduction to Frogmen at Tinian. After almost dying following WWII, UDT had revived, pushed by "Red Dog" Fane. The West Coast now had three UDTs—UDTs 11, 12, and 13. The East Coast had two—UDTs 21 and 22. I showed up at Little Creek with my seabag and some apprehension about starting, at age 31, the toughest goddamned course in the U.S. military.

"Charlie! Charlie!" came that same familiar call that had greeted me when I reported for First Class Diving School. It was becoming a habit, always being welcomed by Lump-Lump Williams. "About time your ass showed up, Roysi. I've been tempted to call the admiral and tell him how you tricked us."

Clements was with him. He and Lump had just graduated from UDTR, Class 12.

"Where's Holloran?" I asked.

"He didn't make it. You just pay attention to your own survival. It's going to be a pleasure watching you hurt after what you done to us."

I was the oldest man of the approximately 140 who began UDTR, Class 13, "Lucky 13," in July 1954. George Walsh was the next oldest student, only two or three years younger than I. He teamed up with the pygmy Lenny Waugh during buddy selections. I stood to one side, knowing the young bucks wouldn't want to be saddled with an "old man." Training promised to be hard enough without being harnessed to Methuselah for a swim buddy.

Two of us were left standing at the end of the selections, like kids unchosen in sandlot baseball. I stared at a scrawny kid who had already demonstrated a tendency to be a smartass. I was to discover he made Lump-Lump look like a preacher.

"It looks like you and me," I said. "What's your name?"

"Digger."

"You got a fucking *real* name?"

"Eddie O'Toole."

"Let me tell you something, Eddie 'Digger' O'Toole. When all the rest of these guys are gone, you and I are still going to be going strong. Understand what I just told you?"

"You got that right, Pappy. We are going to finish."

UDTR proved to be a lot like boot camp, only longer and several thousand times harder. Trainees were assigned 16 each to a row of World War II–era Quonset huts with steel curved walls and rough wooden floors. Heads and showers occupied separate buildings.

We were issued green cotton utility uniforms, heavy boondocker boots, and red-painted helmet liners with our numbers printed on them. My number was 76. I started shouting, "That's the spirit! The Spirit of '76!" whenever I had to drop for punishment push-ups. The liners were worn constantly except inside a building. All a student had to do to quit was take off his liner and place it on the ground. He was gone back to the fleet within the hour, no questions asked. Officers and enlisted men were treated the same, except officers were referred to as "Shithead, *sir.*"

The first four weeks were heavy in physical training and abuse with almost no classroom instruction. No use wasting time teaching those who were going to quit when things got tough. But even when classes started, there was little relief from the physical. UDT trainees went *everywhere* on the run.

"What are you doin', shithead? Run, *run,* RUN!"

It was the same thing in formation. *"Forward! Double-time, march. . . !"* Hard, pounding runs in heavy boondockers, hot uniforms, and bouncing helmet liners. Six or seven miles in the loose sand along the beaches of Chesapeake Bay to Mount Suribachi, the largest sand dune on Beach 7. Instructors ran with us, sometimes *backwards,* harassing and tormenting and torturing us. Push-ups were the penalty for the most minor transgression.

"Get down! Get down! Knock 'em out!"

"How many, sir?"

"Do 'em until *I* get tired, shit-for-brains."

"That's the spirit!"

Digger dropped with me and I dropped with him. "Buddies, sir!" The other buddies started doing the same thing.

The instructors rode us hard, testing us, trying to make us quit if quit was in us. Instructor Kiethline got in my face. *"You fucking lowlife Nazi kraut. You are lower than whaleshit, Boehm, and whaleshit lies at the bottom of the ocean. You ain't gonna make it, kraut. I'm making it my personal mission in life to get your loudmouthed ass kicked out. . . ."*

I surged from ranks to clean Kiethline's clock for him. Lenny Waugh, George Walsh, and Digger slammed me against a tree.

"Boehm, you fucking idiot. That's what he *wants* you to do. He's trying to see if you can take the bullshit. You touch him, you're back in the fleet tomorrow and fucked from now on."

My temper had nearly destroyed for me the opportunity for which I'd yearned for over 10 years—the chance at undersea unconventional warfare. I never lost control again.

Lt. "Whiskey Al" Hodge was the training officer and one hell of an athlete.

"It doesn't make any difference if you come in last every time—as long as you *do* come in," he lectured. "You'll make it to graduation in November and then into the teams as long as you keep going and don't quit."

The first guy quit on the third day. He couldn't take the harassment. He removed his red helmet liner and just quit. That started the exodus. The Quonsets gradually began to empty. Fewer and fewer red liners showed up for *"Forward. Double-time, march!"*

"You bunch of pukes. You whaleshit Pollacks, kikes, spics, krauts, and niggers! You ain't gonna make it. This class will graduate in a telephone booth."

I saw the hurt and strain in the face of my miniature swim

buddy, as he must have seen it in mine. We kept each other pumped up, tried to pump up the others.

"Bastards ain't going to flush us. Right, Pappy?"

"Right, Digger. We don't know the word *quit.*"

Each exercise was called an "evolution" and assigned a name. The *Death Trap* suspended two perpendicular ropes 15 feet above a muddy pond. Trainees crawled across the pond on the ropes while instructors tried to dislodge us and explosions jarred our teeth and splattered us with mud and water.

Around the World was an obstacle course run by a seven-man boat crew carrying an IBL (Inflatable Boat, Large). An IBL was 14 feet long, 8 feet wide, and weighed a staggering 400 pounds.

The evolution began at night with the crew pulling, carrying, or paddling the boat through hundreds of yards of swamp and muck in order to reach a seawall jetty bordering a channel entrance from Chesapeake Bay. The course then led across the slippery rock to the channel, which we paddled across at full speed in order to climb another riprap wall on the other side. Then we paddled a long open stretch of water along the bay, guiding ourselves by landmarks all but invisible in the darkness.

Beaching the IBL, we carried it, running, over barbed wire, ditches, canals, mudflats, and through and around thickets and other obstacles until we gained the final checkpoint—Mount Suribachi. The boat had to be deposited *on top of* the giant sand dune. The loose sand was too yielding to crawl up it and too steep to walk up it. We had to side-crawl up it like a bunch of crabs with the IBL on our heads.

Slide for Life was a tall wooden tower with long ropes angling down from one side across a wide pond of deep stagnant water. You had to straddle the rope and slide down to the ground on the other side of the pond without falling into the water.

The *Obstacle Course* was a series of 26 torture devices through which a trainee scurried while being timed. Zigzag lines of elevated logs; climbing nets 50 feet straight up; the belly robber; the wall climb . . .

The evolution of choice for group punishment was *The Circus.* A *Circus* was nothing but ass-busting, burnout PT done until we dropped from exhaustion.

Biting, gouging, and wrestling were allowed and encouraged in *Murder Ball,* a game of mayhem and brute force something like football without any rules. During one game early in training, George Walsh descended upon me with evil intent to squash and maim. I heard a sickening *pop!* and felt cartilage tearing in my left knee.

The leg quickly swelled to twice its normal size. I hobbled around like a cripple without a crutch. Digger felt certain I was done for.

"I *want* this," I told him. "Don't ever count me out."

They would have to kill me to make me take off my red helmet and quit. I did everything all the other future Frogmen did, it just took me longer. Hobbling but still running, I brought up the tail of the pack.

"You're too fucking old, Boehm. You're an old man!" instructors jeered. *"Old and crippled. A useless piece of shit and the stupidest trainee in the whole U.S. Navy. Come on, Boehm. Why don't you quit? That's all you have to do. Quit before you kill yourself. You don't have to do this shit anymore. You're not going to make it anyhow."*

"I ain't quittin'!"

Standing at rigid attention after a run, knee swollen and throbbing like a toothache. Instructors machine-gunned me with questions.

"What exercises did we perform in Area Two and how many?"

Hell, I was so far back at Area Two that the pack was little more than a memory.

"Can't you read a sign, turd breath? Give me 50 pushups."

"Which arm, sir?"

"Fifty with each, smartass."

"That's the spirit!"

"You're not going to make it, Boehm. You're too old. Give up."

"I'll never give up."

I had killed a goddamned shark with a knife.

Swimming, naturally a large part of the training, offered my knee some relief even after Lucky 13 graduated from pool swims to mile-long swims in Chesapeake Bay. We were issued masks and stiff rubber fins called "duck feet." Eventually we would graduate to open-circuit SCUBA and the more dangerous closed-circuit rebreathers during advanced training. We were in the water every day. That suited me fine. I had been diving for over a decade.

Digger refused to do any navigation on the long swims. That was left up to me as his swim buddy. I berated him about his lack of concern in knowing how to get from Point A to Point B in the water. He shrugged.

"I got an answer to that, Pappy. I follow the ship."

"What ship?"

"The one tattooed on your arm."

Part of the training was *Cast and Recovery,* an old UDT technique for getting men into and out of the water rapidly. An IBS—Inflatable Boat, Small—was made fast to the side of a motor launch. The men climbed into the IBS and rolled—were *cast*—into the water while the launch maintained its speed.

For the *Recovery,* a snare man in the middle of the IBS used a figure-eight loop to snatch swimmers out of the water as the launch roared past.

Digger would have gladly taken some of my pain on himself in order to relieve me, but there was little he could do except offer moral support. While Special Ops stresses teamwork, each man must be capable of handling his part through his own strength and resolve.

"What'd I tell you on the first day, Digger? Nothing has changed. We are going to be UDT."

Sounded good. Sometimes I wasn't sure I could keep going. I stood outside my Quonset billet one late night after training and gazed reflectively toward a scattering of dark clouds looming above the bay. I felt depleted, body and soul. Digger O'Toole stepped outside and stood with me. Lenny Waugh and George Walsh appeared on my right. Silently, the four of us stood shoulder to shoulder watching the clouds.

I turned toward the door. I grinned. "What's the matter with you shitheads? Don't you know UDT has to sleep at least one hour a night?"

Hell Week culminated the first phase of training. A full week of one evolution following another day and night. Running, rubber boat drills, Circus, long swims, Obstacle Course, simulated missions, Around the World. We were already down to about 50 men left from the original 140. Lack of sleep along with constant mental and physical stress promised to take a further toll during Hell Week.

Shortly before the week began, Lieutenant Whiskey Al strolled before the dwindling ranks and flashed us an evil grin. "For Hell Week," he said, "I promised to do something special to instill in you the desire to mend your smartass ways."

He kept his word. Hurricane Hazel blew in on the third day of Hell Week to add her wicked weight to our discomfort. Already forced to carry our IBLs everywhere we went, sometimes with an instructor jumping from boat to boat as we jogged through the surf with the IBLs on top of our red helmets—*"Drop me, shithead pukes, and you'll pay. The earth had better swallow you up if you do"*—the hurricane now beat us, stung us, battered us, stole our rubber boats, and flung them high into the air.

"Just how badly do you whaleshit pukes want to be Frogmen?"

I went into automatic mode. I wrapped my injured knee tight and shut down everything in my body except those muscles actually needed. Damn it, I was determined to finish, even if I had to crawl.

"You're old, but you're a tough old man," Digger acknowledged.

The real UDT training began after Hell Week. I was almost surprised to find myself still surviving with Lucky 13. Demolitions training began. We would conduct a hydrographic reconnaissance of a beach and then return on a demolitions swim to blast obstacles out of the water. Blasting something was more complicated than merely determining that if two pounds of explosives would do the trick, 20 would do it better. We memorized formulas and calculated charges for many different types of obstacles under various conditions.

Small-unit tactical training in patrolling, raids, and ambushes occupied some minimum time, since UDT had not gone fully unconventional. But it was only a matter of time, I thought, until that happened. I might actually be one of the first Navy sea commandos after all.

We learned and then we proved that we had learned and that we could do the job. More simulated missions with our performance evaluated. Graded demo calculations. Leadership evaluations. Five-mile swims in 47-degree water, without wet suits. Boat handling . . .

Finally, in November 1954, the surviving 21 members of Class Number 13 assembled in the auditorium of the Amphibious School Building to graduate. George Walsh and I, the oldest members of the class, were among them. I limped in on my bad leg, limped back out. Grinning. I was UDT.

Lump-Lump was there for the graduation. "Charlie, you old sonofabitch. You fuckin' *made* it."

"You expected otherwise?"

I learned something vital in UDTR that I was never to forget. The men you could depend on most were those who had to work hardest to get what they wanted. The binding of a team through an experience such as UDTR built a band of brothers, elite operational rogues, who would willingly sacrifice their lives for each other.

What more could you ask from undersea warriors?

TWENTY-THREE

★ ★ ★ ★ ★

These tough men of UDT. If it were ever possible, I thought, I would like to see the best of them in one goddamn badass outfit. There would be no fighting unit better anywhere in the world, today or in the past. Although that day of unconventional warfare in the Navy was approaching faster than I expected, my personal path to it kept twisting and turning. Each twist, however, as I would one day appreciate, led me nearer my destiny.

I knocked around in the teams for a few years while UDT struggled to catch up with Italy in equipment and tactics. Italy was the best in the world at the time when it came to diving. The United States lagged 10 years and one war behind in envisioning a need for sea warriors in the Cold War era. At the same time, Frogs kept pushing the envelope in experimenting with unconventional tactics.

During war games around Saint Thomas in the Caribbean, UDT drew the mission of infiltrating a U.S. Marine general's headquarters. The Marine major in charge of security gloated about how UDTs were unable to penetrate headquarters defense. The general smiled and handed his major a note.

"Major, can you explain how this note got on my pillow?"

Red crept out from the junior officer's collar. The note thanked the general for his hospitality in providing UDT raiders with a well-stocked refrigerator of food and beer.

The general handed the note to me. "Boats, is this your writing?"

"Yessir. Palmer method."

"Major," the general concluded, "I have a fine feeling the Frogmen could penetrate the Kremlin itself if they were assigned the mission."

"That's a fact, sir," I agreed.

Being assigned as an instructor for UDTR Class 15 provided me much-needed experience in selecting and training men. I was particularly impressed with one H. L. Ashenbrenner, known as Animal. He was built like a big stump. The man had the kind of grit a sea warrior should have. There were a lot of wanna-bes out there who would like to pass themselves off as hunters, as sharks. But a man can't hunt unless he's willing to go in harm's way. Animal was a shark, even if he couldn't swim a damned stroke.

Rules for the UDT swimming test stated simply that an applicant must "traverse the length of the pool submerged." Lieutenant Whiskey Al Hodge, still the school's training officer, stared in amazement as Ashenbrenner jumped into the pool with complete abandon and bobbed, loped, skipped, and crawled underwater from one end of the pool to the other.

"What the hell are you doing?" I shouted at him. "Jesus! You can't even swim."

"I'll learn," said Animal, then pointed out how the rules said nothing about having to *swim* the length of the pool.

"You'll learn if you don't drown first, you dumbass."

"Roy, we're going to have to drop Ashenbrenner," Lieutenant Hodge decided. "The asshole can't swim a stroke."

"Sir, the book says only that he must complete the evolutions. He has done that so far. That bastard has got to want this program some kind of bad. He's got two things going for him."

"Swimming isn't one of them."

"First, he's too dumb to be afraid of the water. Second, I can't wait to see how he's going to make the five-mile swim. I'm in this man's corner until he quits."

Let the officers and the bureaucrats, the *bu-shit-crats,* make the fucking petty rules. Rules were made for guys who had no ability to think for themselves. Real warriors bent, snarled, tilted, and slanted the rules in order to get the job done.

Animal was among the leaders in everything except swimming. He grinned from the moment I rousted the class for frolics in the sand dunes until he staggered back in after nightfall.

"Animal, you're going to flunk out unless you learn to fucking swim."

"I ain't quittin', Boats."

In-transit fleet sailors housed in a row of three Quonset huts hooted and jeered as my Frogs jogged by on their long morning runs. My disciplined trainees put up with it for about a week.

"Boats," Ashenbrenner suggested one morning, "don't it seem unfair to you that real Frogmen should be insulted by ocean scum?"

"Oh, shit-for-brains, are *you* a *real* Frogman?"

"I *will* be."

The usual jeers greeted my men from in front of the Quonsets.

"Mark time, march!" I called out.

I jogged to the front of the sweating ranks. The sun glowed red on the bay, just coming up.

"Follow me!" I shouted. "Column right, double-time, *march!"*

I led the entire class of Frogs through the first billets like a green tornado. Bunks, lockers, sailors still in their bunks, everything went over and upside down. Still jogging in formation, we crashed into and out of the other two Quonsets and left the same wreckage. Then, in perfect cadenced double-time, without a word being spoken, we circled all three buildings. The awed and somewhat frightened fleet sailors stared in dumb silence.

"That felt *good* to a *real* Frogman," Animal exclaimed.

During long swims, trainees stroked and glided while Animal repeated an odd procedure of bobbing along, disappearing beneath the waves, then reappearing 30 feet on. I pulled the boat up next to him.

"Animal, do you want me to pick you up?"

"What for, Boats? I got it made."

He had it made. He graduated UDT with Class 15.

In addition to working with the teams and training Frogmen, I drew assignment to the Submersible Operations Department (SUBOPS) in the Underwater Demolition Unit at Norfolk, largely, I suspected, because of my performance at First Class Diving School and my experiments with Chief Warrants Moss and Dommagalla. As had become the habit, Lump-Lump Williams managed to draw assignment to the same outfit.

"Who's gonna take care of you, Roysi, if I don't?"

It was exciting to be on the leading edge of research and development in underseas operations. For two years I worked with one- and two-man underwater propulsion units, depth gauges, underwater communications (ANPQC), handheld sonar (ANPQS), mixed gas diving rigs, and other untried equipment and techniques. Dr. Heinz Speck at the Bethesda Naval Hospital used some of us in his Taylor Model Basin for experiments in osmosis, liquid oxygen breathing, seawater oxygen extraction techniques, and the possibility of surgically or mechanically implanting *gills* in animals and, perhaps eventually, in human beings.

Imagine! Waterborne guerrilla troops living and fighting underwater for days or weeks without having to surface for air!

"Would we turn into *actual* frogs if we stayed under too long?" Lump-Lump mused.

"We'll find out someday," I predicted.

While Lump-Lump proved quick to get me into trouble, he was just as quick in saving my ass. I was to owe Lump my life on more than one occasion.

Testing a submersible at Key West called for me to put the fast machine into a steep dive, then pull it out at about 70 feet and surface. The submersible traveled at almost three knots, a tremendous speed underwater almost like punching through a solidified wind. Surfacing, I eased off on the angle when I saw the flat of water against sky. The power of the machine combined with its sudden freedom from water pressure made it leap into the air like a flying fish, with me hanging on to it.

Impact with the water caused the battery pack to short out. Miniature bolts of electricity shot through my body, paralyzing me. Stunned, I sank slowly to the bottom of the ocean. Drifting. It was a hazy, not unpleasant feeling. Everything was liquid gray and off-blue. Fish swam slowly around me. Fortunately, I managed to bite into my air piece.

Silt clouded as I settled to the bottom. *Just let me rest a minute.*

Then Lump-Lump was there. He and Cpt. Karl Hensle of the Office of Naval Research had manned the chase boat. As soon as Lump realized the situation, he grabbed a tank and mask and jumped overboard. He hadn't the time to cinch on the backpack. He carried the tank in one hand while he dived hard. His ears threatened to burst from the rapid increase of pressure.

I recognized the shadowy form. *Good ol' Lump.*

He yanked me off the ocean floor and swam with me toward the bright stabbing of sun rays penetrating the water above. I was starting to come around when he hoisted me into the chase boat.

Captain Hensle hovered. "Are you all right, Boats?"

"Yes, sir," I murmured. Then I managed to crack, "I'm really starting to get a charge out of my work."

Although I had occasionally knocked heads with the bu-shit-crats in the fleet, it was at T&E where I encountered the entrenched bureaucracy and saw how it opposed innovation and resisted new ideas while at the same time appropriating as its own whatever it could not kill. I dug in to fight it with the bulldog intransigence that had marked my career and would almost destroy it in the future.

Cpt. F. R. Kaine, CO of UDT-21 and Commander, Underwater Demolition Units (COMUDU), was a good, soft-spoken man who defined moral courage as "having the will to do what you think is right regardless of the consequences. That's a pretty good definition of Roy Boehm—a hard head and a stinking ass."

A man *had* to do what he thought right, else he wasn't much of a man.

I wasn't ready the first time the bu-shit-crats struck. They blindsided me after another experimental diver, Tom Blaise, and I developed a universal full-face dive mask that eventually became the prototype for modern masks. It had separate intake and exhaust hoses to make it adaptable to both open-circuit and closed-circuit rigs, a divided mask area to prevent CO_2 buildup and make underwater communications clearer and easier, an angled face plate to prevent visual distortion, no dump valve, and a beveled face seal so it would fit most faces.

Blaise drew up the blueprints and we submitted them to the Bureau. Some bu-shit-crat responded that something like it had already been patented.

"Good," I returned. "Send us one for evaluation."

Almost two years later we received a mask for testing that was undoubtedly a copy of *our* mask, except a cheaper version. Some bu-shit-crat had claimed credit for inventing it.

From then on, I eyed everything warily and reacted promptly if not exactly appropriately to all slights. Good training in learning to circumvent the bean counters. When I confronted one of the T&E officers who ordered me to put a quick charge on a propulsion unit when it should have been charged over a 72-hour period instead, the officer snapped, "Don't argue with me, Boats. Do it my way."

His way resulted in damage to the unit. I fired him a memo that concluded with: "Deviating from the manufacturer's charging specifications was pointless and ordered by a dumb asshole. Not very respectfully, Roy Boehm."

The officer punished my insubordination by directing me to clean and prepare his personal Pirelli oxygen rebreather.

"The bag will be cleaned inside and out," he ordered.

"You will clean the face mask. You will complete a safety check on my equipment. You will jack the oxygen to 2,200 pounds, which means a hand pump. You will see there is no dust in the barrel lime."

I complied fully. That evening the officer complained, "Boats, my lung seems to be a little musty. Did you do as I ordered?"

"Aye, aye, sir. Exactly as you ordered."

"I wonder where the musty odor comes from."

"That's easy, sir. I pissed in the barrel lime after I did everything you said to do."

Outraged, he reported me to Captain Kaine.

"Is all this true, Boats?"

"Every word of it is exactly the truth. Officers don't lie."

Captain Kaine eyed the young officer. "I always prepare my own lung when I swim," he said. "I would suggest you adopt the same policy."

Lump-Lump and I evaluated and compared two mixed-gas diving rigs, the Emerson and the Scott, not knowing the decision of which to purchase had already been made by the bu-shit-crats at the center of power. I was to realize eventually that most decisions by higher-higher were made through political power and patronage, not common sense and need.

We determined the Emerson to be superior in design, performance, and engineering principle. The Scott was dangerous and poorly designed. The Navy's Bureau of Ships chief engineer, Mike Foran, pushed the Scott anyhow during the selection meeting. He grew irritated because we divers refused to change our minds about it. I finally requested permission to address the table.

"Our Bureau has evidently made its decision for reasons other than engineering principle or of providing the Underwater Demolition Teams with the more efficient and safer diving apparatus," I said. "Therefore, I suggest this entire charade has been orchestrated to acquire a fleet endorsement. I'm not giving it. As representatives of the fleet, we withdraw from this meeting rather than prostitute our obligations or place our integrity in jeopardy."

Lump-Lump and I walked out. UDTs received the inferior Scotts, as expected.

"You're always in there fighting, Boats," Captain Kaine said. "You'll either get what you want—or you'll get court-martialed and kicked out of the Navy." He laughed. "You're the type who'd tell George Washington, 'Hey, you with the wooden teeth. I don't give a fuck who you are. Sit your ass down before you fall overboard.' "

Several times over the years, disgust, frustration, and raw weariness had prompted me to get out of the Navy. This was one of those times. Congressman Lathan of New York, an ex-UDT Frog and a family friend, had put me in touch with Ed Link, who was building a submarine he called *Sea Link*. Ed wanted me to go with his company in civilian oceanographical research and testing when my hitch was up in the Navy. I was simply biding my time.

Somewhat later, I was scheduled to report to the Underwater Sound Laboratory in New London, Connecticut, to test a two-man submersible called the "Mine Hunter." I stopped by UDT-21 headquarters at Little Creek to write up some equipment evaluations. Cpt. Don Gaither, who had recently relieved Captain Kaine as COMUDU, stopped me as I prepared to leave.

"Where do you think you're going, Roy?"

"I have to be in New London in the morning."

"Negative, Boats. Spend the night with your wife."

"She'd faint dead if I did that."

He threw an arm around my shoulders. "Roy, you *are* staying here tonight. You *are* taking the exam tomorrow for Limited Duty Officer."

I stared at him. "Me? An officer? Do you know what you're saying, Skipper?"

"Fully."

"I'm no gentleman, sir. I wouldn't know a salad fork from a teaspoon. I don't want a commission. I haven't got time for this."

"The hell you haven't. Roy, you've always talked about your sea warriors. There's nothing certain, but there *is* talk that the Navy may implement UW ideas. *Unconventional warfare.* You have a chance to be a big part of it—if you're an officer. So, you either take the LDO test or I will personally transfer your ass to the slowest LST in the Amphibious Force."

Unconventional warfare? *Sea warriors?*

I snapped a salute. "Yes, sir. Get my ass in and take the exam."

Bos'n First Class Boehm became *Ensign* Roy Henry Boehm, officer and gentleman by act of Congress. I changed my opinion that the only things lower than a naval ensign were whaleshit and 95 percent of Congress. In fact, I felt pretty good about myself. While I relinquished the prospect of Sea Link, I revived my dream of one day commanding a *special* combat unit whose warriors were prepared to go anywhere in the entire goddamned world and do any goddamned thing our country demanded.

PART III

SEaAirLand: A Badass Outfit Is Tested (1960–1963)

"Who is like unto the beast?
Who is able to make war with him?"
—Revelations 13:4

TWENTY-FOUR

★ ★ ★ ★ ★

If any single historical event thrust America into accepting the concept of limited unconventional warfare, it was Fidel Castro's takeover of Cuba. The so-called Cold War had bloused fully, along with its companion "domino theory." According to this theory, one country after another would fall to communism until the United States stood alone and isolated in a hostile world. In creating the U.S. Army Special Forces, the Pentagon at least acknowledged the value of covert and overt guerrilla-type operations in stopping the Third World dominoes from falling. It was Cuba that provided a test of wills between communism and the free world.

Plots to invade Cuba began almost as soon as Castro swept out of the Sierra Maestra to take over Havana. The coast of Florida, 90 miles from the Cuban coast, grew into a hotbed of revolutionary and counterrevolutionary activity. Cuban exile organizations vowing to topple the island's bearded *jefe* sprouted like mushrooms; Castro retaliated by seeding Miami with spies and agents.

Vice President Richard Nixon and the CIA fanned the invasion conspiracy. When John F. Kennedy assumed office in 1961, the government's top-secret "5412 Committee" had already conceived a plot for invading the island nation. The plan called for exile forces to establish a beachhead on Cuban soil, behind which a Cuban government-in-exile would broadcast to the world as a government-in-arms. Under international law, the United States would then have an excuse to supply and reinforce the invaders.

Rumors of the impending invasion spread even as CIA

procurement teams scouted the United States and Europe for airplanes, tanks, ships, and other weapons with which to arm the exile army. A CIA reception and debriefing center at Key West directed arriving Cuban refugees to Miami's Dinner Key, where the Frente Revolucionario Democratico (FRD) had established a Cuban government-in-exile and a recruiting office. News broke in American and Mexican newspapers shortly after New Year's Day 1961 that a Cuban attack force known as Brigade 2506 was training on a coffee plantation and a refurbished airstrip near Retalhuleu in the mountains of southern Guatemala.

Cuban recruits all received the same assurance—that the project could not fail because the U.S. government was behind it and would not let it fail. Word leaked out that the UDTs and Army Special Forces would be involved in the action. I didn't particularly trust either the CIA or the State Department; I would learn to trust them even less as time went on. However, I looked to Cuba as a proving ground for unconventional warfare, as a catalyst for turning UDT into behind-the-lines guerrilla fighting units. Like or dislike it, UW often meant snooping and pooping with politicians and CIA spooks.

By then I was a naval lieutenant (jg) and operations officer for UDT-21. The skipper, Lt. Comdr. Bill Hamilton, wore a double hat as commander, Underwater Demolitions Unit, Atlantic Fleet. Tall and bronzed—he could have played a golden-boy lifeguard in the movies—he was a Navy brat who attended the Academy. He had clout, plus he knew how to work the system.

He and I shared the vision of a "commando-type unit" supported by the fleet's full capabilities. We chafed together under the yoke of assholes in the Pentagon who were so slow and resistant to change that they started fighting each new war with tactics developed in the last. A goddamned wonder soldiers weren't still marched onto the battlefield, lined up, and ordered to blast at each other back and forth until attrition decided the outcome.

UDT, a product of the toughest training in the military,

had a great potential for converting to UW in the Cold War situation. But we were hamstrung, not by the enemy but instead by interservice rivalry and locked-in-cement bu-shit-crats in Washington. Each branch of the service jealously guarded its own area of concern and its funds, to hell with overall effectiveness. The Marine Corps, for example, insisted the Navy be restricted to operations below the berm line to keep UDTs out of Marine business. Other service branches imposed similar restrictions against each other. They were like seabirds guarding their nests.

"Use us, turn us loose," I pleaded. "We are the most dedicated small group of bastards in the country and there isn't anything we can't or won't do."

I was unaware at the time of plans at work deep in the bowels of officialdom and of actions Hamilton was already taking to create the commandos we envisioned. All I knew was that the skipper's ideas melded with mine. He turned me loose to bypass the Washington logjam and go directly to the source of the training we needed. I was a former enlisted man who understood how to get things done at the lowest possible level. An old saying described enlisted men as sly and cunning; they needed watching at all times. The name of the game under Bill Hamilton became: Acquire the training, avoid the brass until we can educate them.

I arranged with Cpt. Rudy Kaiser at Fort Bragg, North Carolina, to exchange training between UDT and elements of the 5th and 7th U.S. Army Special Forces. An Army captain was equivalent to a Navy lieutenant. Kaiser and I put our low-ranking heads together and, with a handshake, linked two competent groups of professional men of war.

"I'll set you up with a diving allowance list and increase your training," I promised. "I'll teach you everything we know about water training and demolitions. In exchange, I want my men to know everything you know about foreign weapons, kitchen table demolitions, small-unit tactics, and Ranger-type operations. We both have beneficial training and can increase the operating and killing potential for both. You grease the skids on your end. I'll take care of our end."

I went to Skipper Hamilton and pushed a little farther. "There's a hell of a lot of talent in those two Army Special Forces groups," I said. "I want to open the door wide on parachute jump training, to include HALO and Fulton pickups."

HALO—high altitude, low opening—gave invaders or infiltrators the option of parachuting from airplanes at 25,000 to 35,000 feet and "flying" undetected into enemy territory. A Fulton was a method of snatching soldiers from the surface of the earth with a low-flying aircraft. Both techniques were invaluable to guerrilla-type ops.

"I'm going to need a little latitude to work it all out," I said.

Hamilton grinned. "You are my acting adviser on UDT matters. Get cracking and keep me informed. Tell no one what you are doing. I will fill you in on everything later," he concluded mysteriously.

I sent my Frogs to Army Special Forces schools for training in parachutes, foreign weapons, small-unit tactics, counterinsurgency, espionage. . . . Captain Kaiser's men came to me for training in demolitions, small-boat handling, SCUBA. . . . Both Army and Navy benefited in each branch becoming more well rounded and dangerous in the deadly game that was Special Operations.

After all these years, I could almost *see* my commandos. I had only the barest inkling of what commandos might be called upon to do in the name of national security and defense. The reality exceeded my imagination—everything from political assassinations to waging nuclear war. I felt it to be an exciting time in the rebirth of American guerrilla warfare. The Swamp Fox had practiced UW successfully during the Revolutionary War. So had the American Indians. It had been utilized tentatively in WWII and in Korea. But never had it been used to the extent the Cold War promised. It seemed I might finally be granted my chance at it. Sea warriors.

In March 1961, I obtained a piece of the Cuban action, my first experience in a cloak-and-dagger campaign to oust communism from Latin America. I was assigned as senior instructor in training and infiltrating a band of 14 Cuban revolutionaries into their home island. Naturally, virtually everyone in the United States and the world expected a Cuban invasion. What no one knew was *when* and *where.* Saboteurs, spies, and other infiltrators were being sent to pave the way for it. The invasion looked imminent.

I linked up with my Cubans in Panama Beach, Florida, and flew with them in a CIA-chartered DC-3 to a secret training camp in Virginia. The revolutionaries had been issued civilian clothing with all the labels removed. They were a determined lot, far more political than the Nationalist Chinese I had trained for Chiang Kai-shek in Tsingtao right after the war. Their spirit infected me with the belief that they really *could* retake Cuba.

Training commenced immediately in escape-and-evasion, survival, demolitions, and communications. That we taught no underwater procedures, heretofore the UDTs' specialty and virtual reason for existing, showed how deeply the Frogs had ventured into land-based warfare. Frogmen were becoming much more amphibious in the Cold War. I predicted optimistically that it wouldn't be long before Frogs also grew wings.

The emphasis of my band was on demolitions. My men were ready to go by the first week of April. CIA spooks with first names only—"Carl" or "Tom"—appeared in Virginia to brief the infiltrators on their missions. It was a tense briefing as my men learned they would be blowing up roads, bridges, and railroads when the invasion began.

"¿Cuándo?" the patriots asked. "When will be the invasion?"

"Soon," the spooks promised. "Listen to your radios. You will hear the codes and know where and when to go into action."

An ex-UDT Frog-turned-spook, "Smarty Marty" Martinez, a Mexican American, flew military with my guerrillas and me into the U.S. base at Guantanamo Bay on Cuba's southeastern point. We were hidden in an isolated barracks for a couple of days, then guided to an APB landing craft that sailed us under cover of darkness into the black Caribbean off the island's long southern coast. The Sierra Maestra rose dark and rounded off to starboard. Each of my 14 Cubans gripped an M-14 rifle and a backpack containing dynamite and C-4 plastic explosives, radio, and survival gear. They would hide out in swamps and mountains until D day. They waited silently in the tension until we transferred them to a smaller AVR, a crash boat, and then into rubber boats for their clandestine landings on the coast.

I passed from one to the other before they left, solemnly shaking hands.

"When we meet again," one of them said, "it will be in a free Cuba."

"Remember what I said about the shark," I admonished my guerrillas before I let them go. "Don't give yourself away until it is necessary. Then *strike.* Fierce and deadly."

I watched as the dark Sierra Maestra passed aft and the rubber boats vanished one by one, merging with the black shoreline. I felt that in my not accompanying them I was deserting them. *My* guys, the guys I had trained, were going into action without me.

"Keep your sorry ass off Cuban soil," Hamilton had lectured. "I don't give a damn what happens down there. All Khrushchev needs to start an international incident is to capture a U.S. personnel inside Cuba."

He hesitated, then added, "Roy, you're going to get your chance. Believe me, you *are* going to get your chance."

The AVR dumped the first team 20 miles east of the Gitmo U.S. airbase. Seven more went ashore near an inlet called the Bay of Pigs. Another team disappeared into that moonless night off the Isle of Pines.

I wondered as I flew back to UDT-21 at Little Creek, Virginia, if I would ever see my Cubans again.

TWENTY-FIVE

★ ★ ★ ★ ★

Fidel Castro jerked awake at dawn on 15 April 1961 as two B-26 bombers flew at rooftop level over "Point One," the national military headquarters in suburban Havana.

"What are those planes?" he demanded of his staff.

No one could tell him. He bolted to the window and watched in helpless rage as the American-made WWII bombers dived on Camp Libertad airport nearby. He heard the crump of exploding bombs and the stutter of antiaircraft fire.

He was sure the invasion had begun.

The bombers were part of one of the largest air forces in Latin America: 16 B-26 bombers, 12 C-46 and C-54 transports flown by 45 exile pilots trained by U.S. flyers. Vital to the success of any invasion was the destruction of Castro's air force, estimated to consist of 15 B-26 bombers, 10 Sea Furies, and four T-33 jet fighter trainers. An invasion force was on its way to Cuba behind the air attacks.

Relations between the United States and Cuba had continued to deteriorate within recent weeks. The United States suspended Cuba's sugar quota to the mainland while Castro nationalized American-owned property. Soviet premier Nikita Khrushchev declared the Monroe Doctrine dead and, to demonstrate Russia's commitment to Castro, sent one of his highest-ranking diplomats to Cuba as ambassador. On 3 January, Castro banished all but 11 of the U.S. embassy's 300 employees from the country, the final step before Washington and Havana severed diplomatic ties.

While the CIA promised Cuban patriots that Americans

would ensure the invasion's success, President Kennedy was saying something else. Although he had blessed the project with a qualified go-ahead, he insisted no American be involved in the actual attack since he wanted to create the impression that the invasion was entirely Cuban. On 12 April, three days before the B-26 strikes, he announced to the Alliance for Progress in Latin America that "there will not be, under any circumstances, an intervention in Cuba by the U.S. armed forces or American civilians." CIA operatives assumed JFK's statement to be one of misdirection to lull Castro into a false sense of security.

Vacillating, Kennedy postponed the invasion date from its original 11 April to 17 April to give himself more time to think. He telephoned Richard Bissell, CIA chief of clandestine services, and asked him how many airplanes would fly against Castro's airfields. Bissell told him 16.

"I don't want it on that scale," the President said. "I want it minimal."

During the predawn of Saturday, 15 April, two days before D day, a bomber force sharply reduced to *six* airplanes took off from Happy Valley in Nicaragua. Two planes would strike each of three Cuban airfields—Camp Libertad, Antonio Maceo Airport at Santiago de Cuba 450 miles southeast of Havana, and San Antonio de Los Banos.

All six bombers returned safely to Nicaragua after the raids. Jubilation that Castro's air force had been wiped out soon turned to gloom. U-2 reconnaissance photos showed that only five enemy aircraft were destroyed on the ground. Fidel had anticipated attack and dispersed his planes, using several broken-down ones as decoys. He still possessed a formidable force to use against invaders.

On Sunday in Washington, D.C., the Air Operations officer for the invasion forces was ordering ordnance for a cleanup strike against the airfields when Gen. Charles Cabell arrived. Cabell was acting director of the CIA in Allen Dulles's absence. Dulles was in Puerto Rico.

"What are you doing?" Cabell demanded.

"Readying the follow-up strike, sir. We have to finish them off."

"Seems to me," Cabell snapped, "that we were only authorized one strike at the airfields."

"Oh, no, sir. There are no restrictions on the number of strikes. The authorization was to knock out *all* the airfields."

Cabell's jaw jutted. "I just don't know about that. So to be on the safe side, I'm going to ask [Secretary of State] Dean Rusk about it. Cancel that air strike order . . . until I can get someone to approve it."

JFK scrubbed the cleanup air strikes, but gave his approval for the invasion. Rebel pilots in Happy Valley were revving up B-26 engines for a follow-up attack when they received orders to cancel. Maj. Gen. George "Poppa" Doster, the American commander of brigade pilot training, slammed his hat on the ground and yelled, "There goes the whole fucking war!"

The invasion brigade of 1,453 soldiers in Guatemala was trained and equipped with four-deuce mortars, 75mm recoilless rifles, bazookas, surplus M1 rifles from WWII, machine guns, pistols, and five M-45 Sherman tanks. To transport this vast weapons stockpile and accompanying assault troops to Cuban soil, the CIA leased a six-ship rundown freighter fleet from the Garcia Lines Corporation. The ships were all old and slow; no one would suspect them of being a military armada.

"They'll be given air cover by American combat craft and by U.S. Navy destroyers," the CIA promised Eduardo Garcia. "An American Navy ship will bring landing boats to the freighters to pick up the troops."

To this dilapidated freighter fleet CIA agents added nine landing craft they obtained through the Pentagon.

Invasion plans called for bombers to knock out the enemy's air force, after which a rebel paratrooper battalion would drop into Santa Clara to secure the airfield there and cut the island in half. Maritime feints would then distract Castro while the main seaborne thrust was made against Trinidad on the southern coast. The brigade would march east and west off the beachhead toward Havana and Santiago, picking up local strength as it went. Castro's 200,000-man army would be caught by surprise and conquered.

During the final days, the CIA changed the landing site from the sandy beaches of Trinidad to the Bay of Pigs, more than 100 miles east along the southern coast. CIA intelligence showed the area to be a sparsely populated stretch of territory isolated by the treacherous Zapata Swamps spanned by two narrow-gauge railroads and tricky footpaths known only to villagers. The small 108-man militia detachment at the village of Giron was not considered a real threat. Bissell decided that since there were no rapid communications between the Bay of Pigs and Havana, the invaders could land, capture the airfield at Giron, and begin landing and flying in war supplies before Castro realized what was happening.

Changing the invasion site proved to be simply another planning snafu in a long line of mistakes and poor judgment. *Three* hard-topped roads now crossed the swamp, providing a rapid response route for defending troops.

Early in the evening of 16 April, a U.S. naval task force consisting of the aircraft carrier *Essex* and seven destroyers secretly rendezvoused off the Cuban coast with the ragged vessels of the invasion fleet. Rebels were still under the impression that American fighter planes would fly cover for the invasion while the naval task force stood ready to respond to cries for help from the government-in-exile. Instead, not only had JFK withheld follow-up strikes against Castro's airfields, he reneged on the CIA promise that an "umbrella" of U.S. fighters would protect the landing. The Navy would perform only picket duty off the coast. JFK was keeping his word to the Alliance for Progress that the United States would not openly involve itself in any invasion. The rebels, however, did not know this.

The Brigade landings began shortly before dawn on 17 April with half of the troops unloading on "Blue Beach" at Playa Giron and the other half disembarking on "Red Beach" at Playa Largo 20 miles deeper into the mouth of the bay. Washington dispatched an urgent message to CIA agents at the site: "Castro still has operational aircraft. Expect you to be hit at dawn. Unload all troops and supplies and take ships to sea as soon as possible."

By 6:00 A.M., even while the invasion fleet was still offloading infantry and equipment, Castro's troops and aircraft were in full counterattack against Brigade 2506. JFK's ill-advised decision not to provide U.S. air cover, coupled with his not permitting follow-up air strikes on enemy airfields, exposed the invasion to disaster. Cuban Sea Furies and B-26 bombers pounded Garcia's freighters in the bay, sinking the bulk of the invasion's ammunition, fuel, and medical supplies. American A-4D pilots from *Essex* watched helplessly as Castro's bombers and fighters picked off the freighters and rebel aircraft. Enemy fighters quickly picked seven of the Brigade's 12 remaining aircraft out of the skies and then started bombing the invaders.

U.S. pilot Jim Forgy came upon a Cuban Sea Fury riding the tail of a Brigade B-26. Flames engulfed the bomber's starboard engine. The Sea Fury closed in for the kill.

"I have a Sea Fury shooting this B-26 down," Forgy radioed. "Request permission to take positive action."

"Negative," came the quick reply. *"Negative!"*

By midnight, Fidel and 20,000 soldiers had the invaders trapped on the beaches and were squeezing them into tighter and tighter perimeters. Tanks and infantry battered the Brigade with artillery fire for 48 straight hours. Stalin tanks rumbled against the dug-in rebels.

Abandoned by the United States, surrounded by a force 10 times larger, pounded by artillery and fighter bombers, pushed back to the beaches and swamps, out of ammunition, the invasion commander, Pepe San Roman, ordered his command to break into small groups and try to escape however they could. He shouted his last radio message across the air: "Am destroying all equipment and communications. I have nothing left to fight with. Am taking to the woods. I can't wait for you."

CIA case officer Grayston Lynch, San Roman's contact,

later remarked that this was the first time he had ever felt ashamed of his country.

Brigade 2506 lost 120 men killed in combat. San Roman and about 50 of his followers struggled in the Zapata Swamp for two weeks before hunger and thirst forced them to surrender. Castro eventually captured 1,180 invaders.

Back at Little Creek, Virginia, where I sweated out the invasion with other UDTs, I agreed with Lynch. I too was feeling ashamed of my country for the first time. I paced the makeshift operations room as news filtering out of Cuba grew bleaker with the passing hours and Kennedy refused to heed pleas for help from the Cuban government-in-exile. Nervous energy drove me like a cat. Some of the men I had trained were undoubtedly in the midst of the action. I later learned none of mine was captured or killed.

"We should have been there," I raged, meaning by *we* the United States and the UDTs. "This wouldn't have happened if we had been there. Goddamnit, we *abandoned* those poor fuckers to die when they were depending on us."

"It's politics," Lump-Lump said. "Politics will use you like a condom and then flush you down the stool."

Although I couldn't have known it at the time, Cuba and the Bay of Pigs were about to change the course of American history and my own personal history. Out of the defeat at the Bay of Pigs and the United States' refusal to aid the rebels grew a communist presumption that the United States might no longer possess the moral courage to honor its commitments. Out of this presumption grew the Berlin Wall, the communist intervention in the Dominican Republic, guerrilla warfare in Latin America, the Cuban Missile Crisis of 1962, and, arguably, the Vietnam War.

And out of the Bay of Pigs, too, arising from the memory of those bloody beaches, sprang a *special* unit to wage combat Cold War style with a ferocity, deadly intent, and skill that had rarely been seen on the globe.

TWENTY-SIX

★ ★ ★ ★ ★

UDT-21 Skipper Bill Hamilton summoned me to his office. He reminded me of Gregory Peck in *The Guns of Navarone.*

"Lieutenant," he began through a mysterious smile, "you and I share a vision."

"Yessir. Go back and kick Castro's ass."

"Better than that. Roy, can you make commandos out of our people?"

"We've already been training them. They're the perfect people out of which to make commandos."

"Do it then. Start selecting the men you want from UDT. Start pulling them for training right away."

I had dreamed of such a thing for nearly 20 years. "I'll coordinate it with the executive officer."

"No. This is classified Top Secret. I'm not only commanding officer of UDT-21, I'm also Commodore, Underwater Demolitions Units, Atlantic Fleet. You are now in the UDU chain of command. As such, you are my adviser. You report directly to me. I want you to select and train men as a nucleus for a Special Operations force to be incorporated into the Underwater Demolition Units. You will discuss the creation of this unit with no one except me. You will volunteer information on the purpose of training to no one, not even the men undergoing it. Is that clear?"

"Aye, aye, sir. I'm going to establish a team within a team and not tell even the exec about it. Those are my direct orders. What kind of mission do you have in mind?"

He leaned across the desk toward me on his elbows. His eyes sparked with excitement.

"Roy, do you know what this means? We've somehow been granted *carte blanche* to create the finest band of unconventional warriors in the world. President Kennedy has taken a lot of flak for the Bay of Pigs. He's not going to let it happen again. He's caught up in the unconventional warfare concept and has authorized us to do it the way we want. All he wants to see is results. I'm putting it in your hands because I think you're the most capable man in UDT to do it. You *always* get the job done.

"Lieutenant, I know how you've wanted to see this happen. Now, do it *your* way. Get men who can successfully complete any mission anywhere in the world. I expect you to produce a concept of operations, a mission profile, and a profile of the men you'll need. You've received your orders, Lieutenant. Get cracking."

That was how it began. Hamilton was supposed to command the Special Operations force while I became his executive officer. That wasn't how it turned out. I seldom saw Hamilton after that. He was almost always away in Washington coordinating with the CIA and a special office within the Bureau code-numbered 338. Running interference to keep the brass off my ass while I got the job done.

I realized why I had been selected to form the Special Ops force. It wasn't only because I was the best qualified for it and that I had let it be known my heart lay in unconventional warfare. It wasn't like I had fallen off a tramp steamer in the harbor day before yesterday. In a political world of CYA—*Cover Your Ass*—leadership, I was a junior officer, a mustang who had risen through the ranks and was never going to make captain or admiral. Top brass probably figured they could control me, first of all, and therefore control the unit. Secondly, if anything fucked up, *anything,* Lt. Roy Boehm became the scapegoat in their CYA world.

I went into it with eyes wide and no illusions about who got the credit if everything went right—*the brass*—or who got the blame in the event of a fuckup—*me.* But JFK wanted sea warriors; *I* wanted sea warriors. The commies were already spreading like lice throughout Latin America and you could smell Vietnam over the horizon. What the country used my sea warriors for was up to the commander-in-chief and the Pentagon. What they *could* use us for was up to me. I started the project determined that we could be used for *any damned thing.*

In drafting a concept of operations and a mission profile for my new unit, I recalled with some bemusement the predictions of wise old Li, the Chinese holy man from Tsingtao.

"You are touched by the Orient," he had said during our long afternoons sipping tea in his little hut. "You are a warrior destined for the life of a guerrilla. Remember when the time comes that you learn more from your enemy than from your friend."

Although I had trained in the use of and studied unconventional tactics and strategies for years with the lingering hope that I would use them one day, I suddenly felt inadequate for the task now that it had become reality. I had little time to learn everything I thought I needed to know. I lugged home boxes full of books and manuals, pored over them into the night. History was full of countless examples of successful guerrilla operations in every type of terrain and environment.

I studied Che Guevara, the engineer of Castro's Cuban revolution, and his passion for violent, sadistic actions, sabotage, guerrilla attacks, civil insurrections, infiltrations, and espionage. I learned how difficult it had been for the Poles to resist Hitler because the Nazis started out by forcing gun registrations and confiscating weapons. In his book, *A Different Kind of War,* U.S. Navy Vice Adm. Milton Miles demonstrated through his tales of U.S. Navy guerrilla forces in WWII how Americans could fight and win a guerrilla war, even in Asia. Such a war was winnable if the politicians kept out of it and the State Department didn't bungle it like it bungled most things. I committed to memory the supreme maxim of UW: *The front is everywhere.* I also memorized Mao's clear and concise philosophy:

> When the enemy advances, we retreat.
> When he escapes, we harass.

When he retreats, we pursue.
When he is tired, we attack.
When he burns, we put out the fire.
When he loots, we attack.
When he pursues, we hide.
When he retreats, we return.

The vision I had for my unit was clear in my head, had been for many years. Swift, deadly, like the shark. Capable of infiltrating or striking from the air by parachute or airplane, from overland, from the surface of the sea or from underneath the sea. Competent, strong, *thinking* men able to operate alone or in small groups behind enemy lines if need be, while at the same time proficient enough to perform direct-action missions against enemy targets in combat. Men, in fact, for all seasons. Who could and would do literally any damned thing required of them.

They had to be more than killers, all muscle and neck and attack-dog mentalities. I wanted—*demanded*—creative men who could operate with their brains as well as with their muscles. The UW brand of warfare required men of courage, dedication to duty, sacrifice, personal dexterity, and intelligence. Team and mission must come first. At the same time, they must be individuals, near-rogues in fact. Rough men, tough men, who could kick ass and operate outside protocol. *Desirable* undesirables.

One time I knocked a man down during a fistfight. "You're not going to kick him while he's down, are you, Roysi?" Lump-Lump asked with a sly grin.

"What the fuck you think I've got him down for?"

I wanted officers and enlisted who would kick the enemy no matter what his position. The name of the UW game was *win.* That attitude started with the officers, the leaders who lived the principle: "My men, right or wrong. My men, first, last, and always. *My* men." No sycophants kissing up to the brass at the expense of their men. I didn't give a damn if my officers knew what fork to use or if they had ever attended an Admirals' Ball.

Hamilton gave me a complement of 10 officers and 50 enlisted. I devised a rough guide sheet for selecting names. *My* men, I decided, should be:

Adept at all the skills, the more the better.
Versatile and be a volunteer.
Actors capable of playing any role convincingly.
Strong of character. I preferred sinners. Sinners could be relied on. Saints could often rationalize dog turds in a drinking fountain.
Able to perform.
Loyal with a sense of obligation.
Deeply devoted to duty and team.
Mission oriented.
Drug free.
Quick to learn.
Streetwise.
Creative, sly, and cunning, with a sense of humor.
Able to handle difficult situations and setbacks without undue emotionalism.
Capable of making friends, not be loners.
Free of overwhelming personal problems.

To help me determine which potential applicants met these criteria, I jotted down a list of questions to ask them and myself about them:

What are his strongest/weakest traits?
What is his philosophy on life?
What does he read?
Do I like/dislike him? Why?
How does he handle his liquor?
What is his psychological motivation?
What/who does he fear? Why? Are his fears a liability? Can he control them? Can he conquer them?
Will he kick ass and take names? To hell with the names.
Is he more apt to say "go" than "no go"? Does he have a "We ain't refused a job yet, why start now" attitude?

Finally, would he react to a kill without hesitation? Could he forget the inbred fair play bullshit that could get him killed? Could I train that out of him?

I reported back to Bill Hamilton with a list of names I was considering from among UDT. The officers were all young junior officers, lieutenants (jg), and ensigns. The highest ranking among them, John Callahan, was only a lieutenant who would eventually be our commanding officer. In the meantime, however, I was in charge.

For operations officer, I fingered Lt. (jg) Dante Stephenson. Dante considered himself an intellectual, but had the bad, *bad* loaded-gun-with-hair-trigger streak I could use if I could control it. Then there was "Tex" Hager, George Doran, Dave Graveson, Jose Taylor . . . I wanted a cross section of the best, men more mission oriented than career oriented. Many of them were like me, LDOs—so-called Limited Duty Officers, mustangs who had worked their way up through the enlisted ranks. Special Warfare was like the kiss of death to an officer's career in these early stages of its inception.

From the enlisted ranks, I chose tried warriors whom I knew personally as good operators. Harry Dick "Lump-Lump" Williams, of course. Louis "Hoss" Kucinski, "Leg" Martin, James Tipton, Rudy Boesch . . . Hamilton promised I could get anyone I wanted. The best storekeeper and cumshaw artist in the U.S. Navy, who could acquire *anything* you needed or wanted, was Hoot Andrews, then working for Admiral Rickover with a Presidential Priority One. I put in a request for him.

UDT's Special Operations Force looked formidable, *on paper,* when I presented it to Lt. Comdr. Hamilton. He went down the list, repeating a name here and there. He lifted a chiseled eyebrow.

"Rogues," he commented.

"These are the caliber people I want for what we're asking them to do. I don't want Jack Armstrong All-American types who'll say, 'Yessir, nosir, two bags full, anything you say, sir.' I want sonsofbitches who can and will think for themselves and will get a job done no matter what. We might not win popularity contests—but we'll be capable. I'm here to fight like hell for what I do want."

"That's one of the reasons you were chosen, Lieutenant Boehm."

He suddenly sat up straight. "Make it happen," he said. "Start pulling out these men and training them the way you want. When the time comes for the unit to be activated, you'll get them." He hesitated. "Lieutenant, work fast. I don't know how much time we have."

TWENTY-SEVEN

★ ★ ★ ★ ★

The way I envisioned my new force, UDT was *minimum* basic training, a foundation upon which to build all other training. I started stripping men from UDT-21 and sending them to schools and training courses all over the Navy and the Army, with a few civilian classes thrown in. I had the green light to go anywhere, do anything.

I laid on Ranger training, jungle warfare, martial arts. I dispatched one group to Annapolis to learn how to sail boats. I figured we'd be in Vietnam sooner or later—and the Vietnamese junks had canvas sails. I sent men to prisons to learn safecracking from experts. I ordered people to become auto hot-wire artists and lock pickers. Frogs went to learn trick shooting, photography, and intelligence gathering.

Everyone would be parachute qualified. Not merely conventional hop-and-pop, but also HAHO, high-altitude high-opening, and HALO, high-altitude low-opening. I wanted my commandos capable of jumping from an airplane at

27,000 feet to *fly* a parachute from over international waters into enemy territory.

Gen. "Jumping Joe" Stillwell was commander of all Army Special Forces. I had already established liaison with the Army. The general and my Fort Bragg contact, Cpt. Rudy Kaiser, with whom I had earlier teamed for an exchange of training between Navy UDT and Army Special Forces, helped me lay on all the Army special training my men could absorb. Water entry procedures from low-flying aircraft. Kitchen table demolitions. Foreign weapons. Combat tactics. Survival. Escape and evasion.

Although I had made a "dream list" of men I hoped to recruit, which included a number of former UDT and some who had not yet undergone Frog school, I was at that time limited to training only those currently within UDT—about 60 percent of my allotted complement of 10 officers and 50 enlisted. UDT-21 men on my list became conspicuously absent from the naval base at Little Creek. Men were always coming and going. As soon as they returned from one course, I hurried them out on another. They knew something was going down, that they were being drawn into an orphaned twilight between UDT and something else, but I was prohibited from telling them what it was. I assured them the purpose for all their training would become clear at the appropriate time. Among the teams, East Coast and West, only Lieutenant Commander Hamilton and I knew the true nature of my mission. Important eyes higher up were watching, Hamilton said. Including those of the President of the United States.

I was as much on the go as my men. One afternoon I was boarding an airplane in Bermuda to fly to Washington to give a briefing on my progress and receive my regular high-level ass chewing when Bruhmuller, Gallagher, and some of the others came running out on the tarmac to see me off.

Bruhmuller shouted, "Daddy! Daddy! Please tell us who our mommy is before you leave? Please, Daddy?"

I turned toward them from the top of the boarding stairs. "Children," I said, "I told you once and I'll tell you again.

She was a one-night stand and as ugly as sin. I don't remember her name."

Lt. Mo Lynch, UDT-21's executive officer and second-in-command, was furious at having been excluded from the secret. I was operations officer, third-in-command, and technically worked under Mo.

"Goddamnit, Roy," he fussed, about to bust open for curiosity, "what's going on here? I've got guys scheduled for things—and you're always snatching them up and sending them off on boondoggles. What's all the training about? What in hell are you training them for? The least you can do is consult me."

"Sorry, Mo. I'm not at liberty to say."

He tried every way he could think of to weasel the secret from me. The men couldn't tell him anything; they didn't know anything. Mo went to the commander.

"Skipper, Boehm has just destroyed my Med cruise by taking all the men. Whatever he's doing is not good for morale. The men don't know where they're going from day to day, nor even *why* they're doing all this."

Hamilton looked at me. "How do you feel about that, Boehm?"

"Mo's a good man, Skipper. I agree with him."

Hamilton nodded. "Let me tell you both something," he said. "Boehm is my adviser on UDT matters. What we're discussing now, Mr. Lynch, is UDT matters. You have no need to know. Boehm is instructed to carry out my orders."

"Without informing me?" Lynch protested.

"He's to carry out my orders. That'll be all, gentlemen."

"Goddamnit, Boehm!" Mo exploded after picking up another red herring. "What's this I hear about *astronauts* and *space?*"

"Space?" I'd reply, acting surprised. "Who told you that? I'll have their hides."

I was almost 38 years old, pushing hell out of middle age, and the weeks of building Lieutenant Commander Hamilton's Special Operations unit had my ass dragging. But any officer who couldn't hack it, who couldn't or wouldn't endure the same training as his men, didn't belong in *any* unit in the military, much less a special outfit like UDT or Army Special Forces. Anytime one of my men took a step, it was into my big wide footprint.

Some of the regular Army soldiers found it difficult to understand and accept why the Navy was sending sailors to infantry schools. They found it equally difficult to accept the comradeship that existed between officers and enlisted in UDT. When Lieutenant Driscoll and I showed up together for airborne training at Fort Bragg, all the cadre knew was that the only two sailors in the company were to be treated the same as the soldier trainees.

The senior Black Hat instructor was a black man nearly a head taller than I. "Blood" Burns's shoulders were as wide as Lump-Lump's. The U.S. Army was the only thing in the entire world he professed to like. Everything else he berated in a thick southern Negro drawl. He glared disapprovingly at Driscoll and me, as though putting squid into the ranks of soldiers somehow fouled his beloved institution.

"Suh," he declared, *"nothing* falls out of the sky in the U.S. Navy except gull shit. Suh, it is blasphemy." He pronounced it *blas-feemy.*

And it was *blas-feemy* from then on.

"Lieutenant, suh, you are guilty of blas-feemy."

"Blas-feemy, Sergeant?"

"Blas-feemy, suh. Now get yo' white ass up there in that tower and make a vigorous exit, suh."

"Cleah, Sergeant." Fucking with him and his accent.

"Vigorous exit, suh."

He liked to walk up and place his mirrorlike, perfectly spit-shined jump boots next to mine. "Blas-feemy, suh. Blas-feemy."

As an officer, I was supposed to supervise the enlisted men policing among the big pines for cigarette butts and candy wrappers. In Special Ops, if my men picked up cigarette butts, so did I. Blood Burns rode toward me on his stiff walk, like he was marching in pass-in-review. I was ready for him.

"Suh, officers do not pick up and fieldstrip them cigarettes with the enlisted men. You *order* someone to do it."

He stood his boots in front of mine and looked me over. "Does this tell you something, suh? Our boots should be the same."

"Cleah, Sergeant!"

Then, before he could yodel his *blas-feemy,* I dropped the handful of sand I was carrying on our boots. "They look the same to me, Sergeant," I said.

"Blas-feemy. Give me twenty push-ups, suh."

"With which arm, Sergeant?"

"Twenty with *each* arm, suh. Wiseass."

I gave him 20 with the right, 20 with the left, and 20 more for UDT.

"Blas-feemy, suh." A slight grin edged onto his dark face and he did a perfect about-face and marched away.

Just before my first night-training parachute jump, a Special Forces major strap-hanging for a night qualification jump approached while the sticks of paratroopers were loading onto the C-119.

"Laddy," he said in a thick Scottish burr, "I'll race you to the ground for a case of beer."

"You're on, Scotty."

Once on the airplane, he grinned and moved from seventh in the stick behind me toward the door. "I forgot to tell ya, laddy. I'm actually *first* in the stick."

"You sonofabitch," I murmured. I was *sixth* in line and I had never night-jumped. Still, I was determined he would earn his case of beer.

Once my canopy popped wide, I spotted a big tree growing alongside Bragg's Normandy Drop Zone. I used it for perspective as I pulled my front risers to my knees, then hooked my boots into the risers and stretched them down even farther. That spilled air out the back of the T-10 canopy and reduced lift. I fell out of the sky like a stone, plummeting earthward through all the other jumpers floating below.

I knew I had Scotty beat. I kept one eye on the big tree,

not realizing in my ignorance how deceptive objects could be at night from the air. At the last moment, at just above treetop level, I kicked my boots free from the risers. The chute huffed, popped one time, and immediately set me on the ground. The tree I assumed to be a huge oak was actually only about head high. I had almost ridden a reduced-lift canopy into the earth.

The Scot hit the DZ second, behind me. I swaggered over, not letting on about my tree miscalculations.

"Laddy, I hate to give up a case of beer considering I've also lost my dog tags and will have to buy more. But you earned it fair and square."

Blood Burns shook his head. "Suh, I have to hand it to you. I've never seen a slip better executed in my life."

"Blas-feemy, Sergeant."

"*Blas-feemy,* suh."

In December 1961, Lt. Comdr. Bill Hamilton received orders transferring him out of UDT. I didn't know if his transfer meant the new unit was a go or would be put on hold. I waited, on edge. The program had to go. It just *had* to.

Finally, during the Christmas holidays, an old friend working in BUPERS, Bureau of Personnel, telephoned me.

"Hey, asshole," he greeted. "What in motherfuckin' hell is a SEAL?"

"Furry little creature lives in the ocean?"

"You'd damned well better find out for sure, ol' buddy. 'Cause you *are* one now with a license to steal."

"No shit? When is this to take place?"

"Pretty damned soon. That's all I can say. I probably shouldn't have said anything to begin with. But giving you an outfit like this with a license to steal is going to land your ass in jail, sure as shit. I just wanted to say *adieu* before it happened."

On 7 January 1962, OPNAV made the decision. I didn't know who came up with the acronym SEAL—SEaAirLand—but I liked the concept of what it implied. Backdated to 1 January, the U.S. Navy SEALs were commissioned into service as the Navy's answer to guerrilla warfare and the

Boehm (left, with helmet) during his early days as a hard-hat diver. Dressing Roy is Navy Petty Officer Gene Lewis. The diver on the right is Hugh Lansden. The other people are unidentified. *(U.S. Navy photo)*

Boehm (center), face in mud, during Underwater Demolition Training (UDT), the toughest training in any military in the world. *(U.S. Navy photo)*

"Hell Week" during UDT training. *(U.S. Navy photo)*

Roy Boehm preparing to test-dive a German Draeger closed-circuit oxygen rebreather in the Virgin Islands. *(U.S. Navy photo)*

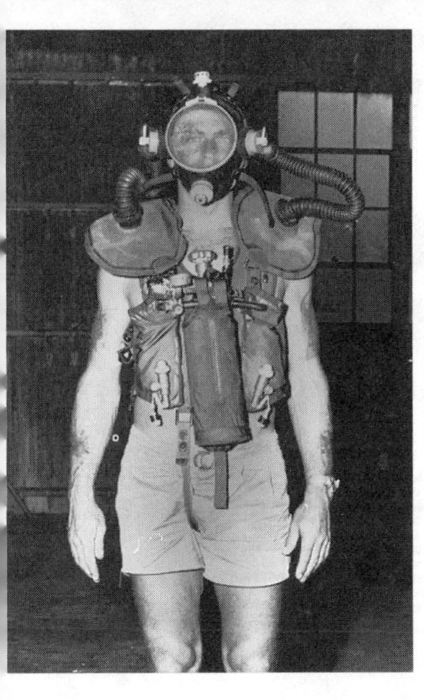

Boehm wearing an experimental closed-circuit diving rig during the early days of testing SCUBA (Self-Contained Underwater Breathing Apparatus). *(U.S. Navy photo)*

Boehm's swim buddy, George Callison (pictured here), also experimented with underwater propulsion units, such as this Sea Sled, while with the Underwater Test & Evaluation unit in the U.S. Virgin Islands. *(U.S. Navy photo)*

A "mother sub" about to recover a swimmer on a swimmer-delivery vehicle in the Caribbean. UDT members were trained to get in and out of submarines up to 60 or more feet underwater. Submarines like this infiltrated Boehm and his SEALs into communist Cuba. *(U.S. Navy photo)*

Boehm (far right) briefing his SEALs as they prepare for invasion of Cuba during the Cuban Missile Crisis. *(U.S. Navy photo)*

LDNN "Frogmen" boarding a PBR (Patrol Boat—River) with a PRU (Provincial Recon Unit) after an operation in the Rung Sat Forest, 1967. *(U.S. Navy photo)*

Boehm (left) and Doc Schultz in one of Lt. Comdr. Jerry Ashcroft's river junks in the Mekong Delta. *(Photo by Jerry Ashcroft)*

This is typical of South Vietnamese junk bases along the Mekong River, like Junk Base 33, which was overrun by Commander Minh's 514th VC Battalion. *(U.S. Navy photo)*

Boehm consults with his Vietnamese soldiers during an operation with his *Lien Doc Nguoi Nhai* in the Mekong Delta. *(Photo by one of Boehm's Vietnamese soldiers, unknown, with Roy's camera)*

Members of Boehm's LDNN prepare for a mission in the deadly Rung Sat. *(Photo by Roy Boehm)*

Boehm with his trademark .357-caliber pistol surrounded by his Vietnamese Frogmen at a junk base along the Mekong River. *(Photo by Doc Richard Schultz)*

Boehm's Frogmen on an operation in the Mekong Delta. *(Photo by Doc Richard Schultz)*

After Vietnam, Boehm helped organize and train U.S. Navy Riverine Forces to fight on Vietnamese waterways. The "river rats" were equipped with PBRs, 31 feet long and capable of speeds in excess of 25 knots. They were heavily armed with twin 50-caliber machine guns forward and a single .50-caliber aft. *(U.S. Navy photo)*

Army Special Forces in the Cold War. My sea warriors had become a reality.

I received orders as acting commanding officer of SEAL Team Two on the East Coast, over a force of 10 officers and 50 enlisted whose names I had been carrying around for months but who had been blindly undergoing training for an unspecified mission. SEAL Team One, under the command of Lt. Dave Del Guidice, would be implemented on the West Coast. Del Guidice didn't even have names yet.

Roy Boehm, now promoted to full lieutenant, received the first SEAL orders. Roy Boehm, salty old sailor and WWII vet, former bos'n mate, was now *acting commander* of the very first SEAL team to be commissioned in the United States Navy.

Goddamn. The *First* SEAL.

TWENTY-EIGHT

★ ★ ★ ★ ★

First priority—obtain the UDT men on my list whom I had been training much of 1961 in anticipation of Spec Ops commissioning. To my surprise, I was assigned a Presidential Priority One in obtaining men and equipment. It was, in fact, as my buddy at BUPERS declared, a little like giving me a license to steal. While Frogs formed the SEAL nucleus, I had to stomp on some important toes, which might one day stomp back, in obtaining some ex-UDTs on my list who were on operations with the fleet. Like Rudy Boesch, whom I wanted for my master-at-arms, and storekeeper Hoot Andrews.

Boesch was a senior chief petty officer, a clean-cut man of average size who stayed in excellent physical shape. He was regulation and commanded the respect of both men and officers. His commander resisted his transfer to SEALs, but to no avail. Boesch reported to Little Creek, immediately asking, "Mr. Boehm, what in hell is a *SEAL?"*

Former Frogman Hoot Andrews had recently qualified as chief of watch in a nuclear submarine. Hoot's skipper fought his transfer to SEALs—"What *is* a SEAL?"—all the way up to Admiral Rickover. Hoot packed his seabag to Little Creek, still wondering what a SEAL was. SEAL teams and our operations would remain largely secret throughout the Cold War.

I still needed more men to fill out my roster. As I wanted first pick, ahead of the teams, of UDT graduates, I burglarized the UDT offices that contained student training records. Using a red-lensed flashlight, I quickly made my shopping list. I heard the night watch coming down the hallway as I was preparing to leave. I had timed him prior to breaking in, but he was a bit irregular. I played broom in a cleaning-gear closet until the sound of his footsteps faded.

I whipped over to BUPERS with the list of names and my Presidential Priority. "Send me these lucky rascals after their satisfactory completion of all phases of UDT training," I said.

"Has this been approved by Commander, UDU?" I was asked.

"Of course. Here, let me call him for you."

No sense bothering the commander. Bruhmuller, one of my original SEAL picks, answered the phone in the decrepit building on the UDT compound where I had established SEAL headquarters.

"Commander, BUPERS wants to verify that you have sent me as your representative," I said.

Bruhmuller caught on and chuckled. I handed the telephone receiver to the suspicious BUPERS officer. Whatever Bruhmuller said, it turned the officer pale. His attitude instantly changed from difficult to kiss-ass helpful.

"Your boss says for me to do whatever I can to fill your needs."

"Yep, he's a great guy," I said. "But I surely wouldn't want to cross him on any deals he's made with your boss."

This transaction produced Ensign Bill Painter, who would become the first SEAL Two man lost when, several months later, he was swept overboard at night off the deck of a submarine; Bob Peterson, who possessed a steadying influence and a generous helping of common sense; Charlie Wiggins, a tough, reliable rogue; and Gordie Ablitt, an unpredictable hell-raiser who needed a tight line on his trigger.

Shortly after Gordie joined the team, some of the guys reported him too drunk to swim. There were *never* any excuses for my SEALs not performing. "Throw his drunk ass in the water," I ordered. "If he drowns, you're right, he's too drunk. Drowning is optional as long as he does it on his own time. Drink he may, but swim he must."

Only one officer wanted nothing to do with SEALs. "If you ever go out on any of these harebrained schemes," he predicted, "you'll never get back."

"Where there's a way in," I responded, "there's a way out."

Thirty-seven men reported aboard in January 1962; 19 more would report for duty as soon as they completed training or returned from operations. The CIA and the Pentagon were already wanting to use them. They were men like Bob "The Eagle" Gallagher who would become a legend feared by the Vietcong; Gene Tinnin, later killed in action along the Cambodian border; J. C. Tipton, who would log countless missions into Latin America and Asia; Bill Bruhmuller, a brave man who would let himself be captured by the VC in order to obtain information and escape; "Hoss" Kucinski; Hoot Andrews; the always-reliable rogue Lump-Lump Williams, who would soon go to Vietnam as adviser to the Vietnamese junk force.

What men! Never had such men gathered in one place before. My long-dreamed-of *sea warriors* to whom, in conjunction with the Army's Green Berets, the American military would forever owe its unconventional warfare roots.

UDTs had traditionally run around in T-shirts and cutoffs, looking like paste-ups of Joe Shit the Ragman. While I believed performance counted over appearance—too many outfits looked strak but couldn't operate their way out of a wet paper bag—I nonetheless wanted to immediately establish pride of unit by creating the impression of tough discipline. That started with appearance. I marched before my newly assembled SEALs wearing spit-shined jump boots, a stiffly blocked fatigue cap, and starched olive-drab fatigues with the trousers bloused into the boots.

I had too much bos'n in me to make any long speeches. I simply explained to my new SEALs that we were *special,* that never had such a combat outfit placed their big capable bootprints on the crust of the earth. We would be involved in international insurgencies and wars, and in training and leading guerrillas in insurrections and actions wherever our nation sent us. Our enemies would be committed, unpredictable, cruel, dangerous, and fanatical. We must not only survive against such enemies, we must *triumph,* beat them at their own fucking bloody games on their own goddamned terms. We'd be ready and available, down and dirty with a round-trip ticket, for whatever mission was assigned us—guerrilla fighting, assassinations, rescue missions, espionage, sabotage, direct action raids, or ambushes . . . *anything.* And *screw* the noncombatant do-gooders and the bean counters and their naive rules of *fair play.* SEALs were created to *win,* goddamnit, to protect the United States of America and to preserve what little freedom remained in the world.

"You *will* live up to my expectations," I growled. "SEaAirLand. SEALs. You will not discuss with anyone what you are, what you do, or who you work for. You will keep a low profile. Do you understand? You had better all understand that."

Bruhmuller subsequently drew up a list of basic survival techniques, which he posted in the new SEAL headquarters under the heading of:

Boehm's Ten Commandments

1. *By sending us off to all these schools, we will be better at our jobs. Before the government knows it, it will have so much invested in us that it can ill afford to get rid of us.*
2. *One of you bastards will be honor man in every school you attend.*
3. *You will represent the United States Navy and both SEAL teams in a professional manner.*
4. *You will not discuss your job with others regardless of their rank.*
5. *You will not surrender your identification card to anyone.*
6. *Should you fail in any of the above, your ass is mine.*
7. *Do not get caught.*
8. *On marriage and duty: If the Navy wanted you to have a wife, it would have issued you one along with your seabag.*
9. *Priorities are, in this order: country, Navy, family. Reasoning for this sequence is that if it were not for this country you would not be free. If it were not for the Navy, your country would not be free. If it were not for the above, your family would not enjoy freedom and their rights under the Constitution.*
10. *About special requests. Any request that starts with the phrase "My wife, she" or "My car, it" is automatically disapproved.*

I wanted my men to have a distinctive emblem, like the green beret for the U.S. Army's Special Forces. I formally requested permission from the vice CNO, Adm. Horatio Rivera, for the SEALs' uniform to include the black beret.

Rivera's boss, CNO Admiral Halloway, was a strong opponent of UW. He wanted aircraft and aircraft carriers. He said the Navy had no business fighting a war in muddy rivers.

"We call seamen 'White Hats' in the Navy," Admiral Rivera roared. "I don't know any 'Black Berets' and I want that term wiped out."

I ordered Hoot Andrews to obtain black berets for every man in the team. We wore them in defiance. I did what I thought best for the team, faced the heat, and waited for the high priority placed on the SEALs by President Kennedy to chain-react its way down through the commands. But if the CNO himself, the highest-ranking officer in the Navy, resisted the concept, it might never work its way down. The Navy SEALs were starting out in stormy seas.

TWENTY-NINE

★ ★ ★ ★ ★

Being a Navy wife wasn't an easy life for a lady. Her devotion to the service could be no less than that of her partner, or she wasn't going to be there at the end of the trail. Since official secrecy prevented my SEALs from talking to their wives about their jobs, the women led by my wife, Ellie, rebelled. They wanted to organize a wives' club to support their men, whatever the hell SEALs were. It wasn't enough that I had to contend with a recalcitrant naval bureaucracy. Now I had a bunch of nosy and irate women snooping around trying to find out what was going on.

Ellie's leadership in the movement had, I suspected, little to do with her concern for me. What little she had picked up about the SEALs prompted her to cry out, "You're nothing but a murderer, a trained killer!"

Our marriage had been on the shoals for some time. We refused to admit it because of the three offspring. My passion was the Navy and, now, the SEALs. Hers was religion, the Seventh-Day Adventists. She had donated her engagement ring to the church and contributed $1,000 I had worked all winter on a diving job to earn, so the church could buy a new furnace. Fluffy the parakeet became a symbol of the underlying hostility between us.

I thought Fluffy brain dead. Even though he immediately lost all his feathers after Ellie named him, he nonetheless thought he could fly. He would spring from his cage with reckless abandon and featherless wings—and bounce his bare ass on the floor. One Saturday morning Ellie asked me to clean Fluffy's cage while she tore out the door to the church in her perpetual search for salvation.

I was also late for a meeting with my teammates. I whipped out the vacuum cleaner and started sucking seed hulls, old seed, gravel, and water out of the cage. Fastest way to clean it. But then, before I could shout *bon voyage,* Fluffy disappeared down the vacuum cleaner hose.

I popped the lid off the vacuum. Out staggered Fluffy like a drunk in Times Square. I thought I overheard him saying something like, "Pretty boy, my ass!" Figuring he could use it, I treated him from a bottle of uncut smuggled rum from Saint Thomas. Now, I had been feeding Fluffy booze in his water for years. I had seen him so happily bombed at times that he hung upside down from his perch.

Fluffy felt no pain by the time Ellie breezed back home. Sticking her face up to the cage, she cooed, "How is Mommy's little Fluffy?"

Fluffy was half drunk and fully pissed off. He grabbed her nose with his sharp beak, drawing blood.

"He pecked me!" Ellie shrieked.

"Must have had a bad feather day."

"What have *you* done? You've turned Fluffy against me!"

She glared. I had somehow *made* the damned bird bite

her to vent my own hostilities. Everything going wrong in our marriage, from the SEALs to the alcoholic bird, was somehow all my fault. Seeing Fluffy every day reminded her of that.

Nevertheless, the fact that we were growing apart and heading for divorce after 14 years of my dragging her all over the world with the Navy could not deter her from promoting a social club for the SEAL wives. Ordinarily, I would not have objected. Family social interaction helped build team bonds. What the woman refused to understand, however, was that my Top Secret SEAL team was a different animal. There was a Cold War going on. It would soon turn hot if the signs from Indochina were an indication. My SEALs were too goddamned busy for this. Let the wives get together on their own, if they had to, but the SEALs were not going to sponsor any social clubs.

"I'll take it under advisement," I hedged when the women called. "I'll get back with you."

Finally, they got through to Admiral Ward, Commander of Amphibious Forces. The admiral called me. "Lieutenant, I suggest you have a meeting and try to pacify these ladies."

A suggestion from an admiral was the same as an order. I arranged for the manatees to have their first and, hopefully, last wives' club meeting. I sent out for three-day-old donuts. Bruhmuller returned with one-day-olds instead.

"That's all they had, boss."

"Okay. Put 'em in a locker with some old sneakers and socks for the rest of the day."

Came the hour of the meeting. Bruh and Lump-Lump served the donuts in rusty hubcaps on paper towels from the men's room. The coffee had been brewing since 4:00 A.M. and was about the color and consistency of road tar. The tea, on the other hand, looked like slightly stained swamp water. On my instruction, SEALs placed rows of chairs so closely together in a small room that kindergartners would have bumped their knees. As a final touch, I left the ladies waiting outside in the sunshine for a quarter-hour before I had them escorted in and seated.

As I entered, Tipton shouted, *"Attention on deck!"* Confusion reigned as the manatees fought to their feet in the cramped quarters.

"Ladies," I promptly announced, "will you please arrange yourselves according to seniority?"

They shuffled about, giggling and twittering. Ellie looked pleased to occupy the most senior chair.

Then I amended it. "Ladies, please return to your original seats. You do not wear your husband's rank or rate. You do not have seniority."

There was a lot of grumbling this time. I waited until they settled down.

"Ladies, the SEALs are a secret organization," I began. "We are not permitted to discuss any of our operations or missions with you. A breach of security could possibly get your husbands killed. I will tell you this, though: For the remainder of the year, you will see little of your man. He will be training in order to ensure that you will have a husband to return to you, in order for your children to have a father to love and care for them. Think of this training as his life insurance.

"Your understanding and your support is the contribution you can make to the SEAL team. I consider this to be the last meeting we will have until I am permitted to tell you more. If I hear any more reports instigating an active wives' club, it will result in the offender's husband being sent so far away that if he goes any farther he will be coming back. That is all, ladies. Please enjoy your donuts, coffee, and tea."

THIRTY

★ ★ ★ ★ ★

I had been informed that I had a grace period of approximately eight months to equip my SEAL Team Two and sign on for ops. Del Guidice asked me to do for his SEAL One whatever I did for SEAL Two. Instead of giving me that time, however, the Pentagon hit me immediately for operators. My men desperately needed equipment—special weapons, diving lungs, modified parachutes, aircraft, boats. I might have had a Presidential Priority One, but that meant shit to the bean counters, who were experts at fouling the system. There was little support in the regular Navy for the unconventional warfare concept. Sympathy for what the SEALs hoped to accomplish could be found in the dictionary somewhere between "shit" and "syphilis." The whole world was senior to the officers running the SEALs; most of the Navy wished we would just dry up and go away. I had nagging fears that we would be tasked with a mission while the bean counters continued to withhold essential equipment.

I rode Hoot Andrews and my other supply people mercilessly, driving them as near armed robbery as I could get away with in order to obtain supplies. It was up to me, if it was to get done. That was how it had been since I first started selecting and training men for Special Ops, before I even heard the term SEAL. Lt. Comdr. Bill Hamilton laid the task of getting the outfit going on my shoulders, then left for Washington. I was now *acting* commander of SEAL Team Two. Lt. John Callahan was the actual skipper, at least on paper. He finally showed up.

"I've been looking forward to your arrival," I told him, meaning it, then gave him an hourlong briefing on the team's status, the problems we were having, and what I was doing about them.

"I'm damned happy the ball is finally in your court," I concluded. "What are your plans and what do you want me to do?"

He stood up. "Roy, keep doing what you're doing. I'm going to Washington."

He left. What was this thing about Washington? I saw him one or two times, briefly, after that over the next year.

Hamilton and Callahan were both good men and good leaders. They realized I was the man best equipped to make the SEALs go. They simply turned me loose. I was a mustang, former enlisted, an unpolished, two-fisted type more at home in a sleazy enlisted barroom than in an officer's stateroom. I was never going to make captain or admiral anyhow. Brash and unorthodox, not knowing the word *quit,* I made a good target for brass waiting around to watch me fail and maybe give me a little nudge over the edge.

I made myself an even bigger target by refusing to lie down and roll over. I raised hell with BUWEPS, Bureau of Weapons, when my requests for .357 magnum handguns were turned down.

"Why do you need the magnums?" I was asked.

"War in Vietnam is inevitable," I explained. "Vietnamese communists use outboard motors for transporting munitions and supplies. The way SEALs will be operating, often behind enemy lines, we'll need a firearm powerful enough to disable and destroy the outboards. A .357 is powerful enough. The .38 you're offering is not."

I received cheaper, less-powerful .38s on the advice of a Bureau "gun expert."

I again confronted Mr. O'Connor at BUWEPS over obtaining firepower for my own team and for Dave Del Guidice's Team One in California. I explained patiently how the current M-14 rifle was a fine weapon, but it was long, heavy, noisy, and possessed limited firepower compared to the new AR-15 manufactured by Colt.

My SEALs did not require the M-14's lethal 1,000-yard range. We would have to do submarine lockouts and other maneuvers that called for smaller, lighter weapons. We would have to move fast with most shooting done at relatively close ranges. The AR-15's .223-caliber, 5.56 dovetailed bullet coupled with an extremely high velocity of 3,300 fps provided excellent killing power, plus we could carry a third more ammunition at the same weight. A combat unit armed with AR-15s could hose out twice the firepower of a comparable unit armed with M-14s.

"My men have run exhaustive tests under extremely arduous conditions," I informed O'Connor. "We need the AR-15. Didn't you get my report?"

"Your report was sent to the circular file since you are not an accepted test facility," he responded.

I felt heat steaming up the back of my neck. "This isn't the first time I've been stonewalled," I grated between my teeth. "You changed my .357s to .38s. My men are training for commando-type quick reaction operations that require lighter weapons and greater firepower."

Mr. O'Connor was a portly gentleman with an aloof air. "That's not my problem," he said.

"Did I mention I have a Presidential Priority One?"

"The M-14 has been approved by the Army. In my opinion, you have no need for anything not in the system at the present time."

"Do I have any other recourse?"

"Not that I can see. That *is* the final word."

I lurched to my feet. Upon O'Connor's desk rested an M-14 rifle cradled in a beautiful wooden stand. I plucked up the weapon, held it at arm's length over the desk, and let it drop. Papers, pencils, file baskets flew. O'Connor reeled back in surprise and fright.

"Asshole *bu-shit-crats,*" I muttered and stormed out.

Several years ago I had gotten crossways of the Navy's Bureau of Ships chief engineer Mike Foran while I was testing equipment in Key West with the Underwater Test & Evaluation Center. Foran had insisted on purchasing inferior Scott diving rigs for UDT in spite of the results of our testing. Since then, he had virtually destroyed any capability of swimming undetected underwater by having all foreign closed-circuit rigs in stock burned and replacing them with the open-circuit lungs. This meant bubbles. I confronted my old nemesis by requesting either the Italian Pirelli or the German Draeger oxygen rebreather for the SEALs.

Experts evaluating the request confirmed that the Scott was vastly inferior in both design and function to imported lung systems. Foran nevertheless insisted on the Scott.

"It's about as hydrodynamic as pushing a cardboard box through the water," I argued. "Didn't *you* notice it when you swam the rig?"

We stood next to an Olympic-sized pool where divers tested equipment. Foran glanced uneasily at the pool. "I don't swim," he admitted.

I stared, taken aback. "What right do you, a nonswimmer, have to decide what we in the fleet will swim?" I demanded.

"I am an engineer," he retorted smugly. "Based on my experience as an engineer, I know what equipment is best suited for your use."

"Sir, the Scott is just barely superior to a Mark I Mod 0 Hypoduchenator."

He blinked. "What is *that?*"

"That, *Mister* Engineer, is a clothespin on your nose and a piece of hose with a mouthpiece on one end and the other end stuck up your ass. You, sir, would be a far better engineer if you learned how to swim."

Fully clothed and nonswimmer that he was, I nonetheless picked him up bodily and hurled him into the deep end of the pool. His assistants rushed to help him.

"Let the bastard flail for himself—or you're next in the pool," I warned. "He's making his first dog paddle into better engineering."

I had the same problems with BUSHIPS as I had with BUWEPS. The Bureau of Ships was responsible for design, procurement, maintenance, and supply of the fleet. In charge of local procurement was Lieutenant Commander Hess, who dug in stubbornly and insisted that many of the supplies requested for the SEALs were either not permissible or were unavailable on the military market. Never mind that standard equipment could not satisfy the SEALs' special needs.

Among the prohibited items were HALO parachutes modified to make them more maneuverable. In an effort to push past Hess, I used my Presidential Priority to arrange a demonstration for the commander-in-chief, Atlantic Fleet, and commander, Amphibious Forces, Atlantic. My men and I personally modified an army HALO parachute to satisfy some of our requirements. We had a lot riding on the outcome.

Lenny Waugh from my old UDT Class 13 was the team's best sports jumper. I wanted him to make the jump. He argued that I should do it since I was the only one to have actually used the HALO chute. Bruhmuller agreed to jump-master while little Lenny stayed on the ground with the skeptical admirals to explain my sky maneuvering.

A strong wind blew in from the bay across the beach at Little Creek as Bruh and I took off in a borrowed helicopter with an agreeable pilot. The pilot flew us about 2,000 yards out over the bay. We looked down upon water kicked up by the wind into white mares' tails over the jetties.

Standing in the chopper's open door and shouting to be heard, I asked Bruh, "Wind too strong?"

He replied with an amphibious salute—arms stretched wide, shoulders shrugged, dumb look on his face. "Beats the shit out of me."

"Fuck it."

I tightened my helmet strap, gave my reserve a last check—and bailed out the door into the wind.

It was *magnificent.* My target was the baseball field. Everything seemed to be going just right. In spite of the wind, the altered parabolic opening in the rear of the chute provided the maneuverability by which I was about to land at home plate, right in front of the impressed admirals. I could almost hear Lenny pouring on the honey and syrup.

Suddenly, an unexpected updraft. I bounced upward on a cushion of air and watched in chagrin as the earth below and between my boots picked up speed. I raced across the ballpark, over Shore Drive and the high-tension wires. All I could think of was that we were going to be fucked getting anything out of BUSHIPS after this fiasco, especially if I landed in the high-tension wires and fried myself into a crispy critter. I saw Lenny and the admirals turning to watch my flight. I wondered how Lenny was explaining *this.*

Then, by some freak coincidence or design of fortune, the updraft let me go and the ground winds died. I guided the parachute back to the ball field, flared, and landed wearing a wide grin on the pitcher's mound. Lenny was calmly explaining that this was what I had *intended* doing all along in order to demonstrate the parachute's maneuverability.

That one jump opened the door a small crack. The Navy was slowly backing into UW. Even though I was gradually gaining higher-ranking supporters who wanted to see the SEALs succeed, I had many more enemies who thought *unconventional warfare* was so many four-letter words and a waste of effort and money that could be better spent on more ships, airplanes, and nuclear bombs. They warred against each other while I warred against the entrenched bureaucracy to launch the SEALs in more than just name.

Such methods pissed off some important people. The sharks started circling. The next thing I knew I faced *five* formal boards of investigation. I was going to be court-martialed, charged with:

Open purchasing the AR-15 by bypassing BUWEPS.
Open purchasing the Lambertsen/Emerson diving rig without its being approved by the experimental diving facility at BUSHIPS.
Patent violations by replacing another company's pop-off safety valve on a closed-circuit diving lung.

Violating safety by training men to dive without the pop-off valve.
Modifying the HALO parachute without going through the manufacturer or the El Centro Parachuting Facility.

I had run a slick side play around the bean counters—and now they were going to slam-dunk my ass for it. I figured my career was dive-bombing. Not even Admiral Taylor could save it.

I might have had a chance if I hadn't crossed so many influentials along the way. I could be forgiven, perhaps, for sidestepping the system. I *could not* be excused for throwing the chief engineer into his pool, frightening Mr. O'Connor at BUWEPS by slamming a rifle on his desk, using profanity and bullying recalcitrant officials into doing what they would have done in the first place. Possibly Lt. Roy Boehm's grandest offense of all was that he was *no* officer and gentleman. Once a lowly enlisted puke, always a lowly enlisted puke.

The proof of this and the final straw for my enemies occurred because of Gen. Lewis B "Chesty" Puller, a genuine World War II Marine Corps legend. Having retired next to the Naval Amphibious Base, he and his friend, Cpt. Fred Myers, the base doctor, often anchored down the end of the bar at the Officers' Club. The general refused to let a Marine drive him home after he had had too much anchoring. He and I had also become friends.

"Call that swabbie," he would say to the bartender, "and tell him I need a ride."

I always came; he was a grand old man. Mrs. Puller would greet me with, "Roy, did you get Lewis tipsy again?"

"Yes, ma'am. It's all my fault."

One afternoon while I waited for Chesty to finish a conversation, I sat on the footstep at the end of the bar. I was tired and it was a convenient place. The bartender brought me a drink. A chunky Marine Corps major and two other gyrene officers walked in and spotted me.

"What are you doing down there?" the major demanded.

It was none of his goddamned business. Sarcastically: "Waiting on a fare."

"You could get a drink spilled on you down there."

I looked up. "Major, I wouldn't recommend it."

"Oh?" Slowly and deliberately he upended a glass of beer over my head.

As I sprang to my feet, I brought every ounce of my 170 pounds to driving my fist into his nuts. He doubled in pain and shock.

I then front-kicked the next nearest Marine in the nuts. He went down on the floor with the major.

The third Marine was a skinny lieutenant. He stood stunned. I hooked a right to his jaw anyhow for good measure. It felled him. He should know better than to associate with riffraff.

I concluded the encounter by pouring a glass of beer over the major as he lay groaning on the floor.

"General Puller, sir, I'll wait for you outside," I said.

He lifted his glass in salute.

The skirmish resulted in my Officers' Club privileges being revoked. Hoot Andrews invited me as his guest to the CPO Club for a sandwich and beer. Several of the chiefs ragged Hoot about banging ears with an officer. It soon got out of hand, annoying even the normally patient and gracious Hoot.

"Let it go, guys," he pleaded. "You're out of line. The lieutenant is my guest and shouldn't be subjected to this."

It continued. Hoot finally turned to me. "What do you think, Skipper? I have half a mind to clean their clocks."

I bowed expansively. "As your guest, I am not allowed to wipe out the bastards personally."

Hoot gave a quick nod. "Kee-rect."

Several people on the team were pure pleasure to watch in action: Lump-Lump Williams, with his effortless grace and devil-may-care humor; Hoss Kucinski and his uncoiled snakelike speed; Hoot Andrews and his gentlemanly precision. . . . It seemed Hoot turned around only three times, punching as he went, before three CPOs lay bleeding on the floor. He lost *his* club privileges.

Brawling in bars like a common enlisted man! Wasn't that additional proof of what kind of man Boehm was? I figured I had a *sixth* court-martial coming.

"That sonofabitch is going to keep me from making admiral," wailed "Whiskey Al" Hodge, former training officer at UDTR and now CO of UDT and my superior in the chain of command.

The chief of staff, COMPHIBLANT (Commander, Amphibious Forces, Atlantic), sent word down: "Do something. Make sure the recalcitrant rogue in SEAL Team Two is taken care of."

It wasn't only me they were out to get. They wanted to destroy the SEALs as well; there was simply no room in the Navy for nonconformists, for *unconventional* warfare. Indeed! Enemies appeared like battleships with all guns blazing in an attempt to discredit me personally, the SEALs in particular, and the idea of UW in general.

During a commander's briefing, COMPHIBLANT's operations officer openly scoffed over the Navy's ever having need for commandos. He asked derisive questions about SEAL training in hot-wiring cars, safe breaking, and the like.

"I would like you to prepare a demonstration to justify all these unneeded boondoggles," he snapped at me.

"Be happy to, sir."

"Let me know when you will be ready."

I grinned. *You stupid fuck. My SEALs are always ready.*

We went into action immediately. The men were eager to showcase their unusual skills. Hoss Kucinski and Leg Martin stole a shuttle bus from the base motor pool. I dressed Bruhmuller in a full lieutenant's uniform while seven other SEALs donned post security watch arm bands, helmets, and web gear. All of them climbed into the shuttle bus as decoy passengers.

Hoss drove the bus across base and stopped in front of the COMPHIBLANT building. It was after hours; three sentries were on security detail. Bruh in his lieutenant's uniform and three SEALs posing as post security guards approached the sentries.

"These men will relieve you men for about an hour," Hoss informed the watch. "There's a special class tonight on security measures. Attendance is mandatory for all watch personnel at the Naval Amphibious Base. The bus will transport you there and back."

Bruhmuller's manner invited no questions. The sentries obediently marched out and joined the disguised SEALs aboard the shuttle. They were all delivered to a classroom where J. C. Tipton, also in officer's uniform, delivered a class on security consciousness and how the Reds would steal your secrets if you didn't watch out.

In the meantime, Bruh and his three "replacement guards" went to work at COMPHIBLANT. Picking locks, opening safes, and unlocking doors, they photographed classified records throughout the building, including the personnel records of the chief of staff and the operations officer.

Three or four days later, the ops officer drummed his fingers impatiently on the table during the next commander's briefing.

"What progress have you made in preparing the demonstration I asked for?" he demanded.

"Sir, we completed the intrusion last Friday night," I replied, fighting to contain a grin.

He looked blank. "Intrusion?"

I handed him a large envelope containing photographs of many important documents in the building, including those from his own locked desk, files, and safe. Other photos showed his watch personnel getting into the bus and sitting in a classroom. They had even signed their names to a classroom roster.

I openly gloated as the red crept out of the ops officer's collar.

THIRTY-ONE

★ ★ ★ ★ ★

President John Kennedy himself had announced that he wanted unconventional warriors for unconventional times. On 25 May 1961, five weeks after the Bay of Pigs fuckup, he had addressed a joint session of Congress in one of the most important speeches of his presidency. He set a goal for rocketing an American to the moon before the end of the decade, and he called for a major restructuring of the nation's military to pull it back from sole reliance on "massive retaliation"—MAD, Mutual Assured Destruction—with nuclear weapons.

"I am directing the secretary of defense to expand rapidly and substantially, in cooperation with our allies, the orientation of existing forces for the conduct of non-nuclear war, paramilitary operations and sub-limited or unconventional war. In addition, our special forces and unconventional warfare units will be increased and reoriented. . . ."

He ordered the Pentagon to set aside $400 million to beef up Special Operations. That was what prompted Lt. Comdr. Bill Hamilton to fire off a letter to the CNO in which he proposed creating a naval commando force capable of operations on land and in the air as well as on and under the sea. Now, five or six pending courts-martial later, I feared my SEALs might be going under for the third time. Even if by chance they survived, it appeared someone other than I would be leading them on their first real-world missions.

I received notification that the President and Vice President Lyndon Johnson were flying to Norfolk in the presidential chopper to take a look at the SEALs. Everything I had worked for these past months, the very survival of my sea warriors, might well depend upon this visit. I rode my SEALs hard, preparing them. To their credit, they rode themselves just as hard.

We presented the President with a typical action-and-danger show. Parachuting, casting-and-recovery from RBSs, insertion from the sea, martial arts, weapons. . . . In addition, we embarrassed hell out of the Secret Service and demonstrated our covert skills by planting a 35-pound sandbag "bomb" under the President's podium. A timed flash bulb went off to simulate an explosion. Kennedy seemed impressed.

I delivered a brief speech about the SEALs and our capabilities, a dramatic demonstration of which the Secret Service had already received. JFK and the Vice President shook hands with me, then browsed through a display of SEAL weapons and equipment.

Lyndon Johnson was a gun nut enthusiast of exotic assault rifles as well as of hunting pieces. He and A. D. Clark, one of my SEALs, became involved in a discussion concerning the points of the Colt AR-15 rifle compared to the standard-issue M-14.

"We need a light weapon with a range of about 500 yards, not 1,000," Clark explained. "The SEALs are not going to fight across a mountain range. We'll fight in jungles, swamps, forests, and in rooms, houses, and streets. The M-14 is noisy, awkward, and heavy. As far as I'm concerned, you can take it and jam it. My boss, Mr. Boehm, knows our needs. But he's getting a court-martial because he ordered the new AR-15s for us."

Johnson eased over and said a few words to JFK's naval aide, who then spoke to Kennedy. Kennedy looked over at the weapons, then looked at me. Two things happened after that during the following weeks. First, President Kennedy sent Clark an autographed picture of himself and thanked him for the weapons briefing. Second, Admiral Taylor telephoned me.

"Roy Boehm, do you own any civilian clothing?"

The *President of the United States* was meeting with Lt. Roy Boehm! I must have really let my bulldog mouth overload my Pekinese ass this time. Whatever it was, I'd take it like a man with real balls, like a SEAL. I could take the President of the United States chopping off my ass; what I couldn't take was having my SEALs chopped off too.

"They can't shoot me, can they, sir?" I asked Admiral Taylor.

John Kennedy entered the room briskly, wearing his famous grin. He shook hands with Admiral Taylor, whom he knew personally, then with me. "Good to see you again, Roy." It impressed me that he remembered my name.

I immediately blurted my confession, for no intelligent reason whatsoever other than it was the first thing that came to mind: "I didn't vote for you, sir."

JFK laughed heartily. Whitey Taylor rolled his eyes. I quickly regained presence of mind and redeemed myself. "But I'd still give my life for you, sir."

The President got right to the point. He said, "I see you've incurred some notoriety, Roy."

"Yessir."

"Do you know what a Presidential Priority is?"

"I know what it's supposed to be, Mr. President," I charged on. "It means I'm supposed to be able to get items for my teams without going through a lot of red tape. It's not happening, Mr. President."

"So you . . . uh . . . *circumvented* the system?"

"I'm used to being stonewalled, sir," I said. My ass was gone anyhow. I might as well let him have it with both guns. "The thing is, they're stonewalling *you* on this. The bureaucracy is locked in cement. These people are not going to budge for anybody. The regular military hates the idea of Special Operations. The bigger things are for them, the better they are. They're going to do away with me, sir. I'm just a nobody. Then they'll wait for you to either get out of office or lose an election so it can go back to business as usual."

JFK looked me over as though trying to decide if this example of what he had created was worth it.

"I'm looking into it," he said finally. "We'll see what we can do. Your SEALs will survive, Roy. I promise you that. Now, let me talk to Whitey."

That was all? I stood up.

"Lieutenant," the President added in farewell, "you'll make your number."

What the hell did that mean—*I'd make my number?*

I never learned exactly why the President of the United States wanted to see me. I figured it must have had something to do with Whitey Taylor's intervening for me. Whatever prompted the visit, things started happening afterwards. All pending courts-martial against me were dropped. Almost immediately, the SEALs were hurled into both overt and covert actions in Latin America and Asia—*with* sufficient equipment, support, and the backing of President Kennedy. The SEALs had made it.

THIRTY-TWO

★ ★ ★ ★ ★

SEALs were being dispersed all over the globe to evaluate and train allied militaries, from Vietnam and Korea to Panama and the Caribbean islands. Lump-Lump, Waugh, and Bill Burbank, for example, were in Vietnam with the Vietnamese junk force. Ostensibly, my government sent me to the Dominican Republic early in 1962 to assess the Dominican navy and evaluate the island nation's underwater demolition team. The true purpose for my travels, however, was far more sinister. It left me feeling ambivalent, tense. My old shrapnel wound headache from WWII returned.

What I had been instructed to do was wait for the CIA's man in Santo Domingo to contact me. In the meantime, I lived my cover story, working with the rusty navy and the comically out-of-shape UDTs who damned near drowned each other on short swims in Calderas Bay.

Two Italian frogmen had been sent over to train the UDT. They were equally out of shape. Maybe the scorpion in my bunk was nothing more than the Italians expressing their resentment against the interfering gringo. One of the Italians, the short, stocky one with the pot gut, hated Yanks. American GIs had captured and held him for a while during WWII. I felt certain it was his shadow I saw outlined against a window in the bunkhouse barracks. The rustling of insect net draped high over my bunk awoke me. Then I caught a glimpse of pot belly against a window. The next thing that demanded and got my attention was an excruciating stab of pain below my navel as the black scorpion dropped onto me found its mark.

The fat Italian wouldn't meet my eyes the next morning. I gave him what I intended to be a truly evil grin as I started the UDTs on a three-hour cross-country run on the narrow, hilly roads around Las Calderas. The little town containing the UDT base was about 50 klicks from the capital of Santo Domingo.

The terrain rose sharply from the UDT base on the bay into rugged, rocky hills overgrown with cholla cacti. Apaches in the American Southwest used to strip their enemies naked and toss them into cholla where they killed themselves on the needlelike thorns while struggling to climb out.

My belly was inflamed from the scorpion sting, but I determined not to let the pain show. Wind sprints going uphill soon had the Latin frogs strewn out over a half-mile. The sullen Italian who liked to play with scorpions brought up the rear, huffing and puffing and sweating in his swim trunks and running shoes. I dropped back from the lead. The Italian navy was about to encounter the meanest sonofabitch in the U.S. Navy.

My fat friend was *walking.* I had picked up enough Italian

to insult him and his ancestry back three generations. He charged me with an enraged bellow. I stepped nimbly aside, laughing, and slapped him open-handed across the face so hard tears flooded his eyes.

"I slap you, for you're less than a man," I taunted.

He lunged again, head down like a bull. I danced aside like a matador and kicked him as hard as I could in the ass as he swept past. The kick added to his own momentum sent him sailing off the road into an arroyo filled with cholla.

At least, near naked as he was, he had the good sense not to struggle and commit suicide. It took a cherry picker to lift him out of the cacti when he was finally missed.

I had had enough of both the Italians and the Dominican navy. I was almost relieved when my contact finally approached me, even though it meant I now had to get down to the dirty work. The spooks in D.C. had told me to call my contact "Raul." They showed me his photograph. That was all I needed to know about him.

"He will provide you with all the information and details you need once you are on the scene," they said.

I had received my orders verbally to report to D.C. The CIA never put anything in writing. I had gone to a phony magazine publishing company as instructed. The receptionist sent me to a cheap motel room where I cooled my heels until two expensive suits with shiny shoes showed up. They double-locked the door and pulled the shade. Spook stuff.

"The night has a thousand eyes," I joked, amused.

"*Everything* has a thousand eyes." They were not amused.

"We have a job for you," the spooks said. "What's the SEAL motto? Go anywhere, anytime, do any goddamned thing your government demands?"

"Cuba?" I asked.

Castro had become a thorn in the State Department's side, a permanent reminder that the evil spread of communism was virtually lapping at our beaches.

"Santo Domingo," the suits said, beginning their briefing. But it had Cuban ties, they added.

President Trujillo of the Dominican Republic had been

assassinated more than a year previously. Rafael Bonnelly assumed control of the provisional government with which the United States had resumed diplomatic relations five months ago in January, the month the SEALs were commissioned. While he was president, Trujillo housed and trained a group of international assassins. From this group emerged the would-be assassin who attempted to slay the Venezuelan president. Spies had now uncovered a plot to kill a Cuban in Havana. This particular Cuban happened to be working for our side to overthrow Castro.

"The assassin has already been selected," the spooks explained. "You may know him."

"Why would I know him?"

Apparently, he had been a double agent pretending to work with the CIA while he infiltrated the Cuban resistance before the Bay of Pigs. He had been among the group of Cuban rebels in Panama City, Florida, from which I had selected the 14 fighters I trained and inserted into Cuba. He looked vaguely familiar in his photo, but I couldn't say for sure. He appeared to be a pudgy Latino of about 40 with dark hair balding on top, a sharp nose, and a knife slash of a mouth.

"He must be stopped before he can kill our man in Havana," the CIA agents said. "He must be neutralized within the next fifteen days."

"Neutralized?" I must have looked stunned. "Would you speak fucking English?"

"Assassinated. Is that clear enough for you?"

Political assassinations—call them *murder*—were still legitimate covert actions in the early and mid-1960s. I realized that spying, dirty tricks, and political killings were all part of the unconventional warfare scenario into which I had bought stock once I committed to training the SEALs. Still, the hard reality of it took a little getting used to. Like most SEALs this early in the unit's existence, I had never killed a man face-to-face.

"We want *you* to neutralize him," the spooks said.

I relished the thought of it about as much as having a

rattlesnake in my skivvies. But I had no doubt I *could* do it. I possessed the unique capability of being able to separate intellect from emotion, action from conscience. I would kill the man because my country demanded it and it was my job.

"You can trust Raul," the CIA spooks assured me.

Right. I had already learned about government types. They used and abused you and didn't respect you in the morning. In Santo Domingo, the CIA had checked me into a hotel room that let for 50 bucks a night; my per diem was half that, including bologna sandwiches. That meant part of the expenses for killing a man came out of my own pocket.

I recognized Raul from his photo when he approached me on the beach at the capital. I was lounging in a beach chair drinking a beer. He walked right up.

"You're Mr. Boehm." It was not a question.

"You're Raul. What took you so long?"

"We've been watching you. You've made your presence known," he said with a flashing Latin smile. "The Italians will be happy to see you leave, I presume. Was your friend able to remove all the thorns from his anatomy?"

He *had* been watching.

"Mr. Boehm, are you prepared?"

"Like a scorpion," I said.

THIRTY-THREE

★ ★ ★ ★ ★

The entire damned affair was beginning to appear as amateurish as a college frat prank. I had entered a foreign country cold turkey, alone, under my own name, with almost no money and under the most transparent of cover stories to murder a national from yet a third country. On top of that,

I trusted no one involved. Not the CIA and certainly not Raul. I should have brought along J. C. Tipton or one of the other SEALs for backup, someone I trusted implicitly.

I was anxious to get it over with and get out of this poor shitbag country. Raul seemed in no hurry. He insisted I accompany him to a club with a Dominican air force general so huge he couldn't have entered a C-130 through the paratroop door. Boys' night out was a Latin thing. The men in the club were mostly married; almost none of the women were. The .38 revolver Hoot had obtained for me before I left offered some comfort snugged inside my waistband. I had smuggled it in-country inside a diplomatic pouch. It could not be traced.

I soon knew Raul's reason for bringing me to the club. He introduced me to a shortish man named Manuel who seemed somewhat familiar. Manuel eyed me too, as though he thought he recognized me but couldn't be certain. He took his leave quickly and avoided encountering me again.

"Did you not recognize him?" Raul asked.

"Should I have?"

Then I knew. Manuel had changed some from his photograph. He was heavier, older, and there was more wear on his face around the knife slash of his mouth. I took a deep, silent breath and looked across the crowded club at my intended victim.

Raul explained the situation. Manuel's amigo, Renaldo, who apparently worked for the CIA, was the one who uncovered the plot to assassinate the Cuban mole working in Havana with the underground resistance. Renaldo, whom Manuel trusted, had set up Manuel for the assassination before Manuel could knock off the mole. Real spy-versus-spy shit, directly out of *Mad* magazine.

"Renaldo is now away in Cuba," Raul said. "He must remain politically clean."

"Of course. How do I get to Manuel?" I asked with forced nonchalance. Raul obviously assumed I had done this sort of work before.

"You have a meeting scheduled with him. It's arranged

that he thinks you are an American friend of Renaldo's. You will meet at Renaldo's residence."

"I thought Señor Renaldo had to remain clean."

"Manuel and Renaldo are close. It is natural that Manuel should be at Renaldo's house, even when Renaldo is away. He will think he is meeting both you and Renaldo. It is very clever. Castro will think Renaldo is also in danger; he will never suspect him."

On the morning of the meet, Raul invited me to his house where he slipped me a 9mm German Luger equipped with a makeshift silencer as long as the pistol itself. I stared at it. I didn't know what I expected, but certainly something more than this. Maybe I had watched too many spy movies. There should have been background music, perhaps, some drama or something.

Instead, everything was so *ordinary,* so *normal.* Some guy gives me a pistol. *Now go kill this other guy.* This was all there was to it?

Renaldo's house was back in Las Calderas. A Dominican military Beechcraft flew me from Santo Domingo to the little airstrip in Las Calderas. A driver in a Land Rover met me. The afternoon was still full of sunshine when he dropped me off in front of one of the more expensive houses in the valley between the hills above the bay. It was a neat, open house painted a shimmering gray. The other houses along the block were also expensive, most of them painted in Caribbean pastels, with palms growing in the front yards and mountains beyond in the distance. Obviously, the elite lived here. The vast majority of the population lived in shacks and hovels.

I got out of the vehicle. I had dressed casual for the occasion in slacks and a loose tropical shirt. Inside the valise I carried were a manila envelope containing my notes and reports on the Dominican navy and UDT, a clean shirt, and the silenced Luger.

"I'll be here when you are done," the driver said, and drove off.

I looked around, not exactly sure where I was. I had little

choice but to depend on Raul and his driver to get me out of here once it was over. I was beginning to hate this shit, starting to get a case of the nerves. It wasn't the *morality* involved in *murdering* the guy; I had confronted that issue already and coped with it. It had to be done. It was more because the mission seemed so half-assed organized.

I marked everything off as last-minute mission jitters.

Manuel rushed outside like the attentive host to greet me. If he was suspicious of me from when we met in the club, he no longer showed it. He was smiling and gracious as he escorted me into a breezy, tile-floored room whose curtains over wide windows breathed with breezes coming from the sea. I repressed a pang of guilt as I noted how Manuel was no warrior, not even an armed opponent sworn to cause me personal harm. He was merely a pudgy middle-aged Cuban with skin like dark walnut, dressed in a loose shirt, baggy shorts, sandals, and a modified fedora to keep the tropical sun from burning his bald spot.

I had to remind myself that he was a professional assassin. At least, that was what I had been told.

"Where's Renaldo?" I asked to make conversation.

"He will return very shortly, señor. That's why we're waiting."

That *wasn't* why we were waiting.

"His wife isn't here?" I asked.

"She is shopping in Santo Domingo. Would you like a drink? A rum or a beer?"

I could have gone for a beer, but I declined. I took a chair across from Manuel. I placed the valise next to my foot. It was already unsnapped. We made small talk for a while as I improvised a plan, such as it was, and we ostensibly waited for Renaldo to make his appearance. I had already looked Manuel over and decided he was unarmed.

Manuel removed his hat. I picked out a spot behind his ear as he lounged in his chair across from me, swirling ice cubes in a glass. A bullet behind the ear was quick, clean, and painless.

"My people have given me some money for you," I announced presently to fill in a silence.

Manuel looked puzzled, but said nothing. Trying to appear casual, I reached into my valise and extracted the manila envelope. I deliberately dropped it on the floor as I reached to hand it to him. He bent to retrieve it.

My hand darted for the Luger. The goddamned thing with its outlandish silencer hung on the inside of the valise. The valise came off the floor with the weapon.

Sloppy. This whole goddamned thing was sloppy.

Still reaching for the envelope, Manuel peered up at me through thick brows. He looked surprised, then startled, starting to frown as I shook the Luger free.

His eyes focused with terror then on the last thing he was to see on this earth—the rough-looking silencer and the little hole at its very end. He started to rise from his chair.

I sprang up in a half-crouch and thrust the pistol toward the little spot behind his ear. He twisted his head. I squeezed the trigger.

The Luger spat with a noise not much louder than that of a Daisy air rifle. The bullet splashed into his forehead. He lunged facedown to the floor, losing all control of his muscles and nerves. His body did the chicken, jerking and flailing weakly about.

The action had turned me cold and emotionless. Mission always came first, ahead of men, ahead of self, ahead of God. I calmly shot Manuel again. This time I did not miss the spot behind his ear. He went still. Blood poured thick and rich and copper smelling from the two holes in his skull.

I was on autopilot. I wiped prints from the Luger and placed it at the entrance to the room where the police would hopefully see it first and pick it up. I recovered my envelope and shoved it smeared with blood back into my valise. It left a clear imprint of itself on the blood-splattered floor. I had been careful to touch nothing else while I was inside the house. I took a last look around, like a criminal at a crime scene, to make sure I had overlooked nothing. Then I mock-saluted the dead man and went out the back door and around to the front. The Land Rover appeared immediately.

My hands had trembled spastically after the hit, not necessarily because I killed the guy but because I had not done it on my own terms. I felt like I had been used. A hit man on a shoestring, susceptible to being disavowed and cast to wolves if anything had gone wrong. Next time, *I* would handle the entire thing myself, make all the arrangements.

The two suits who assigned me the mission, along with a third, showed up at the Washington, D.C., motel to debrief me once I returned to the States.

"How did 'lights out' go?" they asked me.

I had heard about how spies worked. Once they had dirt on a man, they held it over his head to blackmail him into other jobs. They *knew* how the job went; I didn't have to tell them. I figured my best approach was to admit nothing, confess to no one, and evade the issue.

"I don't know what the hell you're talking about," I responded.

"How did the job go? Manuel's departure?"

"My assessment of the Dominican navy and its UDT capabilities is included in my reports."

Although the assassination must have been the *right* thing to do or my government wouldn't have asked me to do it, I still wasn't about to give these lackeys any additional leverage against me. The spooks must have read my mind. They laughed.

"If you're worried about your naval career . . ."

"I never had a naval career," I shot back. "I'm a SEAL."

THIRTY-FOUR

★ ★ ★ ★ ★

The Cold War produced a new style and concept of warfare. Spy versus spy. Covert terrorism, espionage, sabotage, assassination, snooping and pooping to catch your enemy with his pants down. It was underhanded, deceitful, raw, and political. It wasn't as day-to-day bloody as Tarawa or Anzio, but, because of nuclear power, its ultimate potential for destruction exceeded all of man's previous wars combined.

Special Operations forces like the SEALs were designed for the Cold War, designed deadly and efficient like the man-eating shark. War entered the Atomic Age with its face painted black and green, an assassin's dagger in one hand with which to stab you in the back and a peace dove in the other. The dove blew up when you handled it. Twenty years ago when I first went to sea and to war, I nurtured only an uncertain dream of leading the most dangerous and effective band of commandos in the world. That dream had become reality.

The SEALs' first missions were against Cuba, that festering thorn of communism only 90 miles from Key West. I was no stranger to the charts of Cuba that Admiral Ward, COMPHIBLANT, his aides, and a civilian CIA type laid on a table before me along with aerial photos of Havana Harbor. Although it was secret shit not yet made public, I knew Khrushchev might be sending ICBM nuclear missiles to Cuba. The United States was considering landing Marines on the island.

My fledgling SEALs were being assigned to swim into Havana Harbor to reconnoiter the two-mile-long strip of beach east of the Havana jetties for a possible amphibious landing. The aerial photos showed a sea buoy near the mouth of the harbor, beyond which rose the point of a long rock quay wall. The wall curved around to the beach, alongside of which ran a highway that could serve as a rapid avenue of approach in the event of an invasion. It had been such roads that contributed to the defeat at the Bay of Pigs.

"We need updated intel on locations, direction and speed of water currents, depth of water gradient, and obstructions to navigation," Admiral Ward concluded. I recalled from Saipan the blue-green Frogmen with stripes painted around their bodies. Their harbor missions had been conducted under fierce Japanese fire.

"Your cover story if you're caught," advised the CIA spook, "is that you are fishermen who drifted ashore after your boat sank."

I looked at him. "You're shitting me, right? Here we are with fins and K-bars and uniform swim masks, me with tattoos all over my dumb ass, and I'm gonna tell 'em we're *friendly fishermen?* They'll execute our asses as the spies we are."

Each of my men, I said, would carry at least a .38 caliber Combat Masterpiece for defense.

"No," chirped up a suit from the State Department. "We must avoid anything that looks like an invasion."

"You're not the asshole with *U.S. Navy* tattooed on your arm. Maybe I can have my men cut off my arm if I see we're going to be captured."

"We're not sending you in there to be caught, Lieutenant. No one is to know we have been in there. No one is to be left behind unless it's a dead body with no markings or identification."

The mission was classified Top Secret and "vital to the security of our nation." I selected five men to accompany me: Lump-Lump Williams, my right hand man who had returned from Vietnam and who would die or kill for his commander; J. C. Tipton, who played guitar and sang "Bundy, Bundy, Bundy" and said, "Boss, it's a real shame them kids of yours had to have a father as ugly as you"; short, wiry Gene Tinnan; George Walsh, a tall, lanky man and one of the team's best divers, who was almost as old as I when we completed UDT training together in 1954; and Chief Schmidt, a cold, narrow-eyed kraut with a mind as mechanical and impersonal as a calculating machine.

The six of us would lock into a submarine out of Key West, but only two of us would do the actual recon—Tipton and me, using an SPU, a fast Swimmer Propulsion Unit like the ones I tested for UDT when I was with the Underwater Test & Evaluation Center. The other four SEALs would act as backup. I trusted Lump to go through hellfire and the red tape of every bureaucrat in the State Department to get to us if the proverbial feces hit the fan.

In addition to the SPU, I asked for an electronic depth recorder and eight German Draeger closed-circuit oxygen rebreather lungs. In stepped my old nemesis, Bureau of Diving's chief engineer Mike Foran, who had learned not a goddamned thing from my having dunked him in the pool.

"You'll have to take Scott rigs," he insisted.

"How many times do I have to tell you? Those things are a piece of shit."

"Congress is on a buy-America kick."

"I don't give a fuck. I want Draegers."

The equipment was shipped ahead of us to Key West. *Scott* diving rigs, no electronic depth finder, and the submersible hadn't been checked out. It wouldn't work. The only thing that *did* work properly was the electronic homing device that would guide the submarine to us for pickup after we completed the mission.

That sonofabitch Foran!

There was not enough time to send replacement equipment. We had to go with what we had. That meant Plan B. Instead of two men zipping in on the SPU and using the recorder to measure and calculate depth and terrain, the entire team had to swim in with plumbing lines and slates. We may as well have painted stripes around our bodies as the original Frogs had done in the South Pacific. The operation was back to men and basics—stamina, endurance, courage, and dedication to mission. Our chances of discovery by the enemy had also increased about tenfold.

If we were killed as a result of a hazardous mission in the line of duty, so be it.

"But if any of my men are killed because of that bu-shit-crat bean counter," I vowed as the submarine *Treadfin* plunged across the Straits of Florida toward Cuba, "I will personally cut off that sonofabitch Foran's dick and suffocate him with it, if it's big enough."

Treadfin cruised at periscope depth about two miles off the coast of Cuba while my men and I studied Havana Harbor through the periscope. I watched vegetable trucks and a few cars on the highway racing along and around the beach toward Havana. A family brought a picnic lunch to the beach, but left before nightfall.

We locked out of the sub at a depth of 60 feet shortly after nightfall. The boat loomed a darker black shadow in the sea behind me as I finned free of it. We couldn't use lights, not this close to enemy shores. We had smeared our near-naked bodies with a mixture of iodine and glycerine to cover the fish-belly white of our skins under the moonlight.

Suddenly, George Walsh grabbed me as he shot out of the submarine's hatch. His dark watery outline jabbed a hand upward, indicating he had to surface. He started up without waiting for my approval.

I signaled the others. Six dark heads bobbed in the black sea as *Treadfin* slipped silently away into the Gulf Stream; she would lay off Cuba in deep water for the next 10 hours, waiting to recover the team. Walsh explained that his piece-of-shit Scott lung had filled with brine. Goddamn Foran. We would have to surface swim. Our chances of discovery had just increased another tenfold.

I began swimming toward the sheen of city lights shimmering on the liquid horizon. The others pulled up abreast. We swam silently, using mostly our fins, sticking together in the black sea and keeping our eyes and ears alert for signs of the Cubans' Soviet-made Komar patrol boats. The current ran crossways. It forced us to compensate in order to hit the darker strip of beach to the east of Havana proper. I thought of the night the *Duncan* went down and of the sharks.

Lt. Roy Boehm's sea warriors were about to become the first element to step ashore in a likely United States invasion of communist Cuba.

Tipton saw them first. Two blocks of shadow separating from the distant clutter of mainland city lights. He pulled back, treaded water. Then we all saw them. Two stocky, high-beamed Komars highlighted in distinct relief against the lighter sky. Coming toward us and coming fast. The Cubans must have spotted something and sent out patrol boats to investigate.

Distance is deceiving at night. One minute the Komars were moving squares of shadow and the high predatory drumming of engines. They loomed upon us in the next minute, their black V-hulls shooting off phosphorescent wakes. I expected machine guns to start churning the water red with the first loss of SEAL blood.

"Dive! Dive!" I hissed.

I jerked on my breather mask and upended myself, kicking furiously with my fins to drive deep into the sea, below the Komars' deadly prop blades. My mask leaked brine. I breathed salt water with air. My eyes searched for Walsh. He was with us, but he must be breathing more water than air. Goddamn Foran! I eased over next to him, prepared to buddy-breathe him if necessary.

The six of us huddled like a school of stunned yellowfin, looking up with fearful darting eyes. We would never see the grenades falling on us through the dark sea.

The boats cut a wide glowing pathway across the surface directly above us. My adrenaline-spurred brain did the timing on how long it would take before the grenades went off.

Pulling the pins on the concussion grenades . . .
Grenades arcing through the darkness . . .
Striking the surface of the water . . .

Sinking the first 10 feet toward our water graves . . .
Sinking to about 20 feet, our level . . .

On target. I held my breath against the expected explosions. Waited for my ears to blow, my mask to fill with blood and eyeballs. For the final experience of my life during which someone drove an egg beater up my ass and put a wild man on the crank . . .

THIRTY-FIVE

★ ★ ★ ★ ★

Nothing happened.

The Komar engines faded to a distant humming. Walsh must be half drowned. We had to surface. It was dark and quiet again in the gentle lapping of the waves. Wonderful how the dry breezes smelled with their land scents of coconut palms and orange trees.

Leave it to Lump-Lump to ease the tension. "Boss, think you might take your K-bar and loosen up my asshole before it strangles me?"

Another hour's swim and I picked up the whisper and murmur of wave action against sand. There was no time to waste. The beach was approximately two miles long. It ran at a 45-degree angle to the double highway, starting at the thick base of the rock quay wall and ending past a *T* formed by the main road and a hard-topped drive leading to what appeared to be a small apartment building. Castro's rationing of nonessentials, such as gasoline and food, had brought island commerce almost to a standstill; traffic on the highway was so light that a vehicle passed only every 5 or 10 minutes.

Starting at the waterline, the team imposed imaginary grid lines across the surface of the bay, then paired off to take measurements with lead and line across its entire width. Back to Stone Age technology. Tipton and I worked together nearest the shore. The water was about knee-deep to waist-deep. We crawled along on the sandy bottom with only our heads out of the water, to avoid profiling ourselves against the skyline.

I caught a movement in the corner of my eye. Tipton passed my *Danger!* signal along. Everyone froze in place. Tip and I crept through the water like salamanders. He settled against the edge of the beach while I shucked my dive equipment and slithered ashore to investigate. I hid in a grove of palm and low bushes as a horseman reined up not 30 feet away. His face glowed momentarily inside his cupped palms as he lighted a cigarette.

He was probably a guard or a sentry. He wore a sidearm. He worked over his cigarette for what seemed an eternity, its tip flaring red in the night, while he gazed reflectively out to sea. Apparently, he was guarding against a possible gringo invasion. He was so near I smelled his acrid tobacco smoke.

Although my SEALs were downslope and pooled in darkness against his vision, there was still a chance he might spot them. If he sounded the alarm, so long, mission. So long, SEALs. And so long, Roy Boehm. I had heard enough about Castro's gulags to know I preferred to have my bread and water somewhere else.

Slowly, I slipped my long-bladed K-bar from its scabbard. The wicked serrated blade was painted black to prevent reflection. Low-crawling like a serpent, all senses alert and taut as a garrote, I worked my way toward the guard. I merged into shadows within leaping distance of his throat. The horse whuffed and pawed the ground impatiently. I smelled its warm grassy breath, heard the gentle jangle of its bridle. I lay on my belly almost at the animal's feet, ready to spring the instant the guard showed any indication of having seen the SEALs.

If I had to, I would cut his throat and then swim mount and dead rider into the bay, rip open the horse's jugular, and sink both in deep water.

A fish splashed. I held my breath. The bastard's cigarette must have been three feet long judging from the time it was taking him to smoke it.

I watched, coiled like a spring, as the sentry drew a final lungful through his cigarette. The butt arced brightly as he flipped it toward the beach. I heard him sigh, bored. Then he rode from the palms and rode slowly on along the beach toward the apartment building I had noted earlier. He dismounted and went inside. Lights glowed dimly through several windows.

We finished undisturbed our hydro survey of the bay. Then I said, "Wait here, guys. I'm going to check out that building."

It might be important for invasion planning.

A big hand settled on my shoulder. "You know Mama won't let you go anywhere without your baby-sitter," Lump-Lump whispered.

"Not this time, pard. I won't be long."

I approached the building from the side, running silently in light sneakers. The building was two stories with a dimly lighted hallway on each floor. I left wet footprints as I padded from door to door, putting my ear to each to listen.

I heard two different snoring patterns behind one door, three men speaking sleepy Spanish behind another. By the time I reached the end of the short downstairs hallway I figured the building to be a six- or eight-soldier outpost. There were five horses in a corral out back.

Satisfied, I returned to the water and led my men back to the sea from which we came. We swam for nearly two hours against the current. It was a hard swim. I turned on the homing device to call Mom to come pick us up. We continued swimming. It would be dawn in an hour or so. The Komars would be back with the daybreak.

Lump-Lump finally voiced what everyone was thinking: "Maybe they ain't coming back for us."

Walsh jettisoned his rebreather; our other lungs were leaking badly. We swam, held together by the jackstay line we intended using to snag the submarine's buoy when it was released to guide us back under into the *Treadfin*. We faced a 40-foot free dive without air to reenter the sub. *If* she picked us up. *If* the fucking State Department hadn't got cold feet and called her off.

"What if she don't come back?" someone asked.

"Easy," I replied. "We swim to sea and drown."

Lump chuckled dryly. "I knew being a shipmate of yours would get me killed sooner or later."

"Hell, Lump, we've been living on borrowed time for years."

Unknown to any of us, we were swimming over a shallow submerged coral head. It prevented the submarine's approaching to recover us. I cast uneasy glimpses toward the eastern sky. A gray streak against the horizon was beginning to turn silver. It would not be long before I made out the features of the men around me.

Three things happened almost simultaneously. Deep-sea currents whipping around the coral head combined with our fin action to drift us once more into deep water. *Treadfin*'s periscope snorkel appeared almost immediately; she had been waiting for us to clear the obstruction. And, third, the Komars zeroed in on us. We heard their distant humming whine coming our way.

"Just like in the movies," Lump-Lump brayed. "Rescued by the last hair on our macho asses."

"We're not out yet," I cautioned.

Snagging the buoy with our jackstay line was the easy part. Getting inside the boat was a bit trickier. The airlock at the forward escape hatch accommodated only four divers at a time. Lump-Lump, Tinnan, and George Walsh hung on to the exposed periscope while we others dived for the air lock.

A bubble of air remained in the escape trunk just outside the air lock door when a submarine submerged. There was an intercom to the sub's bridge inside the air pocket.

Schmidt, Tipton, and I swam to the overhanging lip of the escape trunk and bobbed up into the air pocket. I contacted the bridge on the intercom.

"Get in!" the captain urged. "Komars are coming like bats out of a cave."

"Captain, I still have three men on the periscope."

It took time to enter a submarine underwater. First, lock into the chamber. Blow the water, replace it with air, and equalize pressure. Enter the sub itself, relock the inner hatch, open the outer door to flood the chamber for the second group. We would have to go through the procedure *twice* in order to bring us all in.

We didn't have that much time.

"Captain, you'll have to surface," I all but shouted into the intercom.

"The Komars are almost within machine gun range—"

"Fuck the Komars. Our breathing lungs are fouled and we can't submerge. I have three men on the periscope and three here. The situation is, you can either surface this boat and recover *all* my men—or you can take her down and drown *all* of us. The ball's in your court."

The captain was old-school cool. He barely hesitated. The nose of the sub went up. The conning tower broke above the waves. The tower hatch opened and Lump, Walsh, and Tinnan tumbled inside. They heard my voice resonating over the intercom on the control deck.

"Captain, it's either *all* of us or *none* of us."

"Mister Boehm. Your men on the tower *are* aboard."

"Roger that," I snapped. "Thank you. We're locking in now. Let's get the hell outta here."

THIRTY-SIX

★ ★ ★ ★ ★

By the autumn of 1962, it became more than apparent that the Soviets were moving intercontinental ballistic missiles into Cuba. SEALs who had been involved in mapping possible invasion sites, training resistance forces, and conducting spy and assassination missions against Castro were naturally committed to proving the existence of these missiles on the island. The events of that summer and autumn, as Secretary of Defense Robert S. McNamara put it, forced the earth to face its "greatest danger of a catastrophic war since the advent of the nuclear age."

I was ordered to pick one other SEAL to accompany me on a Top Secret hazardous mission. The fate of the free world, I was informed with undoubted hyperbole, hung on two SEALs and a CIA spook with whom Lump and I would link up in Key West, Florida. What our mission produced might well prompt a confrontation between the world's two superpowers that could result in the destruction of civilization.

"We paying Papa Fidel another visit?" Lump asked.

"They'll brief us once we're aboard the submarine."

The spook, who said to call him "John," and a State Department goon were already waiting for Lump and me aboard the moored sub *Sea Lion.* John, a photographer, was a fragile Spanish twig upon which hung a pair of thick glasses. He looked like he should have had a pocket protector full of ballpoint pens. Next to him, Lump-Lump looked like a walking man mountain with his broad shoulders, clifflike jaw, and short quills of hair driven like nails into his scalp.

"Charlie," Lump growled at the spook. "That ugly Lieutenant Boehm is the best goddamned operator in the SEALs and the SEALs are the best goddamned operators in the world. We'll get you in to do your job and we'll get you back out. Just listen to us. Fuck up and I'll drown your skinny ass."

Once *Sea Lion* dove in the Florida Straits, John, Lump, and I crowded into the wardroom along with the State Department goon dressed like Mr. Ivy League in shirt, sweater, slacks, and deck shoes. He began the briefing with the subdued relish of a neighborhood gossip.

"Gentlemen, you are about to embark on the most significant mission of your military careers. The forces of communism and the forces of the free world are being compelled into a standoff the outcome of which only God knows. The world may be only days away from nuclear confrontation."

His grim eyes swept the wardroom. Lump nudged me. "Who *is* this asshole?"

"That's your new lord and master."

To Mr. Ivy League, I said, "Can the bullshit. Get down to the need-to-know."

SEALs required no motivational speeches. Ivy League glared, offended. "The United States has good reason to believe the Soviet Union has moved ICBMs into Cuba," he said. "How's that? President Kennedy will not back down, not even from nuclear war. The President will broadcast it to the world as soon as we can confirm the intelligence we've gathered that Castro and Khrushchev are installing ICBMs to target the United States."

Holy shit!

He produced high-altitude photos of Bahia del Mariel, code-named *Pinlon* for the mission. The deepwater harbor lay a few kilometers west of Havana. It bulged into the island like a lopsided balloon with one narrow opening to the sea. Ships were tied up to piers inside the harbor. Trucks with large flatbed trailers appeared to be hauling away long cylindrical objects covered with tarps.

"We must obtain irrefutable proof that they're missiles," said Mr. Ivy League.

Lump-Lump and I would insert into Pinlon with John the spook photographer and protect his scrawny nerd ass while he sneaked up and took snapshots of the missiles. In a *real* war, we would have swum in, attached explosives to the freighters, and blown them up with the missiles still aboard. *Sayonara, motherfuckers. Fuck you very much. Don't forget to write.* In the Cold War, however, it wasn't done that way.

"You're checked out in a diving lung?" I asked John.

He gave me a blank look. I thumped one of the air tanks laid out among the mission gear in the forward torpedo room.

"I'm not," he admitted.

Lump-Lump discharged air from his cavernous chest. "Jesus H. Christ."

"You *do* swim?" I asked.

He hesitated. It turned out he was about as much at home in the water as a hobo in a bathtub.

"You just get me to the beach," he said. "I'll do the rest."

We locked out of the sub off the Cuban coast after nightfall, using a rubber raft as transport. The raft was like an air mattress used by some fat lady on Miami Beach. Surface swimming was a risk, what with the Komar torpedo boats patrolling the coastline, but we had no choice. John sputtered and coughed as we shot to the surface from the submerged boat. The *Sea Lion* slid off as silent as a shark to wait in the black-running Gulf Stream for our signal to return.

John rode the raft with our two waterproof bags while Lump and I swam on either side pushing him. The gear bags contained dry clothing, rations, and fresh water, John's cameras, binoculars, and two .38 Combat Masterpiece revolvers. As when we slipped in to scout the Havana Harbor for a possible invasion site, the State Department forbade our going in armed. It might cause an international incident if we were caught. Fuck me! Just before H hour, the boat's chief of the boat passed me our pistols. God bless enlisted men who don't have to kiss ass.

Gentle breezes from the warm land carried tropical odors seaward. Bananas and mangos and plowed fields and, Lump added, Spanish pussy. The warm sea undulated like flowing oil. Harbor lights tiny and sparking in the distance demarcated where black of sea met black of land. Lump and I swam strong and steady for two hours with John on the raft between us. We kept a sharp eye peeled for Komars, although there wasn't much we could have done in defense if we were spotted.

As we drew near land, the harbor's mouth turned into a narrow black vagina. Deep into it, yellow lights reflected off the water where two Russian freighters rode tied off to long concrete-and-wood piers. Lights draped over the freighters' sides and shining into the water were supposed to discourage underwater saboteurs and spies. Two chunky Komars rode at anchor farther inside the harbor, their machine guns unmanned.

I had been in officers' clubs with more action. I would have been guarding the harbor like Fort Knox were I secretly importing enough missiles to wipe out the eastern seaboard of the United States. I detected *no* security. Maybe Castro had his sentries hidden on the ships and inside the ramshackle warehouses to prevent aerial photo surveillance until he and Khrushchev had their missiles set up and aimed at the mainland. Either that or maybe he *really* was importing cow-feed silos instead of ICBMs.

A flashlight dotted the darkness twice from dead ahead on Punto Barlovento, the harbor's outer lip.

"The contact," John whispered.

I splashed water once in response, like a big fish. The flashlight dotted twice more. We glided through the gently lapping shore surf and slithered onto hostile soil like amphibians breaking free of primordial muck. I couldn't make out the contact's face in the darkness, but his slouching, rather stiff gait marked him as an older man. I eased my hand into one of the sub bags and withdrew the pistols. I slipped one to Lump.

John and the contact embraced each other like long-lost cousins. Then, quickly, we gathered our equipment, wiped out our tracks, and followed the Cuban up the short, steep bank to the dead end of a narrow street. Dilapidated warehouses and other rundown buildings lined the street. They appeared abandoned. The only light came from the freighters nearly 1,000 yards farther along and the growing wedge of the approaching dawn.

We hugged the deeper shadows on the water side of the street. Soon, we came to a small weathered building attached to the water by a tiny wharf on pilings. The single room was about 30 feet long and narrow enough to induce claustrophobia. It smelled of wood rot and fish guts and hemp and seaweed. Old fish nets and fish traps and buoys and canvas and crab traps were piled everywhere. There were two doors. The tiny window in the door that opened onto the wharf let in the weak distant light from the enemy ships.

The tide was out. Sand crabs rattled their quick legs from the crawl space underneath the building. Lump and I checked it out quickly and then changed into jeans and old shirts and deck shoes. The Colt revolver and the K-bar knife felt hard and cold and reassuring against the skin at my waist.

John and the Cuban prepared to leave.

"Where the fuck you going, Charlie?" Lump-Lump rumbled.

"You've done your job. Now I'll do mine."

Dry land seemed to have restored his confidence. He packed his cameras into a worn satchel.

"Don't be seen while I'm gone," he warned, then left with the old man.

I laughed uneasily. "I guess the little nerd put us in our place."

For all Lump and I knew, either John or the old man was a double agent. I visualized Lump-Lump and me lashed to the nose of one of those goddamned missiles as it descended onto Washington, D.C.

"Roysi," Lump grumbled, "it's a fine kettle of shit fish you've got me into this time, lad."

Sent on a mission to protect the future of the free world—and there we sat, hiding in a smelly fisherman's shack, armed with pistols against nuclear missiles. I'd make my number all right.

Suffocating heat seeped into the shack as the sun rose out of Havana to the east and climbed above us. Still no activity among the warehouses. Cubans and their Soviet cohorts must have evacuated the waterfront to help protect the secret of the arriving ICBMs. Lump's sweaty shirt clung wet to the outlines of his muscles.

"You're beginning to stink, sir," he said finally. "No offense, Skipper, but I need a little fresh air."

"No offense taken, you squint-eyed, fish-breathed, whoremongering son of an Arabian camel."

Lump stepped outside just as two teenaged boys swung chattering and grab-assing into the end of the street. They spotted Lump immediately and waved. Lump kept his cool. He waved back and laughed as he tossed them a colorful fisherman's net float. They caught it and played catch with it as they ran out of sight. Lump looked grim as he retreated and closed the door. We hissed at each other.

"Skipper, they seemed to think I belonged . . ."

"All they have to do is let slip one word . . ."

"Jesus . . . I don't think they thought anything . . ."

"You want to bet your life on what two kids did or didn't think?"

I kept watch while Lump erased obvious signs of our presence and made sure our gear was concealed. Then we crawled underneath the shack to hide. It was a tight fit. Sand crabs edged up sideways and eyed us speculatively with their stilted exclamation-point eyes.

"Lieutenant, I ain't going to one of them Cuban gulags," Lump whispered.

"You won't have to. They'll execute us."

"We fight then?"

"Lump, SEALs *always* fight if we're left no choice."

We huddled together in the dark mud with the crabs watching us like hangmen and the strong odor of the incoming tide in our nostrils. I almost laughed at the thought of the fate of the world riding on our shoulders.

"Roysi," Lump murmured sardonically, "tell me again how much glamour there is in this job."

THIRTY-SEVEN

★ ★ ★ ★ ★

Nightfall was a long time coming. Lump-Lump and I, driven from underneath the shack by the incoming tide, finally felt secure enough to venture back inside. The two kids had probably forgotten all about seeing Lump. Sounds of activity began drifting to us from the docked Russian freighters. Truck engines. Winches sounding like chalk against the blackboard of the night. Incredible that security was so lax. The Reds were moving around ICBMs as casually as though they were unloading a grain elevator. Boldness, perhaps, the utter *unbelievability* of shipping nuclear warheads into America's own backyard, as a substitute for subterfuge.

"Someone's coming!" Lump-Lump drew his weapon and spun away from the door window where he kept vigil. I took the other side of the door.

Trapped!

The door creaked open. A dark figure outlined by the lighter outside. I yanked it inside and thrust the muzzle of my Colt against his temple.

"Por Dios, señor! It is only I coming for you."

I pinned the old man against the wall while Lump checked outside to make sure he was alone.

"Where's John?" I asked.

"Near here preparing for the job. It will be tonight. Not for you to worry, *señor.*"

"Easy enough for you to say."

It would be natural for John and the old man to mingle with the locals if the shit hit the oscillator. Together, Lump-Lump and I might know enough Spanish to order a whore and a bottle of *cerveza.*

In broken but passable English, the old man explained, "They move one missile only each night. They hide from—how you say?—aircraft surveillance." He pointed up. Then he flashed a quick grin. "But this night they are seen from more near, *sí?* Come. We have work to do."

He led us up the street to a three-floored warehouse crouching in the dark along the waterfront. Missile-moving sounds came from beyond it. We hid in the shadows of the buildings across from it and watched for a full quarter-hour. The complete lack of enemy security unnerved me. This was *too* easy.

For a second I entertained a disturbing thought that the Cubans had captured John and the old man was now leading us into a trap. But then I released that suspicion. You had to trust the people you operated with; there was no one else to trust.

At last, I nodded at the Cuban. Guns in hand, Lump-Lump and I fast-trailed him across the open street and into the warehouse. The unpartitioned bottom floor appeared littered with old empty packing crates and rusted machinery of some sort. Squeaky wooden stairs immediately to the left led up to the third floor. Our stealthy footfalls on the stairs released mold and dust. The old man knew where he was going. We entered a room at the end of a musky hallway on the third floor and closed the door behind us.

Pale moonlight through the open shutters of a single window illuminated chairs, a table, and a bed with the bare mattress rolled back. The roofs of other buildings obstructed the view through the window.

"You see everything from the roof," explained the old man. "We are to wait here for our *amigo.*"

A quick but thorough scouting of the entire building pinpointed escape routes and defensive points. The window at the end of the hallway opened onto a neighboring rooftop and a ladder that provided access to the warehouse roof. Satisfied, the three of us waited in the darkness of the hideout room and listened to the sobering grind of machinery as it moved ICBMs in preparation for possible nuclear strikes against my country.

Nuke 'em first, I thought. *Nuke 'em until they glowed. Do unto others—but do it first before they did it to you.*

John was in a hurry when he arrived. He wore old sneakers and work clothing and carried his cameras. He jabbed a finger toward the roof. Lump-Lump remained behind to check John's backtrail before joining us where we sprawled on our bellies at the roof's peak and glassed the harbor below with binoculars.

Water lay still and black in its protected land cup. Komars with their running lights extinguished inscribed slow, vigilant rounds at the vagina's opening. The only illumination came from the lights over the sides of the Russian freighters. Stevedores rigged lines and cables around a long canvas-covered cylinder aboard one of the ships. A tractor truck was having trouble maneuvering a long trailer around the sharp corner where the street turned toward the piers. Its engine moaned and groaned in granny gear until a little crane arrived to pick up the end of the trailer and move it around on line. The mundane, I reflected, concealing the profane.

The truck trailer was specially designed with chocks and blocks to receive the missile. John used a light-grabbing telephoto lens to shoot several rolls of film as workers transferred the ICBM from the Russian ship to the Cuban truck.

"Not good enough," he fretted. We had not seen the missile itself, although little imagination was required to know what its canvas covering concealed.

"I've got to get closer," John whispered.

Certainly the Russians had posted security around the missile itself.

"It's something I have to chance," John decided. "You can see it if I get in trouble down there. There's nothing you can do if I'm caught. Just get the hell back to sea before they trap you too. Here. Take these with you." He handed me the film he had already shot.

I took a new look at the little man with the thick glasses. I extended a hand and we shook.

"You've got balls," I acknowledged.

He flashed a pleased grin and said, "I don't intend to lose them in Cuba." Then he was gone, taking only a camera the size of his palm.

I nodded at Lump-Lump. "Cover his ass. Shadow him from a distance."

I waited with the old man, both of us tense and silent as we scanned the piers through binoculars. That was one awesome piece of ordnance down there. It harnessed more destructive power than the entire U.S. fleet had expended against the Japanese during WWII, including the atomic bombs dropped on Hiroshima and Nagasaki. Unleashed against Washington, D.C., it would turn the nation's capital and surrounding Virginia and Maryland into a vast smoldering wasteland incapable of supporting life for thousands of years. Four or five of them would render uninhabitable the eastern seaboard from New York to Miami. *My God indeed, what has man wrought?*

I gave an involuntary start. Was that *John* mingling with the stevedores? It *couldn't* be.

Lump-Lump returned alone, sweating, admiration in his voice. "The little bastard's crazy. I had to drop back. He's right in there *with* the workmen."

We watched, waiting for a commotion to signal John's discovery. Lump called off the passage of each quarter-hour.

"We can't wait much longer," I said.

"A little longer?" Lump pleaded.

An almost palpable sigh of relief escaped the three of us

on the roof when John appeared suddenly from the ladder. He crawled toward us, grinning broadly, clearly on a high.

"I could have *touched* it!" he cried and patted his tiny camera. "We've *got* it now. Let that bearded sonofabitch try to deny *this* evidence. Gentlemen, let's get the hell out of Cuba. In two or three more days, there may not be enough left of this island to support a goat."

THIRTY-EIGHT

★ ★ ★ ★ ★

Escaping Cuba proved anticlimactic, nothing like the SEALs' first visit. A long swim out to sea where the *Sea Lion* picked us up for the fast run to Key West. Photos John took added to the mountain of evidence accumulating against the communists. Examination of both air and ground photography by the nation's intelligence community revealed several missile installations under construction in Cuba to accommodate at least 16 and possibly 32 ICBMs, each with a range of over 1,000 miles. Military experts advised the missiles could be operational within a week. Released against the United States, they were expected to destroy an estimated 80 *million* Americans within the first few minutes after being fired.

On 20 October, U.S. armed forces around the world, including the SEALs, were placed on alert. Missile crews stood with fingers literally on the nuclear button. Troops moved into Florida and the southeastern United States. The First Armored Division began moving out of Texas into Georgia, while five more divisions made ready for deployment. The base at Guantanamo Bay was reinforced. The Navy deployed 180 warships into the Caribbean. SAC, the Strategic

Air Command, dispersed its aircraft to civilian landing fields around the nation to lessen its vulnerability to attack. The B-52 bomber force took to the air fully loaded with nuclear weapons. As one plane landed to refuel, another immediately took its place.

The crisis was so real, danger so imminent, that some political types in D.C. loaded up their families and sent them north to Canada. On Monday afternoon, 22 October, President Kennedy gravely went on the air to inform the nation of the crisis. He said he would enact a blockade around Cuba. His speech was broadcast through loudspeakers on most military bases. Servicemen gathered in hushed groups to listen wherever they could find a TV or radio.

"Let no one doubt that this is a difficult and dangerous effort on which we have set out," he said. "No one can foresee what course it will take or what costs and casualties will be incurred. Many months of sacrifice and self-discipline lie ahead, months in which both our patience and our will will be tested, months in which many threats and denunciations will keep us aware of our dangers. But the greatest danger of all would be to do nothing. . . .

"The cost of freedom is always high—but Americans have always paid it. And one path we shall never choose, and that is the path of surrender or submission."

Although Lt. John Callahan was CO of SEAL Team Two, he was assigned to the staff of CINCLANTFLT for the duration and I was left in command of the team. Secret orders placed me in charge of utilizing both Team Two and Team One from the West Coast, roughly 120 men, in capturing Pinlon harbor and keeping it open in advance of the anticipated invasion of Cuba.

Old rivalries between the teams boiled to the surface when Team One's commander, Lt. Dave Del Guidice, arrived at Little Creek from California with his operations staff. The rest of his men would be flying in shortly.

"There are changes I want made to your op plan," he informed me.

"Oh?"

I had assigned my Team Two the more hazardous missions. I *knew* my men were well trained and ready. Part of my force would parachute onto the heights above the seaport near the Cuban military academy, secure the terrain around the harbor, and seize any ships at the piers to prevent their being sunk at the mouth of the harbor to block it. The rest of my SEALs would launch at sea in 16-foot gunboats armed with machine guns and 3.5 rocket launchers with which to take out the Komars and any security forces.

Del Guidice's Team One would provide backup support, security, and recovery of troops from the water once the invasion began.

"I want to integrate my people with yours," Del Guidice insisted.

"No. I've trained my people for over two years to work together. You've trained yours. I can't downgrade my people by integrating yours."

He flared. "I'll see the skipper."

That did it. "Asshole," I growled. "Don't you know anything about the fucking Navy? I represent my commanding officer, who is senior to you. Therefore, that makes me senior."

He backed off.

"Look, here's what I'll do," I offered in conciliation. "I'll give your team any of the assignments that you want from my team. I'll replace my jumpers with yours, if you care to lead them."

Del Guidice squirmed with sudden discomfort, knowing I intended parachuting in with my air element to maintain positive control and leadership. No more *sneaking* into Cuba.

"Well, uh . . . ," he stammered. "I thought I should remain aboard the ship—for better command and control."

I blistered him with a sarcastic grin. A commander couldn't *push* his men from the rear; he had to *lead* them from up front.

"Have someone else lead the jumpers then. Do you want the job?"

He wavered. "I'll contemplate it."

"Do you want the gunboats?" I asked, still willing to accommodate.

He looked them over. "Have you ever fired a rocket launcher from any of those?" he asked uneasily. A 3.5 launcher emitted a tremendous back blast.

"It might blow up the boat," I admitted. "But if it has to blow, I'd prefer it blow up on a mission where it will do some good first."

"I think that's unsound."

"Unsound or not, do you want it? Make a decision so I can retrain my people to take over whatever position you have left over."

He fidgeted, finally muttering, "It's too late to make any changes now."

"What you're looking for is a fucking way to weasel out. Cover your own ass by mixing your guys with mine and letting me take all the responsibility in case something goes wrong. Mister, there will be none of this bullshit of 'It wasn't my guys, it was *his* guys.' My guys will not fail. If you guys fuck up, it's *your* fault."

"Boehm, your mouth has made you a lot of enemies. Sooner or later, you're going to get your ass chopped off right behind your neck."

He was correct there. For nearly two years now I had done everything I had to do in order to acquire equipment for my SEALs and train them the way sea commandos needed to be trained. I had pushed, shoved, raised hell with the bean counters, circumvented and bent the system, tweaked the noses of officialdom. Along with my courts-martial, I had collected an impressive list of enemies and contributed my name to some even more impressive shit lists. My enemies wanted me out of the SEALs and replaced by someone they could control. I was simply too abrasive, too forward, to play the brand of internecine politics necessary at that level. I was learning again that it didn't make any difference how good you were at your job if you couldn't play the kiss-ass game. *Wash your ass for me, sir, 'cause I'm gonna kiss it a lot.*

As commander of the invasion spearhead, I was probably the hottest goddamned lieutenant in the U.S. Navy. Having tweaked the lion's tail in its den so often in behalf of my beloved SEALs, I fully *expected* the hammer to fall on me. If I lived through the crisis, I would probably be replaced afterwards.

Nonetheless, I continued to push. It came to the point where my old nemesis, Admiral Rivera, Vice Chief of Naval Operations, wouldn't even look at me when we met because of disputes over how my men should or should not be equipped for the mission. I wanted weapons to counter Soviet handheld nuclear missiles reportedly supplied to the Cubans. Instead, my unconventional warriors who traveled and fought light were loaded down with steel-plated flak jackets and the like while the real problems were ignored.

"How about checking on the handheld nukes?" I requested. "Don't you think it's important for us to know that when we go in?"

Staff declined to either confirm or deny the weapons, typically leaving me in the dark when it came to contingency planning.

Hoss Kucinski and Lump-Lump spoke out on behalf of the team. Hoss said, "Mr. Bo, the bastards'll have us so loaded down with gear it'll take four men to throw our asses out of the airplane and a six-by truck on the ground to haul us around."

"Don't worry about it, boys. We'll go to the airhead with all that useless shit, then dump it into the Dempsy Dumpster before we get on the plane."

The hammer descended a lot sooner than expected. I suddenly received orders assigning me to SERVRON 8, a rear-echelon service-and-support outfit that would tear me away from both the SEALs and the fleet. I reported to staff.

"Who shall I turn the operation over to?" I asked. Del Guidice would literally shit if he had to take it. "Navy regs say I have 72 hours to report to my new duty station."

You didn't have to *like* a man to know he was the best qualified for a job.

"We can extend you here until after the crisis," I was offered.

I dug in. "No extensions. You either cancel the goddamn orders or I'm gone in 72 hours."

I forced the fucking Navy Bureau at CNO level to back down one more time. The transfer orders were canceled immediately—but I suspected they lurked still in the bowels of the bureaucracy where nonoperators and bean counters waited for the opportunity to pounce.

On 24 October my SEALs went into final rehearsals as President Kennedy's quarantine took effect. The entire world watched with bated breath from the brink as two Russian ships, the *Gagarin* and the *Komiles,* steamed the last few miles toward the quarantine barrier. Interception by American warships should take place shortly before noon Washington time. Poised in the operations ready room, all weapons and gear ready to go, we SEALs waited hushed and expectant for the word. In the vast expanse of the Atlantic Ocean, 1,000 miles away from Washington, the final decisions were going to be made within the next few minutes.

A Soviet submarine moved into position between the two inbound ships. Kennedy ordered the aircraft carrier *Essex* supported by antisubmarine helicopters to intercept. If the USSR sub refused to respond to signals to surface, depth charges would be used to force it up.

"I felt we were on the edge of a precipice with no way off," Robert Kennedy wrote later. "This time, the moment was now—not next week, not tomorrow."

The world poised peering into a nuclear holocaust. Then, suddenly, *Gagarin* and *Komiles* stopped dead in the water. They turned back. Khrushchev had blinked.

The crisis passed, although the danger was far from over. The SEALs went on stand-down at the end of the week. Although I was expecting it, SERVRON 8 orders coming out of hiding knocked the wind out of my sails, left me feeling angry and bitter. I should have known, though. This was the way it always was. Bring out the warriors and dust them off when they were needed; shove them back into the closet out of sight when it was over.

My enemies had apparently decreed that I would be hidden from the rest of the Navy until they saw fit to forgive my misdemeanors. I was stripped of my team, no longer to lead it in combat. I had defied the noncombatants once too often in fighting to launch my sea warriors. Now, I must pay the fiddler.

But even as I reported to Commander, Service Squadron 8 at Norfolk, I heard the rumbling and grumbling of more trouble on the horizon. Vietnam. I figured the closet door wasn't shut too tightly.

PART IV

Vietnam: Unconventional Warfare in the Delta (1963–1964)

The U.S. has broken the second
rule of war. That is, don't go
fighting with your land army on
the mainland of Asia.
—Chalfont, *Montgomery of Alamein*

THIRTY-NINE

★ ★ ★ ★ ★

I missed my SEALs. I missed Lump-Lump and Hoot and Hoss Kucinski and all the others. There had never been such men. Once, when I asked for volunteers for "an extremely hazardous mission," the entire team, to a man, stepped forward at the same time. It was the greatest honor I had ever been paid.

My commanding officer at SERVRON 8, Commodore Nash, was a wiry human dynamo with a firm grip and a warm smile. I liked him immediately.

"Roy, the people who do nothing seldom get into trouble," he said. "But they seldom get anything accomplished either."

I was assigned as squadron engineer in charge of propulsion plants. I knew little about engineering; I was an ex-bos'n mate. Nonetheless, I tried to hide my displeasure in "shore duty," a polite way of saying I was being turned out to pasture, while I threw myself once again into the books and manuals. By this time Ellie, Fluffy the parakeet, and I had split and I had few distractions. I became reasonably competent in propulsion plants, but I often stood looking out to sea and wondering, as my old man had, who put the ocean so goddamned near the shore. I was accustomed to the high activity level of the SEALs and, before that, UDT.

Although Vietnam was heating up to a true little guerrilla war, it seemed I had been consigned to its sidelines at SERVRON 8. As I was unable to continue development of the sea-warrior concept I had first envisioned over 20 years earlier, I once again considered civilian life. If the U.S. Navy no longer wanted me, others did. The long-standing offer from Ed Link and his deep-diving submersible operations remained open. Dupont and Hercules Powder offered me similar positions. Then there was always the CIA. I even considered transferring to the U.S. Army Special Forces.

Bored and disgusted with the chickenshit, I finally fired off my letter of resignation to the Secretary of the Navy, requesting to retire to the Fleet Reserve. I received a phone call from BUPERS, the Bureau of Personnel.

"Roy, what in the hell are you doing?"

"Sir, if you don't know, you're not in the know. How about my walking papers? I got places to go and things to do."

"You can bet your ass you got places to go. Your personal likes and dislikes are at the convenience of the government. Convenient for the government at this time is a new set of orders."

The orders came, dated 6 July 1963, assigning me to MAAG, the U.S. Military Assistance Advisory Group, Vietnam.

> Dear Lt. Boehm:
>
> Welcome to a most energetic and purposeful command!
>
> Navy section, MAAG, is responsible for the Navy effort here in Vietnam and I think you will find your tour to be challenging, interesting, and rewarding.
>
> Information received from the Chief of Naval Personnel indicates you will report in October 1963 for duty as numerical relief for Lt. Peter W. Willits, USNR. For rotation purposes and quarters, you will be assigned to the billet of UDT adviser . . .

UDT! *Underwater Demolition Team.* Damn. I was back in the game.

FORTY

★ ★ ★ ★ ★

Vietnam had been smoldering for years, ever since the French were driven out of the country at Dien Bien Phu in 1954. As early as October 1957, Hanoi communists had organized 37 armed companies of guerrillas in South Vietnam, most of them in the impenetrable forests and marshes of the Mekong Delta where I would be "advising" and operating with my Vietnamese UDT. Uncle Ho discouraged armed attacks while he enlarged the traditional communist infiltration routes known collectively as the Ho Chi Minh Trail. Instead, he concentrated on political terrorism and assassinations. The number of assassinated Vietnamese government officials soared to an average of 4,000 a year between 1959 and 1961.

South Vietnam president Ngo Dinh Diem made it easy for the communists to recruit and gain strength by cracking down on civil liberties and appointing military men as province chiefs. These soldiers, mostly Catholics, characteristically neglected the economic and social needs of the local populations. Buddhists felt especially oppressed.

In December 1960, Hanoi took another step in escalating the conflict by announcing a new organization in the south—the National Liberation Front, the NLF, the *Vietcong,* designed to coalesce the disparate collection of elements opposed to the Diem regime. It was under the NLF that the communists planned and conducted increased military pressure against the government.

Persecuted by ancient Confucian emperors, the French, and now President Diem's Catholic administrators, Buddhists staged a series of brutal protests against the government a few months before I landed in Saigon. The protests began after Buddhists assembled in Hue on 8 May 1963 to celebrate the 2,527th birthday of the Buddha. The deputy province chief, a Catholic, prohibited their flying the national flag and then ordered soldiers to fire upon them to disperse a crowd listening to a speech by a Buddhist leader. The gunfire killed a woman and eight children.

On the morning of 11 June, an elderly Buddhist monk in saffron robes climbed out of a car at a busy Saigon intersection and sat down cross-legged on the asphalt. Other monks and nuns encircled him while one of their number doused him with gasoline and then ignited him with a lighter. He went up like a human torch in protest over Diem's policies.

Diem blamed the Vietcong. "Let them burn," he exclaimed of the grisly spectacle of monks immolating themselves on the world's front pages, "and we shall clap our hands."

Partly because of the Buddhists, partly because of Diem's oppressive measures against the people in attempts to stop the NLF, plots to overthrow the government sprouted among Diem's administration. On 2 November, only days before I arrived, Diem's generals rebelled and assassinated Diem in a successful coup. The military revolutionary council headed by General Minh was in charge when I got off the airplane at Tan Son Nhut airport in the sweltering heat of a Vietnam afternoon. Otherwise, all that had changed was that Vietnam, that "splendid little war," that "not much of a war, but it's the only war we have," was about to turn up the griddle.

NLF guerrillas were growing like weeds all over the Mekong Delta and kicking ass; the government was in shambles; Buddhists had just finished making pyres of themselves; North Vietnam was sending troops and supplies south on the Ho Chi Minh Trail; Saigon was rife with spies of all sexes and political loyalties; and political assassinations were common. It was, to use the old military term, a *clusterfuck*.

I hoisted my seabag onto my shoulder as I got off the

airplane and breathed in for the first time the tropic-heated air of Vietnam. It smelled and tasted of ocean salt and rotted fish sauce, of human excrement and wet things growing. Streets teemed with bicycles, cyclos, mopeds, Hondas, rusted trucks filled with vegetables, pigs, and people. A water buffalo lay down in the middle of the road and refused to get up. A policeman drew a raucous crowd by threatening to shoot the beast and have it dragged away.

Vietnam, I believed almost from my first sight of it, was a disaster that had found its own place to happen. Few conventional military and political leaders understood the extent to which unconventional warfare involved literally every component of a society—military, political, economic, religious. . . . Anything, *everything,* was a weapon and a tool to further political goals—terrorism, assassination, intrigue, boycott, propaganda, disinformation, threat, spying. *Grab 'em by the balls and their hearts and minds will follow.*

The insurgent *always* had the advantage. The only way to stop him was by using unconventional *tactics* within a conventional *strategy.* Unfortunately, American politicians had no realistic concept of limited warfare. Even at these early stages, Vietnam was becoming a war led by administrators such as the senior naval adviser at MAAG, Captain "Progress Is Our Most Important Product" Drachnik, who shackled professional warriors with stupid and unworkable rules of engagement.

But politics wasn't my game. Never had been. I figured that since Lt. Roy Boehm had whipped the U.S. Navy SEALs into a formidable outfit whose team presence would soon be experienced by the VC in the Delta with fear and trepidation, I could do the same thing with the Vietnamese Frogs, the *Lien Doc Nguoi Nhai.* I was about to have a real little war going to test, hone, and temper their skills.

And my own skills as well.

FORTY-ONE

★ ★ ★ ★ ★

I had heard about Commander Minh of the 514th Vietcong Battalion almost as soon as I stepped off the MAC flight at Saigon's Tan Son Nhut International in late 1963, before the U.S. military buildup. It was still the pretense era of "advisers." My assignment was to "advise" the LDNN, train, and direct them on combat operations in the VC-infested Mekong Delta.

"Commander Minh is like a ghost in the swamps," I was informed. "He is seen only when he wishes to be seen—and then it is to his enemy's misfortune."

By the time I arrived in Vietnam, my U.S. SEALs had been commissioned and operating for about two years. They proved to be everything I planned and trained for—guerrillas, spies, assassins, good fighters to have on your side, terrifying enemies. My kind of unconventional warriors. Vietnam, however, was to be their first true test in a *real* war. The war in the Mekong Delta was especially suited for them.

The SEALs I envisioned operated as true commandos anywhere there was a link to water, whether ocean blue or river brown. It was a standing joke that SEALs considered themselves in a maritime environment as long as they had water in their canteens. It didn't take nearly that much imagination to see the Mekong Delta where Commander Minh and the other VC warlords operated as a maritime environment.

The Delta encompassed the entire southern tip of the country where the average rainfall was 80 inches a year.

Two wide rivers split the Delta and formed the largest of a network of streams and canals that drained the lowlands into the South China Sea. The southernmost river, the Bassac, ran generally northeast to southwest; the Mekong to the north ran nearly west to east. VC used the streams and canals—arteries of flowing, thin mud that seeped out of swamps and pools swarming with mosquitoes—to ferry men, arms, and ammunition into the major war zones north of Saigon.

While the Delta was a sleepy place where rice grew well, it was also thousands of square kilometers of heat, wet rot, mangrove swamp, nipa palm, and jungle. It was alive with snakes, spiders, scorpions, crocodiles, jungle cats, and VC.

I wanted my piece of the action as commander of a SEAL platoon deployed on hostile soil. Instead, since I had received orders to relieve Navy Lt. Peter Willits as adviser to the *Lien Doc Nguoi Nhai,* I was to take South Vietnamese ARVNs and turn *them* into UDT/SEALs.

I soon understood why Willits's nickname was *Out to Lunch.* He showed up to meet me in Saigon carrying a briefcase that he never let out of his sight. It contained automobile brochures and contracts. He was more dedicated to selling cars than killing VC.

"I work for Cars International," he explained with his used-car-salesman smile. "I can get you a good deal on any kind of car you can name. Buy it here and you can beat the taxes."

I returned his smile with a withering look. "I'm not here to buy or sell cars."

His superior, now mine, at Military Assistance Advisory Group (MAAG) was Captain Drachnik, who plastered signs all over his Saigon office proclaiming: PROGRESS IS OUR MOST IMPORTANT PRODUCT. Reminded me of General Electric or GMC. I immediately recognized that the good administrator and manager took precedence in Vietnam over the combat leader. Had I uttered "kill" or "maim" in either Willits's or Drachnik's presence, they would have probably filled their skivvies and fainted.

MAAG had filed no reports about LDNN actions. Were the *Nguoi Nhai* SCUBA qualified? I asked Willits. Were they parachute qualified? Had Willits observed them in combat? The lieutenant shuffled from foot to foot and found something in his briefcase to occupy him.

"How many men do I have?" I asked.

Willits blinked. "Well, it's hard to tell."

"What the fuck do you mean—it's hard to tell? Do I have any men or not?"

"I think about . . . about 40. . . ."

I had never had much patience. "Pete, I want a roster of my men. Understand? I also want to meet my Vietnamese counterpart and I want to know when the next operation will take place. Meet me with them in Nha Trang tomorrow morning. I'll be out to take morning physical training with you."

Willits looked sullen and put upon. "Their PT is usually over by the time I get to see them."

"How often *do* you get to see them?"

"A couple of times a week. As my schedule permits."

About 20 of the 42 Vietnamese assigned to my LDNN appeared the next day at an old rock quarry training camp outside Nha Trang. Only about seven or eight seemed to have had any combat experience at all. Their commander, my counterpart, Captain Ninh, wasn't among them. Khe was the senior enlisted man, a wiry 22-year-old of less than 100 pounds in weight with a hawklike face as wizened and wise as an emperor's monkey. He stood back, aloof, while the other Viets giggled and held hands. Most of them wore only remnants of uniforms. Some were barefooted or wore shower shoes purchased from the local military PX. Their equipment was almost in the same shape—rusted unmaintained M-14s and carbines, French-made open-circuit Aqua-Lungs frozen, rotted, and unworkable. Many had lost their weapons, forgotten to bring them, or maybe sold them to the VC.

I shook my head in disgust. To send this bunch of giggling,

hand-holding kids into the bush in pursuit of VC warlords the likes of Commander Minh would be akin to sending goats out to catch tigers. Willits must have seen the red creeping out of my shirt collar and remembered he had an appointment elsewhere.

"I have to meet an army colonel about a Mercedes."

He hopped into his jeep and was gone.

Although I had organized and trained American SEALs, this, *this,* was an entirely new matter. I would have to start from the ground up—"This is a diving mask, these are fins, and this is a carbine"—before my Viet Frogs dared infiltrate the muddy waters of the Mekong to meet ghost rider Minh.

"Christ! Let's get started," I said to Khe, the senior NCO.

I had selected a day of test training to determine exactly how far I had to go in turning the LDNN into, first, soldiers and only then into competent *sea warriors.* The day turned out to be pathetic comedy. First of all, I caught one of the Viets dragging a heavy box using detonating prima cord. He had it wrapped around his wrist.

"Boom!" I attempted to explain, my English against his Vietnamese. Frustrated, I demonstrated by wrapping a length of the cord around a board and detonating it. The board burst apart. Pieces of it whistled through the air. That impressed him.

"That could have been your arm," I said.

While constructing a hand grenade net linking frag and WP grenades with prima cord, another little Viet pulled a grenade pin before taping the spoon. I heard the gut-hollowing *Ping!* activating the little bomb.

"Incoming!"

The Viets might have misunderstood the cry; they couldn't have misunderstood the action. They turned frog, hopping in all directions. Bits of shrapnel caught a couple of them in the ass. Otherwise, they were unharmed but shaken.

By the end of the day, I had determined half my unit couldn't swim well enough to begin basic underwater work. Their endurance was limited and their silent underwater stroke nonexistent. As for tactics, they couldn't have sneaked up on a sawmill going full blast. I had one hell of a headache.

They started to load into the six-by truck I had commandeered for the ride back to the base at Nha Trang.

"Out! *Out!*" I bellowed. "Get out of that goddamned truck. Follow me!"

I led out in a wind sprint for the five-mile run back to base. I was damned near 40 years old; if I could run it, *they* could run it. Vietnamese soldiers huffing and wheezing scattered along the road for two miles. Khe, straining and serious faced, kept pace with me until the last mile, when I left him behind. He looked at me with a new open respect I'm certain my predecessor had never seen.

"Papa-san SEAL numbah one," he declared.

It was a start.

That evening, out of courtesy to a fellow American officer, I had dinner with Pete Willits in Nha Trang at a popular French-Vietnamese restaurant widely known for its lobster. What a fucking war. A nine-to-five war, nothing like the years I had spent in the South Pacific against the Japanese.

Willits carefully avoided the topic of his selling cars. He knew my feelings about that. However, halfway through lobster he made the mistake of remarking in all earnestness, "Roy, I'd be glad to extend in Vietnam to help you whip those little men into shape."

I exploded. "You've had a fucking year to do just that, Pete. All you've done is fly around Vietnam on free military air eating lobster and plucked duck and getting rich selling cars. You and that idiot Ninh, who's supposed to be a commander, haven't pulled a single goddamned operation. The only reason you want to stay in Vietnam is so you can continue your car scam.

"Mr. Willits, if I come across you anywhere in Vietnam after tonight, I will blow your fucking head clean off. Get your affairs in order and get out. I pull the trigger the next time I see you—and I won't miss. I'll make it look like you committed suicide. Now, Mr. Willits, get out of my sight. This SEAL has a war to fight."

FORTY-TWO

★ ★ ★ ★ ★

I resolved to make SEaAirLand commandos patterned after the SEALs out of my Vietnamese, rather than straight UDT Frogs. SEALs were more versatile when it came to guerrilla tactics. I explained to Captain Drachnik what I intended doing. I figured I should at least attempt to get an official stamp of approval. It turned out Drachnik and the new Vietnamese CNO, Drachnik's counterpart who had followed the generals' coup d'etat into power, were at odds with each other and on nonspeaking terms over the assassination of the previous CNO.

"Welcome to a most frustrating command, Boy-san," Commander Jerry Ashcroft greeted, inviting me for a drink at the Majestic Hotel where he roomed. The stocky naval officer was senior adviser to the Vietnamese junk force. He and Lt. Jim Vincent and a small cadre of U.S. officers and enlisted advisers had taken a ragtag bunch of river pirates, mostly former VC called *Biet Hai* whom no one except Ashcroft wanted or trusted, and turned them into a formidable band of cutthroats whose exploits were beginning to catch the attention of both foe and friend in the Delta.

"The old CNO and 'Ol' Progress' Drachnik were good buddies," Ashcroft explained. "Now, Drachnik won't have anything to do with the new CNO. He'll block or stonewall anything that has to go through Vietnamese operations channels. So, handle things the way the Vietnamese do. Better to beg for forgiveness after the fact than to ask for permission first."

He laughed. We were going to get along.

I began training my LDNN. While Captain Drachnik pursued *progress*, I would pursue war. I started with basics. Firing ranges. Demolitions. Physical conditioning. Swimming exercises. Small unit tactics. Leadership. Team building. Any Frog who failed to attend training or who showed up late had his pay docked. That took care of further truancies—except for Captain Ninh, over whom I had no control and whom I still hadn't met.

Like most Asians, Vietnamese are accommodating people eager to please, like children in many respects. During the next few weeks I would drive them relentlessly to transform them from straight UDT, for which they were unqualified, to SEaAirLand guerrillas, for which they were also presently unqualified.

"But you will not be unqualified long," I boomed at them as I ran them mile after mile between the rock quarry and the base at Nha Trang. "You will be ass-kicking, tiger-baiting, shark-riding, VC-throat-cutting, bad, *bad*ass motherfucking killers. No more holding hands."

"Numbah one SEAL!" they responded with more enthusiasm than ability.

Khe took me aside. "We have VC spies," he announced.

"Do you know who they are?"

"VC everywhere."

"It's okay if some of our men are spies as long as spy is all they do," I decided, knowing the word would spread among my diminutive troops. "But when we start going out on missions, they had damned sure better fight like SEALs and show loyalty—or they won't be coming back."

"Very good," Khe approved.

Jerry Ashcroft and his junk force were already kicking ass in the Delta. He stood square and stocky in his dungarees whenever he stopped by to observe training. He seemed impressed. My men were shooting pop-up targets on a combat course—and not missing.

"You were *serious* about making SEALs out of them, Boy-san."

"Is a heart attack serious?"

"As serious as a fart in church. What's next?"

"Parachutes."

"You about ready to fight them against Commander Minh?"

"Minh had better know there's about to be a new bad dog on the block."

While my men might have had little stroke in the water, I discovered I had even less stroke on land when it came to support. Supplies, I was curtly informed by both the Americans and the Vietnamese, were either unavailable or delayed somewhere in the pipeline.

"Funds are short," the MAAG supply officer alibied. "We've had to buy more typewriters and office supplies to keep this operation going at all."

"War's hell," I retorted, flaring. "You could get a bad paper cut."

"Lieutenant, this war's not being run just for your benefit."

"Sorry. I forgot myself. A war ain't won until the paperwork's done."

I went to the Vietnamese CNO with a list of recommendations for supplying, training, and utilizing the LDNN. I still had not met my counterpart, that elusive Captain Ninh whom the troops called "Butterfly." I required more authority to make decisions in light of his continued absence.

"A request from you to MAAG would carry more weight," I suggested to Commodore Chung Tan Tang, the CNO.

He laughed. "Unfortunately," he said, "I have very little influence with your Captain Drachnik."

"Me either."

"Mr. Boehm, I see no problem here. Handle things the way you see best. Any advice from you is the same as an order from me."

Almost like another "Presidential Priority One," a free rein like I had had under Lieutenant Commander Hamilton to get the U.S. Navy SEALs moving. Killing Vietcong was the name of the game, and it was the only game in town.

Whether the war was a clusterfuck or not wasn't my concern. My job was to train and "advise" the South Vietnamese to kill North Vietnamese. My LDNN were going to be the best at it along the Delta.

I fell easily into the role of getting what I needed without waiting for the bureaucratic paper mills. After all, the five courts-martial quashed by JFK attested to my unorthodoxy. This time I was even better at it, coming up with increasingly innovative procurement schemes. My men joined in with relish, keeping me informed of the whereabouts of needed equipment we could "liberate." Soon, we were wearing new uniforms and carrying the latest U.S. weapons and training with the best equipment. We sometimes ate steaks while less privileged units subsisted on canned C rations. Morale soared. I had happy campers eager to fight. I felt like Ali Baba at the head of a band of 40 inscrutable Oriental thieves.

During a recon mission to the U.S. Army's Caribou Airlines at Tan Son Nhut airport, I got to know the outfit's first sergeant.

"Hey, Sarge. How would you like to be half-owner in a jeep? I'll be gone a lot; it'll be yours when I'm not home."

He cocked an eye. "That don't sound half bad."

"Will a jeep fit into one of them Caribous?"

"It will if you break down the canvas top and windshield."

"My hoods'll do it. I'll get us one in a day or so if you'll have a Caribou ready to pick it up when I call and take it to Nha Trang."

I already had a jeep in mind. It belonged to the same MAAG supply officer whom I had insulted about the paper cut. He had turned me down when I requested personal transportation. My *Nguoi Nhai* grinned wickedly when I explained the plan. They were excellent actors and thieves.

During normal business hours, drivers for the various senior U.S. military advisers sat ready with their parked jeeps in front of the MAAG compound in Saigon. Khe waited until I occupied the supply officer. Then he approached that official's driver and told him his boss wanted to see him right away. Khe and a couple of other Frogs jumped into the abandoned vehicle and lit out for the airport. I kept the supply officer busy for another 30 minutes, his driver cooling his heels outside the door, then excused myself with a grin and telephoned my contact at Caribou Airlines.

"It's on the way."

"We're ready."

By Monday morning, the supply officer's formerly navy gray jeep had turned unrecognizable army OD green. It was my great perverse pleasure to give him a lift in his own vehicle a few days later.

"Fucking thieving gooks stole mine," he complained bitterly.

"You can't trust nobody in this shitbag country," I commiserated.

Captain Drachnik shot me an odd look at his next mandatory-for-officers get-together at the Circle Sportif. "We've had a lot of government property stolen recently," he said. "It all started after Mr. Boehm arrived."

I tried on my most innocent look.

"People are starting to watch you, Mr. Boehm," he warned.

I hoped my smile annoyed the hell out of him. "In another week, sir," I said, "they'll have to watch me out in the Delta chasing Charlie. I doubt many paper shufflers will be out there counting beans. Sir."

The *Nguoi Nhai* were turning cocky and confident, especially after parachute jump training with the Vietnamese 6th Airborne Brigade. That was the way I wanted them. They were also becoming semicompetent divers and stealthy jungle fighters. I gathered them on a beach at nearby Vung Tau.

Port cities in Vietnam dumped their garbage directly into the water. People even built their outdoor toilets with the holes over the water. All that refuse attracted fish, which in turn attracted schools of sharks.

"We're going for a test swim," I announced to my young troops. "We're swimming across the harbor."

Even Khe cast an uncertain glance toward the sea.

"Sharks in water," he faltered.

I had faced my shark. It was time they faced theirs.

"We," I declared, "are the biggest, baddest sharks in the ocean. Shall we be afraid of fish like women with their cooking pots?"

"You go with us, Boss-san?" Khe asked.

"What have I taught you? A leader cannot lead from the rear."

Khe looked at the other Frogs. They all stepped forward.

"We go," said Khe soberly, "where numbah one SEAL go."

FORTY-THREE

★ ★ ★ ★ ★

Training was, after all, only playacting. I needed a real test for my Viets, a little shakedown in an environment where I might evaluate their training under realistic conditions. An Air Force pilot named Jack Benington scrounged up an L-19 Piper Cub for a reconnaissance flight to Hong Tre, a small island in the South China Sea off Nha Trang's coast. Intel reports listed it as "friendly." Intel reports were about as reliable as a politician's word.

I wondered how Benington could cram all his tall, lanky form inside the cockpit of the L-19 and still have room for his grin. The airplane was tandem seated, like a bicycle built for two. I climbed into the backseat. It had an auxiliary control stick secured with a toggle pin to the left side of the deck.

"Maybe I can get in a little stick time?" I said. "I took a

few flying lessons in Panama City, Florida, on a GI Bill boondoggle."

He eyed me with mock suspicion and stowed an AR-15 rifle next to his seat. "You SEALs *jump* from airplanes, right? Are you sure that makes you smart enough to *fly* one?"

We took off and flew out over the sea. It was littered with trawlers, junks, sails, and craft of every conceivable shape and size. The island was covered mostly with mangrove and palm jungle. Hills rose in the center with marshes around the edges. It was about three miles across at its widest point, big enough to support a fair-sized hamlet of grass-roofed hootches and a small fleet of fishing boats. I made sketches on my notepad.

I pointed out larger hootches around the edge of the village. They were obviously storage buildings. "Make another pass for a closer look-see," I suggested.

"Want I should bounce a wheel on the roof and see what scurries out?"

"I want you should keep this thing in the air."

Benington banked the Cub. As it whined in low above the jungle, approaching the suspicious structures, twin shafts of light suddenly shot through the floor fuselage. Bullet holes! Then another beamed miraculously between my feet and on out through the top.

"We're taking small arms fire!" I shouted.

"No shit, Dick Tracy."

The plane's wings waggled, as though stricken. A smear of bright blood splashed onto the pilot's left side window. His left arm jerked, then hung useless next to his seat.

"Jack?"

He yanked back on the stick with his good hand. The Piper clawed for altitude.

"Jack, you okay?"

"Fuck no. I'm not okay. I've been shot. I sure hope the hell you paid attention before they shitcanned you out of flight school."

The island grew small in our climbing slipstream.

"Am I going to have to fly this thing home?" I asked.

"God protect us. I hope not."

"Me, too," I rejoined in all sincerity.

I studied my controls with renewed incentive. Trying to remember what little I had learned about flying. Sweat popped out on my forehead like hives. Benington was also sweating. I leaned forward to take a look at his wound. It seemed a clean flesh wound through the meaty part of his arm. He was losing blood. I started to tear my jacket for a pressure bandage.

"Not enough time," Benington gasped. "Let me concentrate on getting us down."

Ahead of us lay Nha Trang sprawled along the shit brown coast like well-used children's playing blocks.

"Can you bring it in?" I was almost pleading.

"We'll find out."

He radioed our situation to the base tower. The sight of military ambulances and fire-crash trucks scurrying out to line the runway caused the cheeks of my ass to clutch the seat with a death grip. Benington seemed to get shorter and smaller in his seat, like he was closing in on himself and fading out.

"Jack?"

I hated this shit. Hated someone else having control of my life.

The runway rushed at us on final approach. The wings waggled dangerously as the one-armed pilot worked pedals and fought the ailerons to line up the aircraft for touchdown. Ground rush suddenly, and crash trucks racing to keep pace.

We were coming in too damned fast. Benington couldn't let go of the stick to ease the throttle.

Wheels kissed concrete with a screaming smack. The Piper bounced high into the air. But it was bleeding off speed. It dropped again, with the sensation of topping a steep hill with a fast car.

It bounced again, but not as high this time. Benington struggled desperately with the controls, his one hand darting.

Another bounce. Then the airplane dribbled down the

runway like a basketball in a series of diminishing bounces before it finally stuck to the concrete. Benington pulled back power. He slumped forward over the stick.

"Jack, you are either worse off than I thought—or you are one lousy fucking pilot."

He held up his good hand, middle digit extended. "Fuck you very much, sailor."

"You, sir, are an *adviser.*" Captain Drachnik scowled.

"I'm advising to go after the enemy on Hong Tre."

"You're advising too far. A combat mission on a friendly island is unauthorized."

Okay. Then I would call it a "training mission."

I borrowed a landing craft to transport nine of my mob to the island. Khe, the senior NCO with the hawk face, took seriously the duty of his first foray into Charlie country. He was pumped up for it. He was fast turning into a leader and my trusted left arm. It was he who actually commanded the LDNN; Captain Ninh was commander in name only.

The excited little Frogmen scrambled into the LCM and we plowed the sea across to a wall of cliffs on the island's north side where we couldn't easily be spotted making a landing. After concealing the landing craft in overhanging reeds and ferns, we slipped unopposed into the low, thick undergrowth that furred the island like a dog's back. I warned Khe not to engage unless we were discovered and had no choice.

The "friendly" island teemed with VC. Makeshift installations hidden in the jungle supported a training camp and a resupply point. These were probably what the riflemen who shot up our L-19 had been protecting. After determining that we may have inadvertently stepped into a vipers' den almost within sight of our own base at Nha Trang, I directed Khe to order the patrol back to the hidden LCM. *Di di mau.*

Chanh on point suddenly slashed a hand signal: *Danger near!* Frogs disappeared silently into thick palmetto and rushes alongside the trail. I peered through the foliage, finger on the trigger of the 30-caliber M-2 A-1 carbine I carried with a full-auto adapter. Three 30-round magazines brazed together gave me 90 rounds.

I watched expectantly as I got my first closeup of the enemy. A scrawny little man in black peasant pajamas, sandals, and a straw cone hat was the first to come into view on the trail. He carried an ancient bolt-action rifle. The next man in line carried a light machine gun at the ready. There were six others, all moving stealthily, eyes darting, all equipped with bolt-action weapons. Probably trainees, I thought. Sunlight and shadows from the trees played mottled tag with their thin forms. I was almost disappointed, they seemed so small and, if not for their weapons, inoffensive.

They flitted through the jungle like shadows, crossing our line of march like the top bar of a *T.* My men ached for a fight, but I hoped they had enough willpower to hold off. Discipline was crucial in hostile territory.

One of the VC paused near the hiding point man Chanh. Chanh's nerves simply snapped. Discipline went all to hell in an instant. Chanh sprang to his feet with a shrill scream and sprayed the line of VC with automatic rifle fire.

The blasting chatter of the rifle sucked in the rest of the *Nguoi Nhai.* A mad minute of blazing lead scythed through the enemy patrol. Twigs and leaves exploded from trees and bushes. Tendrils of acrid smoke squirmed violently in the hot air.

VC vanished, leaving two of their number behind lying crumpled on the trail like small bundles of old clothing. Chanh pumped rounds into the bodies, making them jerk and twitch like mad, broken puppets. Some of the others started to chase the escaping survivors.

"Cease fire!" I shouted. "Goddamnit, cease fire! You little pricks hold your ground. Stay here. *Stay!"*

Khe took up the call. The LDNN had expended five times the amount of ammo needed. I was disappointed in their fire discipline, but I couldn't help feeling pride in their willingness to fight. Other ARVN outfits had been known to haul ass when the first hostile gunshot rang out.

My LDNN, South Vietnam's first guerrilla fighters patterned after U.S. SEALs, had drawn first blood with a body count of two. It wouldn't be last blood. Other blood trails led through the jungle toward the hamlet on the other side of the island. Once survivors spread the alarm, we could expect to have trackers on our ass.

Khe and I reconsolidated the jubilant Frogs and beelined for the boat, leaving a small security patrol lagging behind. The men were virtually busting with the glory of their first victory when we came across a farmer roasting corn over an open fire. Nothing would please the Frogs but they haggle prices. There was no hurrying the Oriental.

Frustrated, anxious to get the hell out of Dodge, I dragged out a handful of piasters. Khe picked out what he thought the corn was worth. I was relieved to reach our docking site and find the boat still there and no trackers on our backtrail.

Captain Drachnik went into orbit when he learned what happened. "You can be court-martialed for conducting an unauthorized operation in a friendly zone without going through proper channels."

"We were *training,* sir," I insisted, "when we came upon a VC training camp."

"On top of everything else, you stole food from a farmer."

"Who registered *that* complaint? The Vietcong? I paid the bastard. Maybe I should have killed him."

"*Mister* Boehm . . ."

Commander Arnie Levine stepped in. He was Drachnik's second-in-command, a tall man, stocky, almost portly, who refused to post Progress slogans in his office. "Captain Drachnik, sir. Let me take care of these matters for you. It won't happen again."

"Well . . . it better not. Boehm, this is not over with yet," he said, shaking a finger at me.

That evening over dinner in Ashcroft's hotel dining room, Jerry and Levine decided that the less the good Captain Drachnik saw of me the more progress we could make all around. After all, progress was our most important product.

"The brass and the politicians don't want to know what's

really going on in this country," Ashcroft said. "It belies the tone of progress they're pushing. You have to learn to fill out their chickenshit reports in terms they want to hear. You'll learn that anything you're *really* doing in Vietnam will have to be on your own. MAAG is a joke. Military Advisory Assistance Group. Damned little military, damned little assistance, piss-poor advice, and the group is more properly a clusterfuck. The only way we can make an impact in this country, Boy-san, is if we field soldiers, pool our forces and resources, and *advise* properly. Get my drift?"

"I don't have to sell cars?"

They laughed. We stood up. "A toast," Levine boomed. "To winning this splendid little war in spite of the brass and the politicians."

FORTY-FOUR

★ ★ ★ ★ ★

My *Nguoi Nhai* were fast becoming fully qualified as SEAL-type fighters. It wouldn't be long before I transferred them from Nha Trang to the fortified junk base called Cat Low where Ashcroft and his Vietnamese *Biet Hai* were fighting Commander Minh's 514th VC Battalion on the dark, marshy flats along the Mekong River known as the *Rung Sat,* the Forest of Assassins. I was already anticipating working with Ashcroft by slipping a few of his junk force Viets into my SEAL training. We didn't need official permission or sanction. Things needed to be done; we would do them. Kicking ass was our most important product.

"Welcome to Shit City," Ashcroft greeted when I made my first scouting visit to Cat Low. "With your SEAL types and my thieves and killers, we can make a good attempt to control the river and the Rung Sat."

Cat Low lay on a spit of land 12 miles from Vung Tau near the broad mouth of the yellow-brown Mekong. The compound was a typical fortress of the war—a triangle enclosed in concertina, razor wire, and fighting bunkers. One side of the triangle extended piers into the Mekong to which were tied the fleet of armed junks operating to interdict VC shipping and movements. Vietnamese defenders had moved their families into grass, mud, and tin hootches in the middle of the compound.

As I would be operating out of two locations, I secured quarters both in Saigon where I had to report regularly to Drachnik for my ass chewing and in Vung Tau to be near Cat Low. I shared an apartment in downtown Saigon at the Government Tax Building, not far from MAAG headquarters, with Doc Shultz, a tall easygoing internist, and Ted Reilman, a communications adviser who was short and wiry with reddish blond hair.

Fortunately, they had a sense of humor. They were both gone the evening I moved in. I stripped and had a bourbon and water and a cigarette while I shaved and showered. Then I rigged a dummy hand grenade to the Old World toilet so it would fall hissing and smoking to the floor when the flush string was pulled. I attached a sign to it that said, *You got five seconds.* I stretched out on my bunk.

Reilman and Doc came in later and had a couple of drinks together. I heard Reilman in the toilet grunting and sighing and farting. The pull string released a flood of water.

"Kee-rist!"

Out tumbled Reilman, holding his head with both hands, waiting for the explosion. After a moment, he got up with a foolish grin and brushed himself off.

"You're Boehm, right? What the fuck you laughing at? I knew it was a dummy."

Doc Shultz often accompanied Commander Ashcroft's junks onto the waterways to treat junk force families, civilians, VC, and whoever else showed up needing medical attention.

Ashcroft asked me, "Boy-san, can you train the doc to fire his carbine so he doesn't blow off his own head?"

I linked up Doc with a Special Forces master sergeant who soon had him fieldstripping the carbine blindfolded and shooting it like a combat pro. When a U.S. Army general from the Pentagon showed up on a fact-finding junket, Doc accompanied the general, Ashcroft, and me out onto the river in Ashcroft's command junk. Doc was eager to demonstrate his newly acquired proficiency. I pointed to a stump on the riverbank about 150 yards away. Doc pumped a full magazine into it.

"Damn! Look at Doc," the general exclaimed, impressed. "If somebody were to toss a grenade at us, I'll bet Doc could shoot it out of the air."

"Yep," Doc drawled.

Junk Force Base 33 near the village of Vam Lang lay in the heart of Commander Minh's AO, area of operations. Green tracer fire lashed out at us from the jungled banks as we approached. Bullets geysered in the water. Ashcroft ordered Trung Si', his boat captain, to slam full throttle to the heavy diesel.

Doc hooted like a bronc-riding cowboy as Ashcroft made roaring passes near the bank from which we had attracted fire. Doc and I worked out on the bushes with our carbines. The general joined in with a Stoner.

Afterwards he insisted on taking us all out to a late breakfast. We tied up at the Saigon piers near the statue of the Trung sisters, whose history lay buried deep in Vietnamese lore. The news came while we were eating. A messenger handed the general a Teletype. He looked at it, stunned, before he passed the message on. Then we all looked stunned.

President John Kennedy had been assassinated in Dallas.

The Special Warfare community would miss him immensely. He was a champion for the U.S. Army Special Forces. And, of course, the SEALs had been commissioned on his watch. He had befriended me personally during those trying days. Maybe I would have voted for him the next time.

"This war," said the general, "is going to change. Unconventional warfare will evolve into conventional ground troops. We can't win this war the conventional way."

In Vung Tau, I acquired a cold-water room from Madam Vinh, who operated a rundown combination maternity hospital, orphanage, and rooming house. The room came equipped with a bunk, a desk, a straight-backed chair, and orphans running up and down the hallway, playing. There were always plenty of orphans in Vietnam, what with the war.

My LDNN were spending more and more time at Cat Low as I prepared them for combat the SEAL way. Madam Vinh gradually grew to know and accept me. She was an attractive woman married to a Vietnamese *bac 'si,* a doctor, but occasionally shacking with an American Army officer. Bowing politely in the gentle and gracious way of most Vietnamese women, she began requesting that I drop off bundles of clothing, food, and medicines to a French Catholic priest named Father Dupree.

"Roy-san," she would say, "if your duties take you near Father Dupree's mission, will you please drop off this package?"

Father Dupree was a painfully thin Frenchman with a soul that had turned Oriental gentle from long years lived in Vietnam. However, he liked his bourbon as much as any Irish priest. I always contributed a few Army C rations for the good father's flock and a bottle of bourbon for the father's earthly soul. In this manner, I unintentionally inserted myself into the local Vietnamese community in a way that would eventually save my life and involve me in an unusual friendship with a VC warlord.

"The activities of all who live in a Vietnamese community are known and evaluated," Madam Vinh explained.

"Does that include Americans?"

"Especially Americans. Enemies are of two types. There

are enemies who are enemies personally and who you do not respect. Then there are enemies who are enemies because of war but who are not personal enemies. You can respect them."

It soon became a tradition that I stop by Father Dupree's whenever I could. We sipped bourbon while lounging in a little walled-in garden in front of the imposing brown-mud mission. I found myself oddly drawn, considering my indifference to Western religions, to Father Dupree's island of peace in a world of deceit, turmoil, and death.

One afternoon, the father and I were sitting in the garden working on a bottle when a tiny Buddhist monk with a shaved head and saffron robes stopped at the wrought-iron gate. His round face, neither old nor young, was a marvel of inner peace. Father Dupree jumped up and hurried to greet him. They were obviously old friends. The priest introduced us.

"Lt. Roy Boehm, please have the honor of meeting Thay Wu Chung."

Thay was the respectful Vietnamese form of addressing all monks. It meant "teacher."

"Thay Wu and I were very close friends on a plantation near Da Nang," Father Dupree explained, his face gone suddenly grave. "That was before this dreadful war. . . . Thay Wu is an accomplished artist, talented beyond belief."

Thay Wu bowed gracefully, not flattered but simply acknowledging the fact. I learned he was a Hinayana Buddhist whose followers exalted individual austerity and salvation by personal example. His only possession was a bowl, which he carried with him. He immediately reminded me of old Li, the Chinese holy man who befriended me in Tsingtao after WWII. Li was a Confucianist whereas Wu was a Buddhist, but both were holy men who found sanctuary in inner peace while war raged without.

Father Dupree, Thay Wu, and I became a regular threesome at the Catholic mission whenever I chanced to be in Vung Tau. The priest and I would split a bottle of bourbon while the three-way conversation spirited itself far into the night. I was captivated by the monk. What a waste had he burned himself when the monks were self-torching.

Shortly after Kennedy's assassination, I led my LDNN on one final shakedown mission into Indian country, an uneventful one, then informed Captain Drachnik that we were ready to face the VC on their own terms.

"I'm flying to Cat Low right after the staff meeting," Jerry Ashcroft said. "Care to come along? It's about time you joined the war, Boehm."

FORTY-FIVE

★ ★ ★ ★ ★

By this time in the war, U.S. Navy SEALs, primarily SEAL Team One, were making their own history in Vietnam. As SEALs remained a small, specialized unit, there were never very many operating in Vietnam at any one time. At the height of the war in 1967 and 1968, when the United States was deploying nearly a half-million troops, there were only about 60 SEALs in-country. However, their reputation and their effectiveness far outweighed their numbers.

Unlike the U.S. Army Special Forces, whose primary mission was pacification and troop training, SEALs concentrated on direct action contact against the enemy. Operating in small patrols of seldom more than 14 fighters, the "men with green faces" struck terror into the hearts of the enemy of the Mekong Delta. Night after night, the silent, clandestine warriors of the U.S. Navy's unconventional warfare branch slipped into the jungle to ambush, raid, prisoner snatch, assassinate, sabotage, and harass the enemy, denying him unlimited access to terrain he heretofore considered his own backyard.

There was not simply one war in Vietnam. There were a dozen wars, maybe even a hundred, all being fought simultaneously with minimum communications between them. Everyone fought his own war, convinced that if *he* won *his* war, the war itself was won. The war had to be fought that way, almost in secret, to keep the politicians and bean counters off your ass.

In late 1963 and early 1964, the LDNN, using SEAL tactics, took *my* war for the first time into the Vietcong's home territory. The *Nguoi Nhai* were well trained, motivated, and kick-ass confident. The first of their kind. Working with Jerry Ashcroft's *Biet Hai* and his junk force out of Cat Low, we kept Commander Minh and the other warlords off their feed and on their feet, striking at the enemy along the waterways from Saigon to the South China Sea and for 100 miles up the Mekong River. No longer could the NLF move its supplies and troops freely by day or night without fear of being hit. As my men grew bolder with each successful operation, we ventured deeper and deeper into the forest.

We commonly developed the intelligence for our own ops and jealously guarded that intel until we could act on it. We would *win* our war. Fuck everyone else.

The trip upriver was like moving along a dark hallway. I sensed the walls, but could not touch them. Ashcroft's two junks loaded with his *Biet Hai* and my *Nguoi Nhai* traveled in tandem. The muffled burbles of the engines sounded like a roar in the night stillness. Ashcroft, Khe, Doc Shultz, who had come along for the ride, and I huddled in the cabin of the lead boat using a red-lensed flashlight to study a map.

"We'll be at the drop-off in about ten minutes," Jerry said, bulldog face set in drooping stern lines. "Give us a radio check on the hour. It'll give Doc and me on the boat something to look forward to while we're waiting on you."

Our target was a farmer's hootch near the junction of two canals. Recent intel said a cadre of VC officers would be meeting there that night for operational planning. The Vietnamese CNO provided us with a guide named Phan, a broad-faced, restless little man with nervous eyes.

"Keep an eye on him," I told Khe. You had to always suspect a trap when working with strangers.

A thin smile twisted Khe's lips. "No trap, Boss-san. Phan not want die if captured."

Trung Si', Ashcroft's boat captain, throttled back to slow idle and turned into an even more narrow canal. A rising sliver of moon separated tree line from sky. The boats nosed into the dark bank and cut engines. We sat there in deafening silence for five minutes listening for anything that was not jungle or river sound.

"Khe, let's do it," I whispered finally.

Unloading 18 heavily armed men over the sides of the boats in near total darkness was a feat in itself. I flinched at every sound. Once ashore, a little force chambered rounds and armed their weapons with a muffled volley of metallic clattering. I carried a .357 magnum revolver and my 30-caliber carbine with the 90-round braised magazines. My face was blackened and I wore jungle-filthy fatigues and boots from the previous mission. I never washed them. I simply hung them out to dry, then rewet them before the next mission so that I would smell like the jungle.

What a difference a few years and a different war made. Twenty years ago I fought the Japs at sea from a five-inch gun mount. Tonight, I patrolled thick jungle expecting to shoot the enemy face-to-face. *I* was now the shark.

A well-used pathway ran alongside the canal in both directions. *Biet Hai* set up rally-point security. The rest of us followed Phan. He selected a spur off the main trail. We felt the way with our feet. Eyes were virtually useless beneath the forest canopy.

The moon was a little higher and providing more illumination by the time we reached our destination. A long grass-and-mud hootch sat in a small packed-dirt clearing flanked by 20-foot-tall bamboo on one side and a small grove of banana trees on the other. Low brush and elephant grass clogged the backyard for 30 meters or so before giving way to a patchwork of small rice paddies. The open space in front between the structure and the jungle presented a clear field of fire.

The hootch remained dark and lifeless. Khe escorted the *Biet Hai* into concealed security around the hootch and placed our *Nguoi Nhai* ready to make the actual assault and prisoner snatch. He kept Phan next to us. Then we settled down to wait.

It was shortly after midnight before we detected movement. A shadow suddenly materialized. It glided across the clearing and entered the hootch. Moments later, a candle flickered to life inside, its yellow glow edging the closed door.

Four more armed men arrived one at a time in 30-minute intervals, like thieves and conspirators, and joined the first inside the hootch. Apparently, they felt so secure they didn't bother to post a guard.

At 2:00 A.M. I decided it was time to move. No one else was coming. At my okay, Khe set the plan into motion. He and two other *Nguoi Nhai* circled and darted for the right side of the hootch, running low and quietly in their sneakers. Chanh and three others approached from the left. I crept across the clearing straight toward the door with another contingent of fighters, prepared to cover the assault party and conduct follow-up search and recovery.

The VC proved more cagey than we expected. One of them must have detected a stealthy footfall or the sigh of a fern as a body brushed against it. Dim candlelight flooded in an elongated rectangle across the clearing as the door opened and he stepped cautiously outside with his AK unslung. Someone inside rattled off an interrogatory phrase. He didn't reply.

Instead, alerted by movement, he pivoted toward Khe's element, bringing up his rifle. Candlelight silhouetted him.

I fell into a crouch, tipping the muzzle of my carbine toward him.

Before I fired, a tracer from Khe's group streaked into the man. It took him low, above the groin. He spun to his left in a complete circle. Another tracer caught him in the shoulder, spinning him back the other way.

I unlimbered my carbine and stitched him across the rib cage with a burst. A pink mist of pulverized bone, blood, and flesh clouded the light from the doorway. The guy vibrated on his feet, like a puppet manipulated by a puppeteer with a heart attack. He was dead by the time he hit the ground, but his body continued to twitch.

A second man bolted to the door. He barely hit the ground, felled by a hail of bullets, before my *Nguoi Nhai* vaulted over his collapsing corpse and filled the hootch with a sound-and-light show. Vermilion tracers punched through the hootch's thin walls and either arced across the black sky or spangled into the bamboo and banana trees.

I glanced at the dead man as I charged past. Tasted the copper odor of blood drifting in the air.

The shooting ceased. The candle inside the hootch remained burning. Tension crackled like lightning. *Nguoi Nhai* held at bay one wounded VC who writhed on the floor and screamed in Vietnamese and another who remained surprisingly unscathed. He cowered kneeling in front of his captors. He looked about 40 or so. Flickering candlelight tattooed fear across his face in large script.

The remaining VC sprawled dead across an ankle-high table off which tea, teacups, and cigarettes had spilled onto the floor. Thick cupfuls of steaming blood gushed from his open mouth.

I pointed at the kneeling man. "Khe, ask him if one of these guys is Commander Minh."

The terrified officer shook his head vigorously.

"I *make* him talk, Boss-san."

"Later, Khe. Let's get outta here. Gimme a count."

"All here, Boss-san. No one wounded."

"Good." I made the sign of the "fuzzy nuts," fingers up, hand rotating, which designated an officer or senior enlisted prisoner.

Khe and Chanh bound the prisoners' hands behind their backs with tape and then taped their mouths while I searched the dead and the hootch for documents and other intelligence. I shoved captured papers into my map case, then swept the scene with a final look. The mangled dead resembled automobile victims in a don't-drink-and-drive film.

"Di di mau."

As we vacated the hootch, a spattering of gunfire erupted from down the trail toward Lyn Nhan where *Biet Hai* had set up a security detail. That spurred the assault and snatch troops to greater speed, pushing the stumbling captives ahead of us. The village had apparently dispatched a VC reaction force. I dropped to one knee in the trees and unslung the radio.

"River Rat, this is Frogfoot . . . River Rat, *we are hot.* Leaving position and headed yours. How copy? Over."

"Roger. You are hot. Do you require assistance? Over."

"Negative at this time. ETA your position 20 minutes."

Khe dropped next to me, one eye sweeping back toward the sound of fighting.

"Boss-san, wounded VC more bad hurt we think."

"Kill him if he can't keep up."

"Already done that, Boss-san."

We flew down the trail single file in the dark. The firing behind slackened, then quit as stay-behind security broke contact and folded in behind us. Chanh on point found the canal pathway but then in his haste overshot the hidden junks. We returned. This time we found them hugged against the bank under foliage.

The prisoner was tossed aboard like a sack of rice. The trailing *Biet Hai* soon filtered through Khe's security detail and hurriedly clambered aboard not five minutes ahead of a swarm of pursuing pissed-off VC. Miraculously, no one had been wounded. Our team had done better than their team.

Minutes later, the two junks were riding the middle of the Mekong out of effective small arms range, bound for Cat Low. The men laughed and jabbered. The scene was from a winning team's locker room.

"Those hoods of yours fought like there was no tomorrow," I complimented Ashcroft.

He laughed. "There *would* have been no tomorrow if they were caught."

He had some of his men, former Vietcong, show me the tattoos on their chests: *Sat Cong.*

It turned out Khe had had the same slogan tattooed on Phan's chest to ensure his loyalty. *Sat Cong. Kill communists.*

FORTY-SIX

★ ★ ★ ★ ★

Operation *Hai Khau I* introduced WWII amphibious operations to Vietnam. Watching invasion planning and rehearsals at the junk bases along the Mekong, I deja vu'd back to the South Pacific during U.S. Marine preparations for landings at Iwo Jima or Saipan. The invasions were to be Gilbert and Sullivan extravaganzas upriver in VC strongholds controlled by Commander Minh's 514th Battalion. *Fucked up.* Conventional tactics in an unconventional war.

Leave it to Saigon and the American Pentagon.

Although I argued that the VC would not stand up and resist, that set-piece battlefield warfare was not even in their strategy lexicon, I was nonetheless ordered to cooperate with the Army and provide *Nguoi Nhai* for classic UDT ops to "clear the beaches."

"Clear the beaches! There won't be anything there to clear."

I had to go along with it. I disgorged Frogs predawn in the middle of the river to swim ashore where they were greeted by silence, a few sand crabs, and a wild boar. I watched in bemusement as an artillery bombardment "softened up" the invasion site by chasing out tigers and wild pigs. The VC had already unassed the AO.

Amphibious landing craft plowed wide glistening wakes across the river and disgorged heavily armed ARVN troops who were met not even by the wild boar. The only shot fired was an accidental discharge.

While the ARVN pushed inland without resistance, I arranged transport for my LDNN into the deep interior, where we not only found ample evidence of VC forces but also stepped on the Army's sensitive toes by encroaching upon their hunting grounds. I broke my 40 troops into three patrols and grid-searched the jungle. We came upon caches of ammo and foodstuffs, which we burned or carried away, and upon abandoned training camps that the VC would reoccupy once the invasion troops returned to Saigon. In the late afternoon, the element I accompanied came upon seven armed VC unconcernedly eating and resting in a clearing.

"I want a prisoner," I whispered to Chanh, making the sign of the fuzzy nuts.

The assault was a turkey shoot that left five enemy soldiers KIA and two wounded and captured. *Nguoi Nhai* collected weapons, intel, and souvenirs from the blood-soaked corpses. We leapfrogged back out of the area. My men were the only unit to make enemy contact during the operation.

"There's been a complaint from the Army," Ashcroft laughed. "It seems you were not operating in a maritime environment."

"Our canteens were full of water."

I was ready for the second invasion. My LDNN inserted deep into the interior the night before and turned Charlie's own tricks against him by planting trip-wire booby traps all over his avenues of escape. My men unassed the AO at dawn when, all distant sound and fury, the invasion began. The only contact the landing force made was in picking up wounded VC from our tripped booby traps. We had inflicted more casualties than all other units involved in the operation and we hadn't fired a single shot.

Operations like these, laid on top of the growing body count from the nightly raids and ambushes my little men conducted, inevitably attracted notice, not only from the VC, who soon offered rewards for the capture or death of *Biet Hai* and *Nguoi Nhai* troops and their American advisers, but also from the U.S. Army, which also operated advisers in the Delta.

An Army lieutenant colonel planed out from Saigon to sniff around. He encountered Doc Shultz on the piers at Cat Low waiting for Ashcroft.

"What's going on out here with the Navy?" he demanded. "Seems like you guys might be poaching on Army AO."

The Doc pulled his hardheaded kraut routine: "I know nothing. I tell you nothing."

That pissed off the colonel. He wanted to know what *in hell* was going on. *Now*.

"As a medical doctor," Doc Shultz replied, unruffled, "I prescribe that the good lieutenant colonel return to the comforts of Saigon, take two Ex-Lax in the morning, and leave the fighting to *real* warriors."

FORTY-SEVEN

★ ★ ★ ★ ★

My *Nguoi Nhai* were kicking ass and gaining infamy in the Rung Sat. We had run more ops during my first weeks as adviser than during the entire previous year under Out to Lunch Willits. Nothing major yet. Prisoner snatches, recon patrols, and ambushes. My men begged for a big action. None of them realized just how *big* things were about to get.

The more successful our operations, the more paranoid I became. Was it paranoia if they really *were* out to get you?

In this kind of war, anyone could be a spy, an assassin, or a saboteur. Although the war stopped at the city limits of Saigon, except for an occasional bicycle bomb rolled into an outdoor bar or café, an undercurrent of intrigue and conspiracy ran through the city like black Delta mud. Jerry Ashcroft's own maid, Co-Van, at the Majestic Hotel was a suspected spy, although a goddamned living exotic doll with a gorgeous ass.

"She can be useful," Ashcroft explained. "She provides an open conduit to Minh and the other Delta VC. All you have to do to feed Commander Minh a little disinformation is let a few words slip out in front of her."

The undercurrent of intrigue originated in Saigon and flowed thick into the hinterlands. I discovered a bunch of it even flowed into Father Dupree's mission in Vung Tau.

As usual, I spent spare time in deep discussions with the priest and Thay Wu at the mission. After a session during which the Thay expounded on Siddhartha Gautama, who became the Buddha back in the sixth century BC, and the Buddha's Four Noble Truths of man's condition and his Eightfold Path to "Enlightenment," Father Dupree walked me to the gate as I prepared to leave. I had an appointment with MAAG in the morning. The priest and the monk knew I generally drove my jeep.

"I believe I have lost a potential convert," Father Dupree said, laughing. "You lean toward Buddhism, Roy."

His thin face then changed, becoming grave. As though an idle comment, he said, "Thay Wu thinks Vietnam must be beautiful to see from the air."

It was a strange message. I looked at the priest.

"We think it might be particularly beautiful tomorrow," he added casually.

I took the subtle warning and hopped a Caribou to Saigon. Charlie shot up the convoy of ARVN I would have accompanied on the road to Saigon. The holy men might have saved my life. Certainly that was their intention. A foreigner in this kind of war could never have too many protectors.

A few days later, I parked my jeep in front of Madam

Vinh's while I trotted up to my room to gather up some gear for Cat Low. I noticed the hood latch on the vehicle was sprung when I returned. I lifted the hood. Attached to the motor was a bomb that resembled a giant firecracker. A wire underneath the vehicle ran from the bomb to a Willie Pete grenade underneath the gas tank. A trip wire to ignite both explosives led to the steering column. One turn of the wheel—*boom!* Instant crispy critter.

"The war's starting to get personal and dirty," Ashcroft said. "You've pissed off somebody."

I figured it had to be Commander Minh.

Khe and Ashcroft assigned two men as my permanent personal bodyguards. One was a *Biet Hai* Cambodian I called Bode because I couldn't pronounce his real name. He was a dwarfed, evil-smelling man with a broad face and a cruel, unchanging expression. On stand-down, his idea of a good time was to slip out of base camp at night with a knife and kill VC. He wore a string of dried VC ears around his neck while in the field.

The other, Nguyen, was the perennial happy child with the happy child's innocent cruelty. He could smile and giggle while slitting an enemy's throat. He liked to steal my toothpaste and eat it.

I split my combat pay of $55 a month between the two and gave them a crash course in bomb detection and ordnance disposal. They checked out my jeep before I drove it and took turns sleeping outside my door.

Ashcroft took them aside. "If one of you guys falls down on the job and the Boss Frog buys the farm on your watch," he said, "the other guy gets an extra $30 for wiping him out."

In spite of its intrigue and plotting, Saigon offered a periodic much-needed respite from the war. Clambering off the junk at the Saigon piers, I shouldered my submarine bag and trudged through the crowded fish and vegetable vendors and past the statue of the Trung sisters, heading for Khuyen My's barbershop and bathhouse. Glimpsed in the windows I passed was the image of a man approaching middle age, gaunt from the pace of the war but still in fine physical condition, face and arms burned by the tropical sun. I limped a little from the old Murder Ball knee injury sustained in UDT training. My fatigues and bloused combat boots were muddy from a late-night ambush of three VC moving supplies by sampan—all three were killed—and red mud had hardened into the grip of my holstered .357 and the stock of the carbine I carried. My bones ached and my muscles were sore.

I bought ears of boiled corn from an open kettle and ate them on the way. At Khuyen My's, I shifted my carbine and the submarine bag to the same hand and opened the door. Khuyen met me with a teasing Eurasian smile. All the more beautiful Vietnamese women were part French. Khuyen was no exception. She was a head taller than the average Vietnamese woman and her eyes were almost round and not black but brown. She was perhaps 40, but she still wore the lovely bloom of her youth. Caste and birthright made the difference between the city ladies like Khuyen and the peasant women of the hamlets with their red betel nut–stained lips and their bodies stooped and worn out at 30.

"I'm filthy, Khuyen," I said.

"You have come to a most appropriate place where you are well received." She took my hand and led me to the sunken bath in the back room, leaving the shop to an assistant. Steam escaped from the bath.

My weary fingers fumbled with buttons. Khuyen stepped near. I smelled the blossoms in her glossy black hair, smelled her as woman. She tenderly grasped my hands and placed them by my side. My bag, carbine, and holster belt lay on the floor nearby. She slowly stripped me, teasing. I felt myself aroused. She laughed, looking, and placed a bourbon and water in my hand.

She bathed me, luxuriously, cleaning every crevice and protrusion and scar. Hot water seeped into my pores, penetrating to the core. I leaned back and let the water and Khuyen's caresses work. Closed my eyes.

She pressed a coin into my hand. It was our way of breaking silences.

"What am I thinking? Khuyen My. That is what I was thinking."

"You were thinking of *me?*"

"I'm naked in a hot bath. What else would I be thinking of?"

"Of the war perhaps. About another woman perhaps. You have other goodtime girls in Saigon, Roy?"

"Hundreds."

She giggled. "So many? You are much man indeed."

"I love to hear a woman laugh."

"Why?"

"It pleases me."

"It is different than other things?"

"There is nothing in the world like a woman's laugh and a woman's touch. . . ."

"To make you forget there is a war?"

"Yes."

"You have killed much, Roy?"

"Enough."

"Roy?" she said. "Open your eyes. Look at me."

Her dark eyes lifted me floating from the hot bath. She enveloped me in a silk robe as soft as the lining of a cloud. I followed on bare wet feet up a carpeted stairway to the small apartment upstairs. It was decorated in silk and expensive furs and soft carpet and Oriental art depicting water buffalo and Asian girls. The faint sweet scents of oils and perfumes, the soft look of the room itself, told me few men had been there before me.

She released my robe, then dropped hers to her ankles. Slipped slender and smooth into my arms, tilted her head to let our lips find each other.

"At this place, Roy," she whispered, "there is never war."

FORTY-EIGHT

★ ★ ★ ★ ★

My *Nguoi Nhai* finally had their big battle, had met the elephant, and the elephant in the form of Commander Minh stomped hell out of us at Junk Base 33. Ashcroft's *Beit Hai* left three dead in the flaming ruins of the base before we loaded the survivors onto junks to flee across the river. One of my own men had been wounded, although not seriously. The resident junk force of defenders lost 30 to 35 dead grotesquely strewn among the ashes.

With Minh's victory over the junk base at Vam Lang, he now controlled much of the Rung Sat. I knew that one day my *Nguoi Nhai* and I would return to retake Base 33 from Minh. Until that day, however, we had other missions to run as my LDNN rebuilt their confidence singed by Minh's flamethrowers and mortars.

One thing that came out of the battle was my meeting in Saigon with my enemy, Commander Minh, and the beginning of one of the war's oddest friendships. After dinner in Cholon, the forbidden Chinese section of the city, Minh drove me back to the Tax Building in his taxi. We shook hands. I dreaded the day when I might have to kill this man I already admired and respected, warrior to warrior.

"You won't know when or how," I told him truthfully, "but I'll have to come back to Junk Base 33. SEALs always come back."

"I could never expect anything less of you," he said.

A thought occurred to me. "You haven't said who told you I wanted to meet you."

"It gets around."

"There's only one person who could have told you. Co-Van."

I saw it then. Ashcroft had no idea of how direct his pipeline to Commander Minh really was. Minh and Co-Van, the family resemblance. The same distinctive good looks. Aquiline nose, well-formed lips and jawlines. Virtually identical eyes, dark brown and only slightly slanted.

"Co-Van," I said triumphantly. "Co-Van is your *sister.*"

FORTY-NINE

★ ★ ★ ★ ★

World War II shattered some of the cartilage in my right knee. I exacerbated the injury with Murder Ball and other subsequent injuries and minor surgeries over the years. A bone joint disease called genu varum further complicated things by causing gradual bowing of the legs and periodic severe swelling and pain. The bowing was noticeable even as far back as UDT days.

Joe DiMartino, who also had bowlegs, and I were strolling along a beach on Saint Thomas island in our swimming trunks when a vacationing New York secretary whose acquaintance we had made took one look at the pair of us and started laughing.

"What manner of men are these Frogmen," she cried, "that they wear their balls in parentheses?"

"The pain is trying to tell you something," Doc Shultz preached whenever I had an attack. "It's trying to tell you you're *really* going to screw yourself up if you don't slow down."

I was a SEAL. A SEAL kept going.

Even so, all the paperwork required by Drachnik and then

his relief as senior naval adviser at MAAG, Cpt. "Sweetie Pants" Hardcastle, provided a legit excuse for me to hole up in Saigon at my Tax Building apartment whenever the pain grounded me from the field. Like Drachnik, Hardcastle was a do-nothing commander who preferred not to shake up the status quo. He assumed Progress Is Our Most Important Product as his own motto. It continued to require the mounds of erroneous reports intended to put the best possible light on even the worst disaster.

I was a nervous two-fingered typist on a rickety Underwood, always behind in my reports. Reilman and the perpetual evil child Nguyen ragged me about it good-naturedly. Nguyen, grinning broadly, would pound on the door when he kept bodyguard over me. Brandishing a fire extinguisher, he would exclaim, "Daiuy Reilman say you typewriter on fire." Then he would keel over with laughter.

One afternoon after three or four beers had picked up my speed to about five words an hour, a gangly kid in Navy fatigues rapped on the door.

"What the hell do you want?" I growled.

He took a step back. "My name is Edward Porter. I'm a radioman for Mr. Reilman."

"So?"

"I got dropped out of BUDS training at UDT. A couple of the instructors told me you were over here and that I might be able to work for you."

I glanced at the table upon which crouched the malevolent Underwood and a mountain of papers. "Porter, can you type?"

"Yes, sir."

"*All right!* Sit right down here, boy."

Reilman assigned the kid to me as my yeoman. He doubled the size of my command element; hell, I was building an empire. Porter freed me for even more field time. By now, the *Nguoi Nhai*'s reputation was such that my continuing war against Commander Minh's 514th frequently had to take second place to mission requests for our services from throughout the Mekong Delta and along the coastline of the South China Sea.

"Doc," I complained to Shultz, "draw the fluid off my knee or something to stop the pain and swelling. I depend on you to get me through."

"Roy, you're going to cripple yourself."

FIFTY

★ ★ ★ ★ ★

Squall lines blew in fierce and rattling over Saigon from the South China Sea. They whipped up whitecaps and sent them flying in rolling silver ranks one behind the other across the open water. The seas out past the breakers at the mouth of the harbor at Saigon were rolling at seven to nine feet. My men had never operated in such angry waters.

"The VC will never expect us in this weather," I said.

Ashcroft bent into the wind and slashing salt spray. *"I* don't expect us."

He had volunteered to go along to make sure the Vietnamese navy didn't abandon my team while we were ashore on the peninsula. Colonel Marky, the senior U.S. Army MAAG adviser, had requested my *Nguoi Nhai* recon a sandbag-bunkered warehouse on the Ca Mau Peninsula. A flyover showed it to have a red cross painted on the roof, probably as a deception to camouflage a VC rest area. For transportation, the Viet navy supplied a rusted WWII LSI (Landing Ship, Infantry) that once belonged to the U.S. Navy. It rode bouncing tied up to the pier.

I carried my carbine and holstered .357 as Ashcroft and I waited for Khe, Nguyen, Bode, Chanh, and two other volunteers to show up for the dusk-hour departure. Doc Shultz drained my knee, but I still limped a little. Ashcroft looked worried.

"Boy-san . . ."

"It has to be done, Jerry."

Night settled quickly underneath the cloud cover. It was full dark by the time the wildly bucking boat crashed past the breakers and took to the open sea. Even the ship's crew started heaving over the sides and upon each other. The lashing rain washed them off between bouts of seasickness.

"Not a good sign," Ashcroft observed wryly.

I hung on in the wheelhouse as seas lifted the boat and dropped it jarring into the following troughs like one endless roller-coaster ride. I grilled the captain to make sure he understood.

"We return in six hours after drop-off. If something happens and we have to evade, pick us up at the alternate site at midnight tomorrow. Repeat to me the grid coordinates. . . ."

Ashcroft nodded, as though saying, "I'll be here to make sure he's there."

The storm continued unabated, even in the lee of the peninsula. Visibility was almost zero in the boiling night of darkness, sea spray, and driving rain. I had to take the captain's word that the peninsula lay 500 yards north of the drop-off site.

Twice the sea and wind hurled the IBS-7 (Inflatable Boat, Small, 7 passengers) back at us, like a football kicked through the goalposts. Khe threw himself into it as ballast. The rest of us tossed him and the boat over the lee-side gunnel of the LSI in the wake of the retreating seas, then scrambled over on top of him in a grunting, cursing mass of men and weapons. While the Viets unscrambled themselves and grasped anything they could to keep from washing overboard, I cranked over the silent outboard and gave it power. I tillered it toward the unseen landfall.

It was a wild, surfboarding ride. I heard the men around me, felt their presence, listened to Chanh dry-heaving, but I could have shut my eyes and seen as much as I saw with them open. I rode the bucking cold rubber and held on and followed the needle of the compass I palmed as close to my eyes as I could focus.

All of us were shivering and chattering from exposure by the time land appeared unexpectedly across our bow. There was no time or need for stealth, what with the darkness and the howl of wind, drum of rain, and the pounding surf. I nosed the raft toward shore. Khe and Bode went over the side and pulled the rubber raft into overhanging mangroves and concealed it.

Drenched and miserable, we huddled like chicks underneath a nipa palm while I took compass readings. Everything depended upon, first, the captain having discharged us from the correct grid, then upon my own dead reckoning in bringing us ashore. My calculations placed the warehouse at no farther than 400 meters from our present location.

"Check it out, Khe."

Khe and Chanh disappeared while the rest of the patrol circled into a tight defensive perimeter. We waited for an hour. I thought I detected a slight lightening of the eastern sky.

One moment I stared into a near-total blackout. The next, Khe materialized in front of me. I recoiled.

"It is ammunition depot," he reported without fanfare.

"You found it."

"Boss-san, there are no sentries."

"You're shitting me."

I felt Khe grin. "Never shit Boss-Frog. It is a rule. The target is a squatting pigeon."

"Sitting duck. But close enough."

Charlie must have felt exceptionally secure in his little sanctuary with his red cross ruse. We encountered neither security patrols nor booby traps on the approach to the building. Apparently, the VC hadn't counted on my tiny Frogmen landing by sea in a storm. We soon came to the clearing surrounding the building.

Bode and another man established outside security. Khe led the rest of the band through the driving rain to an entrance whose lock he had previously checked for sabotage.

I wrenched off the lock, eased inside ahead of the others, carbine ready. Rain howled on the building's tin roof, covering our presence. I listened for any sound other than the rain.

Hearing nothing, I flicked on a red-lensed flashlight. The first thing I noticed was pallets of fertilizer bags with the clasped hands logo on them. "Hands Across the Sea" do-gooders back in the States sent the fertilizer, along with outboard engines and other supplies, to the "poor peasants" of Vietnam. The outboards became "shrimp tails" pushing sampans delivering VC supplies in the Delta. The bags of fertilizer containing sodium nitrate and sodium potassium were turned into explosives.

Among the fertilizer were cases of small arms ammunition, grenades, and mortar rounds. Chinese manufacture mostly, but some Russian as well.

Colonel Marky had wanted only a recon before sending in troops to destroy the warehouse if it contained war materiel as he suspected. I could do him one better. Feeling like a burglar in a house whose owner was expected to return at any moment, I rigged the warehouse with booby traps. I wedged grenades with the pins pulled between fertilizer bags. I set trip wires throughout and at every entrance. The triggering of a single trip wire set off a chain reaction that vaulted the entire building into orbit like a Sputnik rocket.

Nguyen the happy child giggled in anticipation. "You should have been a fucking pirate," I told him.

"Yes. Mean pirate like Old Frog."

Our withdrawal was orderly and swift, still covered by heavy rains. Only luck and the improved vision of a dawning wet sky led us back across the boiling sea to the LSI. The captain didn't know how to coordinate engines and rudder in order to provide a relatively calm lee slick out of which to recover the raft. We had to board the hard way, jumping for the deck of the LSI when the waves lifted us on a level with it. Although we lost the IBS to the sea, all seven members of the patrol scrambled to safety. Ashcroft greeted me with an understated slap on the back.

Then the engine of the LSI sputtered, backfired, and quit. The ship's engineer hurried below and pounded away at the tub's old engines, trying to get them started again while the heavy boat wallowed in the sea's troughs and gradually washed toward shore. By now the day had dawned, gray and watery, making us visible from land. We couldn't have been more noticeable had we hired a band and marched in. We would soon be within rifle range of VC AK-47s.

"I feel like Robinson Crusoe," Ashcroft remarked gloomily, hanging at the ship's rigging. He had scrounged an extra carbine and ammo from somewhere. We were about to be shipwrecked.

"It ain't just boy Friday on *that* landfall," I pointed out.

The engines suddenly cranked, spitting and popping. At almost the same instant, the horizon exploded. Brilliant rocketlike fingers and rays and beams and smoke contrails filled the sky, overpowering the dawn. The VC ammo dump went up in fireworks. Explosions in series clapped against our eardrums. Charlie had probably noticed the LSI and hurried to check his cache, triggering our booby traps. *So solly, Charlie.*

Aboard the landing craft, I couldn't distinguish the relieved cheering that the engine had started in the nick of time from the celebration of the destruction of the VC cache. Ashcroft threw a companionable arm around my soaked shoulders.

"Did you do *that,* naughty Boy-san?" he asked, grinning.

The next time I saw Commander Minh, he said, "You caught us by surprise, Roy."

"Oh?"

"On the peninsula."

I grinned. "I did, didn't I?"

FIFTY-ONE

★ ★ ★ ★ ★

A landing craft towed our three IBS-7 rafts upriver under cover of darkness to within three klicks of the target. Six of my LDNN and me had linked up with a nine-man PRU (Provincial Reconnaissance Unit) advised by an American who called himself Hicks. Hicks was bronzed and leathered and Latin, about 35. He talked and carried himself like a soldier, probably Special Forces. I figured he had been chopped over to work for the CIA and that his name was more appropriately Martinez or Sanchez.

Hicks had brought along remote-controlled explosives such as I had never seen before. He nearly filled one of the rafts with them. We loaded the other two rafts with the 15 Vietnamese and ourselves at the release point and set off upstream towing the one raft. Thick fog hung low over the broad Mekong, muffling the sounds of the outboard engines. There would not be a moon until late. It was a good night. Darkness and fog masked most of our activities.

Our destination, our target, was a village lying next to the river just this side of the Cambodian border. It was suspected of harboring large numbers of Vietcong supporting the Ho Chi Minh Trail in Cambodia and Laos. Our combined LDNN-PRU force had been tasked with securing the outskirts of the village to prevent VC escaping when South Vietnamese Rangers in Flying Banana helicopters attacked at dawn.

I ordered the engines cut to idle as we approached the hamlet, hugging the opposite bank. Then we killed engines and took up paddles. The fog was thinner now; I detected a star now and then through low diffused clouds. Different intensities of black separated river from forest shore from sky. I listened to the river sounds, listened for anything *different.* I heard mosquitoes and other insects, a fish splashing, birds interrupted in sleep, the disturbed low howl of a rock ape.

Across the river, squares darker than their surroundings marked a large settlement of 100 or more hootches. The dying coals of one or two cooking fires made red pinprick eyes in the night.

The current flowed gentle this far up the Mekong. We paddled on upriver in order to ride back what current there was. My *Nguoi Nhai* and I slipped overboard into the warm water in the middle of the river, like sunning turtles sliding off a log. We carried only our fighting knives and wore fatigue trousers, light canvas shoes, and black T-shirts. Hicks and his PRU returned to the cover of the overlapping foliage on the far bank while my team searched out a landing site near the village.

No swimming patrol was ever made as silently as I wished it to be. I was going slightly deaf, what with two decades of being around the guns of big ships, small arms fire, and aircraft engines, but even to me the soft ripples we made slicing through the water sounded like the crashing of breakers against rocks.

The river shallowed near the hamlet. Water grasses coiled around my feet like snakes. In the darkness, I mistook for the shoreline a bed of tall grass rising above the smooth surface. We slithered into the grass like giant salamanders, then through it before I realized the grass formed a natural boundary around a wide tidal pool. We were not alone in the pool.

An unexpected raucous din of hideous honkings!

Chanh nearly climbed up my back. No sentry was ever as alert as a gaggle of village geese. The outcry must surely have brought every VC in the village to arms.

I signaled desperately, then led the way with long below-surface strokes back into the river, expecting the hamlet to take up the cry of the geese. Instead, one lone gander continued to bleat out his ringing inquiry, ignored by the villagers. I would have strangled the bastard and eaten him raw if I could have laid hands on him.

After a few minutes, the gander drifted back to bird lullaby. A sleepy voice shouted at a barking dog. The night fell silent once more. Village occupants must have assumed their geese reacted to a swimming boa or to some other natural intruder. Charlie, you had fucked up by not listening to the night sounds.

Nosing along the shore like feeding catfish upriver of the watch geese, we soon detected a narrow inlet partially concealed by twisted mangrove. Khe and Bode scouted for obstacles and sentries. When they returned, signaling all-clear, Nguyen and I swam across and brought back Hicks and his PRU in the rubber boats.

"We had to change landing sites," I whispered directly into Hicks's ear. "Fucking geese."

"I heard them."

Hicks and I loaded our rucksacks with his marvelous experimental explosives. The village slept on, unaware of silent invaders setting up powerful charges on all the trails and avenues of escape from the ville. A miniature radio control panel enabled Hicks to selectively activate the charges from any location.

"You wouldn't believe what our technology is developing," he whispered. "Mines that resemble water buffalo turds. 'Sniffer' detectors that look like dogshit and tell us when troops pass."

Christ. I had trouble obtaining even 50-caliber machine guns and Claymore mines. MAAG hoarded weapons out of fear that issuing them to troops in the field, where they could be used, might result in their falling into the hands of the NLF. *Fucked up.*

By dawn, the village had been ringed in hair-trigger steel and riflemen, each assigned his sector of fire to trap the villagers in the kill zone. I felt almost like a voyeur as I hid in a coconut palm grove on the outskirts and watched the village come peacefully to life with the barking and fighting of curs and the crowing of roosters.

Women were the first to stir. They rekindled cooking fires and set tea and rice to boiling. They were followed by the older men and women, who squatted on their haunches next to the fires for warmth and chewed betel nut leaves. Then emerged the children and the young men to get ready for work in the surrounding fields.

A skinny bare-chested man carrying his cone hat in one hand came out of his hootch. I watched him go through his morning ablutions. He inspected the sunrise. He kicked at a hen with a bare ass. He stretched and yawned, scratched his balls, and watched some geese stroll honking up the dusty street, haughty heads held high above the world.

This tranquil morning scene came abruptly apart at the sound of boat engines on the river and the *whump-whumping!* of helicopter blades. Villagers paused, looking about, their faces suddenly tensing. The skinny man stopped scratching his balls. He darted inside and returned with a homemade rucksack and an AK-47.

Double-ended Flying Bananas popped up from behind the jungle line. Their appearance had the same effect on the village as dumping gasoline onto a red ant hill.

The popping of rifle fire began all at once, immediately reaching a crescendo. Hicks brought down the skinny man with a first burst from the Chicom AK he carried. A frightened flock of chickens stampeded across his fresh corpse.

Helicopters touched down in vegetable gardens. Viet Rangers in helmets, rifles blazing, poured out of the Bananas. More soldiers joined them from a landing craft that rammed its nose ashore where the village's main street ended at the river. The slaughter began.

I wanted no part of it. Nothing wrong with massacring VC. That was why we were here. It was just that this did not seem to be my fight. It was Hicks's fight, and the Viets'. I cradled my cold carbine in my elbows, leaned back against the segmented bark of a palm, and watched dispassionately. It was like watching a war movie. I thought I heard the throbbing beat of the score music. I half expected to see John Wayne.

Fusillades of rifle fire reverberated in waves through the poor hamlet. Men, women, and even a child here and there fell before the deadly hail of tracer lead. Gunfire shredded two men and a kid of about 10 or 11 and left their bodies piled bleeding in a doorway. Some of the VC had time to arm themselves, but to little avail. They kept falling like ragged bundles of discarded clothing all over the village. They would come out of their hootches no further mornings and stand scratching their balls and waiting for tea and rice.

No doubt the hamlet was infested with VC. But there were also many ordinary peasants, rice farmers, and small-time traders and merchants, who were apolitical and merely cooperated with whichever side controlled the village at any particular time. It seemed the neutrals must suffer most in this crazy war. The VC killed them, the ARVN killed them. Poor bastards.

Villagers poured toward the south side of town, trying to escape.

"Watch this!" Hicks cried, hovering over his remote control panel.

He pushed a button. Torn bodies flew as an eruption of yellow smoke and dirt blew a crater in the trail the size of a jeep.

He systematically closed off all avenues of escape with his explosions. Terrified people milled wailing and screaming in the village center as the ring of Rangers, PRU, and *Nguoi Nhai* closed in on them. The firefight dwindled in intensity to an occasional shot here and there. Then it was all over except for the excited crackle of running chickens, dogs barking, geese railing with indignation, and Rangers yelling orders as they waded among captives with their boots kicking and their rifle butts falling against yielding flesh.

One toothless old hag had to be wrenched off the corpse of her fallen son. Laughing Rangers kicked her in the belly until she let go.

Prisoners were thrown into a poultry fence guarded by

Rangers with bayonets. Dead people were dragged to the center of the village and heaped into a grisly pile. Blood cooled and mingled and coagulated, soon drawing swarms of flies and sniffing dogs. The body count numbered 22 suspected Vietcong; of course, anyone killed in a fight automatically became a suspected VC.

"Nice operation," I told Hicks.

"Successful," he said.

I limped into the village on my bad leg. I had not fired a shot. Bode strode past with bloody trophies in his hand. He thrust his prizes aloft.

"This one him have big ears," he chortled. "*Big* ears."

This operation had created a whole batch of fresh Pratas.

FIFTY-TWO

★ ★ ★ ★ ★

The Vietnamese people. The way I saw it, they were caught between the anvils of a corrupt and repressive government on one side and the goddamned communists on the other. I would likely have fought alongside Commander Minh were I Vietnamese. After declaring victory over the government, I would then have gone after the communists to drive them out.

The Vietnamese, however, were so splintered with hate that the factions would never be able to cooperate with each other for a common cause. I saw it wherever I went. Take Captain Hua, commander of the ARVN battalion with whom my *Nguoi Nhai* and I invaded Ilo Ilo Island.

As far as Hua saw it, all villagers between the ages of 10 and 80 were NLF; they were collaborators if nothing else.

He took the lead of many U.S. advisers and contemptuously referred to his own people as "gooks."

The North Vietnamese had murdered Hua's entire family—his wife, sons, and mother. After that, his hatred for the communists became a burning, calculated obsession to rid the planet of their ilk. He believed it his destiny to kill or maim any VC he encountered.

Ashcroft's junk force inserted me and a small patrol of my Viets as scouts to find and fix the VC on their island stronghold. His boats then patrolled the island's perimeter to prevent the enemy's escape by sea while Hua's battalion invaded in landing craft. Sharp firefights erupted here and there as VC fled the hamlets and scattered into the jungle. Prisoners, wounded or not, were thrown into a tiny barbed-wire animal cage on the beach. Hua personally kept guard over them. The intensity of his malice was so palpable that merely approaching him whenever enemy was in the AO was like walking up to a hot stove. Captives cringed in terror.

"Perhaps you would try to escape?" he said, smiling coldly and fondling his captured AK-47.

One of the suspected VC was female and about 80 years old. She set up a howl of protest when government soldiers *liberated* her ancient pedal-type Singer sewing machine after finding NLF flags stuffed into one of its drawers. A skinny old bag of bones in too-big black PJs, she dropped to her knees in the middle of the ville and in a keening wail begged soldiers not to take her machine.

"What are you doing with it?" I demanded of the ARVN. Khe interpreted.

"Burn it," came the reply.

"And the old woman?" I asked.

"She maybe VC. She must be evacuated to a safe village." That meant the animal cage first.

The Vietnamese government had established the "Strategic Hamlet" program in attempts to win people in the countryside away from communist influence. Selected villagers were often forcibly removed from "unsafe" villages and resettled in a strategic hamlet where they could be protected—and guarded—by South Vietnamese troops.

"You're not burning the mama-san's sewing machine," I protested. "If you assholes evacuate her, you're taking her sewing machine too."

"Shall I translate the 'assholes' as well?" Khe asked, deadpan.

"Word for word, Khe. They ain't stealing the old hag's sewing machine."

Hua and I struck a deal. He would protect the old woman and her Singer and not throw her in the cage if my LDNN and I hunted out the VC, treed them, and radioed for his troops to wipe them out. Sounded like a fair trade to me, since that was why we were there.

No wonder the ordinary people, especially the villagers, hated *both* sides.

Ashcroft's heavy voice rumbled from the PRC-10 radio I carried on my back. "Frogfoot One, this is River Rat One. Over."

"Go ahead, River Rat."

"Roy, I have six commie junks stranded by low tide, my location. Repeat—six Victor Charles junks on a mudflat."

The boats were located on a small island separated from the main one by a narrow channel. Ashcroft beached, picked up my men, and dropped us off on the opposite side of the island from the stranded craft. Several of his *Biet Hai* joined me, bringing my force up to about 16 fighters.

Fuck Hua. We had been bird-dogging VC for him most of the day. Now it was our turn to get in on the action.

Ashcroft staked out the channel to prevent escapes while my band crossed through the jungle to approach the beached junks from behind. The terrain was low, suck-boot muddy, and thickly grown over with tangling mangrove. We had to wade muck to our waists in places. It had the stench of dead, rotting things.

Chanh and the evil child Nguyen ran point as we neared the junks. The footing became somewhat dryer and firmer, although mangrove roots continued to twist and twine in foot traps above the ground. The green brush thickened to limit visibility.

My spotting the sentry was a fortunate accident. He swatted at a mosquito on his face and I detected the movement. He wasn't 10 feet ahead of me, standing in a minute clearing. I flashed the *Danger!* sign to the patrol behind and froze. Apparently, the point men had slipped past the guard in the undergrowth without either side spotting the other.

I observed the guy for several heartbeats. Only my eyes moved. He was a little man, not much over five feet tall. Traditional black pajamas, straw cone hat, canvas sneakers. Young face and eyes. Teenager. He carried a carbine and smoked a roll-yer-own cigarette.

The *First* SEAL must be getting old to have *unintentionally* approached an enemy so close. It troubled me. I knew my knees were going and my ears weren't as sharp as before. Still, I should have heard or seen or *sensed* the bastard. I should have smelled his cigarette smoke at least.

I carefully drew my K-bar. Bode kept the blade honed for me. Just a few days ago I had witnessed Bode take out a sleeping VC sentry with *his* K-bar. He came up behind like a stalking leopard, grabbed the man's chin with one hand, and jerked his head back. Butting his knife against his belt, he used the enemy's own weight to drive home the steel. He twisted the blade, severing the man's spinal column.

"Slit throat, slit spine. Same-same," Bode said. "Then take ears."

I waited for Charlie to turn his eyes away. I had killed men before. The man whose ass I assassinated in the Dominican Republic was a personal enough killing—shooting him in the face while he looked at me. But killing a man with a *knife.* That was *personal.*

Bored, the Vietnamese paced his tiny clearing. He finished his cigarette and stripped it to save the remaining tobacco for later. It was going to be his last cigarette.

I sprang, knife poised.

I kneed him hard behind the knee to throw him back into me. I caught his chin with my free hand. Brought my blade swiftly across his throat, slicing through flesh and cartilage and grating on deep bone. I thought his head was coming off in my hands.

Hot blood geysered over my hands. The stench of it. The stench of the sonofabitch's diet—rotted fish heads with rice, fermented cabbage. I almost retched from the awful stench as I dropped the body and stepped back. It lay pouring blood at my feet, muscles twitching involuntarily.

Nguyen on point returned, slipping back through the thickets to report enemy ahead. He stared at the nearly decapitated corpse. He looked guilty that he had not discovered the sentry himself. Bode cast a quick longing glimpse at the dead man's ears before I hand-signaled the two of them to check for other sentries.

Some of the men dragged the body into the bushes. I didn't look at it again. It was a job. SEALs were paid for doing such jobs. I wiped my blade and my hands on my fatigues.

Of the six junks marooned by low tide on the mudflats, one was a motor junk much larger than the others. It lay tilted to port, its cabin with its stubby lantern mast angled away in the opposite direction. Peering from the foliage, I saw no movement. Surely the sentry had not been guarding abandoned boats.

Bode and Nguyen rejoined us. They had found no additional enemy surrounding the boats. Khe consulted with me, then silently spread our fighters into an assault line. The ragged line advanced across the mudflat toward the junks. The boats looked like a row of beached whales.

Slogging through ankle-deep mud. Moving into the open among scattered mangrove. I kept my eyes on the big junk. I had a feeling. . . .

Rifle fire. Unexpectedly. Cracking and popping in a sudden fusillade. Ringing sharp in the sultry afternoon air. Flying lead kicking up gouts of mud, splattering the air.

A man dropped, screaming as he fell.

We were in the open. There was little cover. Only one way out—straight ahead.

Khe saw it too. He shouted a stream of Vietnamese. I mingled my shouts with his, urging the *Nguoi Nhai* to charge. *Charge!* Compelling it.

"Goddamnit, go! *Go, go, go!*"

There was a surge forward, marked by a returning fusillade of rifle fire, carbines stuttering in clamoring auto fire against the harsher barking of Chicom AKs. Bullets popped like popcorn against a pan lid as they riddled the defenders' big junk from which the ambush originated.

The wind seemed right. I popped smoke and hurled it ahead of the skirmish line. Yellow smoke clouded ahead of the attack, concealing us from accurate aimed fire. The VC desperately tried to fill every square inch of the smoke with burning lead.

Running, caught up in the violent thrill of the charge. Sinking knee-deep in places. Smoke acrid and raw in my throat. Sweat pouring. All we needed were mounted bayonets.

Many of my men were barefooted and had rolled up their trouser legs above their knees. They scurried to the attack, high-stepping through the mud like fast chickens, firing carbines and an occasional AK from their hips as they ran.

I emerged through the smoke, startled to find the big junk looming over me. A black-clad figure of death leaned over the gunnels pointing a rifle at me. I popped it with my low-carried carbine. It disappeared.

I dashed alongside the boat's hull toward the bow, intending to catch the defenders as they fled off the opposite side. A sudden, blinding pain knocked me flat on my ass in the mud, dazed. Nguyen and one of the *Biet Hai* laughed in glee as they stampeded over my outstretched body, trampling me deeper into the muck. Then I saw why they were laughing. I hadn't been shot. I had failed to see wooden boxes of cargo extending over the junk's gunnel. My head protected only by a fatigue cap had collided with a wooden crate.

It was what American SEALs would have done—laughed at something funny or absurd in the middle of battle. Damn it all, I felt *proud* to have trained these fighting little bastards.

About six VC defended the big junk. Three or four others were hiding on or behind the smaller junks. Those not dead or seriously wounded took off running as my mad Frogs descended upon them.

I sprang to a high perch on the big boat. Two men lay dead on the deck. A third man, wounded in the thigh, grabbed the back of his head with both hands and cried, "*Chieu Hoi!*" again and again. One of my men shoved him facedown on the deck and yelled at him in Vietnamese.

Yellow smoke thinned and rode the breezes into the forests, exposing the mudflats all around. A dead *Biet Hai* lay in the mud to the right; a wounded *Nguoi Nhai* attended him. Defeated VC raced for the safety of the distant mangroves in the other direction.

Bode, Chanh, and another fighter had followed me onto the junk's deck. They dropped each to one knee and took aim at the fleeing soldiers. They systematically picked them off one at a time.

The last VC alive tumbled like a wounded rabbit. He clawed at the mud and tried to pull himself into the safety of the mangrove thickets less than 50 feet away. Bode finished him off.

The fight ended in sudden silence. I collapsed wearily and let my legs dangle over the side of the junk. Bode leaped down and jogged across the muck toward the fallen enemy soldiers. He reached for the knife at his belt.

FIFTY-THREE

★ ★ ★ ★ ★

The fighting, already savage on both sides, became even more vicious as the war rapidly expanded. The growing string of VC ears Bode either carried in his pouch or wore around his neck in the field attested to just *how* fast and *how* savage. Requests for the special services provided by my Asian sea warriors poured in from throughout IV Corps as the *Nguoi Nhai*'s reputation grew and the VC increased the bounties on our own ears. In a way, I took consolation in conducting operations outside Commander Minh's territory in the Rung Sat. It delayed my return bout with the wily Swamp Ghost who had, oddly, become my friend. With the fall of Junk Base 33 nearly two months ago, Minh's troops virtually controlled the Mekong north of Vam Lang.

My *Nguoi Nhai* continued to hop about all over IV Corps. We choppered to the air base at My Tho as a ready reaction force to defend it against a heavy VC assault. We spearheaded another amphibious assault for the hate-filled Captain Hua at Cu Lao Ban. The LDNN suffered three WIA, one seriously, during seven different firefights.

We dove into a canal near Soc Trang to salvage a downed South Vietnamese AD fighter plane, then had to blow it underwater in place when VC appeared. The next day we choppered to the ARVN River Forces junk base at Ly Nhun to help defend it against an impending attack. Bode slipped out that night, returning at dawn just as I dropped a couple of "survival" bouillon cubes into a canteen cup of hot water. I handed the cup to him. He bowed politely, then informed me the understrength base would be hit that night from both the east and the south. I didn't question him on how he knew that; he wore fresh trophies on his necklace.

I brewed up a batch of homemade napalm by shaving brown saltwater soap into drums of gasoline until the mixture reached the consistency of thick syrup. My Frogs ladled the concoction into jars, cans, and whatever other containers they could find and planted them with igniters at strategic points around the base. That night, I lit up the VC when they came crawling through the grass. It was an awesome sight, amusing in a macabre way, to watch human torches dashing madly all over the field, colliding with each other and running into trees while my *Nguoi Nhai* and the base junk force picked them off with rifle fire.

One night, Ashcroft and I combined our forces to attack two motorized junks unloading VC war supplies. We placed six rockets into the junks and two into the staging area. Small arms fire opened up on our junks from a lookout position, along with a *flamethrower.* I lost one man killed. Ashcroft lost two *Biet Hai* KIA and one wounded. The flamethrower lit up the river, reaching for us with its fiery tongue.

"Holy shit!" I yelled. "Papa-san, let's get our unroasted asses out of town."

Army and Navy Intelligence in Saigon refused to believe us.

"The Vietcong do not have flamethrowers," they insisted.

"Okay." I walked over to the coffeepot. I had been through all this before with Captain Drachnik. "The VC don't have flamethrowers."

"Does our side have flamethrowers?" Ashcroft asked.

"We have them."

"Then, sonny boy, I suggest you check your inventory. You might be missing a few."

I was growing weary of what I already recognized as a no-win war generaled by politicians, car salesmen, and "Progress Is Our Most Important Product" mentalities. I dutifully filed my fictionalized progress reports, typed now by Porter my yeoman, fought my own personal war as best

I knew how, and sought solace whenever I could in either Khuyen My's bed or in Vung Tau at Father Dupree's Catholic mission.

The priest was also suffering due to the increased pressure of the war-displaced needy and of war orphans. Already painfully thin, he had become a war-ravaged reed of a shadow. He had joined common cause with my landlady, Madam Vinh, in expanding her combination rooming house, maternity hospital, and orphanage. It had now become more orphanage than anything else. Sometimes at night in my tiny room with either Nguyen or Bode standing guard at the door I overheard the smallest of the orphans sniffling and weeping in their lonely quarters.

Thay Wu often joined Father Dupree and me in the garden. He took a long look and reminded me of Buddhism's Universal Truth: "Suffering is universal. . . . Your spirit struggles, my son."

"It's because of being here in Vietnam," I admitted. "Fighting on the one side while seeing the merits of both sides."

"This country has for much of its history fed upon itself," he said. "May I tell you a Vietnamese joke?"

"Please do."

"Once there was a scorpion and a turtle," he began. "The scorpion wanted to cross a river. He said, 'Mr. Turtle, will you be kind enough to take me across the river?'

" 'I would like very much to take you across the river, Mr. Scorpion,' said Mr. Turtle, 'but if you sting me I will die.'

"Mr. Scorpion replied, 'But, Mr. Turtle, if I sting you and you die, I will drown.'

"Mr. Turtle considered this. He said, 'Okay. Get on my back and I will take you across the river.'

"Halfway across the river, the scorpion stung the turtle. The turtle cried, 'Mr. Scorpion, why did you do that? Now I will die and you will drown.'

"Said the scorpion, 'Ah, Mr. Turtle. This is Vietnam.' "

FIFTY-FOUR

★ ★ ★ ★ ★

Commander Minh almost always chose the location and time for our visits. The only way I had of contacting him was to drop a subtle hint in front of Ashcroft's sullen housekeeper, Co-Van, Minh's sister. Otherwise, Minh simply appeared, waiting for me outside the Tax Building in Saigon. At other times, he left a message for me in the bar, or he sent one of his teenage children in the taxi to escort me to Cholon. His children were also members of the National Liberation Front. I always tried to bring him a carton of American cigarettes or a jar of *nhouc mam* from Phuoc Quo Island, where he dared not go because of the possibility of his being recognized. The islanders at Phuoc Quo, he said, made the best *nhouc mam* sauce in Vietnam.

Although Minh was Catholic, he approved of my friendship not only with Father Depree but also with the diminutive Buddhist monk, Thay Wu. From what I gathered, Minh played an active role with the mission in directing orphans to Madam Vinh's. He was also one of the few VC warlords who strived to win the hearts, minds, and loyalties of local villagers rather than abusing them. He sometimes recommended a particular village or area whose inhabitants were infested with toothaches, infections, or chronic respiratory ailments. Doc Shultz, escorted by Ashcroft and me, made as many medical jaunts as he could to bring the poor populations needed medical care. Even had Doc and Jerry known about Minh and me, it would have made little difference to them that Minh received credit for the visits; we also received our share of it. We had nothing to fear from the

NLF on these visits; Minh lent us the personal protection of his name.

The strain of the escalating war showed no less in Minh's features than in my own.

"Congratulations, Roy," he said over dinner one evening in Cholon. "You now have a substantial price on your head. Our side will pay a grand bounty for your death or capture."

"And our side will pay for yours. Are you going to collect the bounty on me?"

"No more than you would collect on me, old friend. Besides, I am an officer in the People's Army. The bastards wouldn't pay me even if I killed you."

"Then why kill me, huh?"

"Precisely." He chuckled dryly. "We must be prepared for a long war. Already, you look fatigued."

"And you as well, my friend."

He studied me with his intense brown eyes.

"Roy, we sit here across from each other as friend and friend, but also as enemy and enemy. Each is a reflection of the other. We are the same, yet we are opposites. We shake hands and are friends when we are in Saigon." He paused to wave a hand in a general direction to indicate all that was outside Saigon. "Out there, should we meet," he continued gravely, "we are obligated to slay each other. Your country once had such a war."

"The Civil War."

"Brother against brother, father against son, friend against friend. Such wars breed exhaustion."

Later, as we were parting, he said as though in warning, "Take care, friend. We are both vulnerable."

FIFTY-FIVE

★ ★ ★ ★ ★

Two days before I parachuted my little Frog *Nguoi Nhai* onto Duong, pronounced *Dung,* Island in support of a joint Junk Force/ARVN seek-and-destroy operation in III Corps, I sent word to ask Doc Shultz to come to Vung Tau. My right leg had swollen to twice its normal size. I waited for Doc in my room at Madam Vinh's by elevating my leg and pouring a bourbon and water for the pain. Bode knocked on the door.

"What the hell is it now?"

"For you leg," Bode explained.

"What?"

"You need *bac'si* for you leg."

I hobbled to the door to find six of my LDNN surrounding a wizened old man with a wispy gray beard. My first impulse was to turn the witch doctor away, until Chanh explained that the *Nguoi Nhai* had chipped in more than a month's pay to hire the soothsayer. What could I do? I was starting to feel half Asian anyhow.

"Bring the bastard on in—as long as he don't cut it off." My stock immediately doubled in value in the Viets' eyes.

I limped back to bed. The *bac'si* solemnly turned off the lights, lit some candles, and began his rituals with a chanting litany of incantations. He had bells and chimes, seaweed and hot cups and foul-smelling salves, all of which he administered in one form or another. He pinched my neck and forehead to get the evil spirits moving, then used the hot cups to suck out the evil. While he was sucking evil, I sucked on a bottle of Jack Daniel's.

Finally, after more than two hours of ritual, the *bac'si* pronounced me "cured" and left. I drifted into exhausted slumber.

I was still sleeping the next morning when Doc Shultz arrived to tap the fluid off my bad knee.

"Who treated you?" he asked.

"What do you mean?"

I stared at my leg in stunned silence. The swelling had gone down. My knee looked normal. I half expected Doc to laugh when I reluctantly explained about the *bac'si.* Instead, he said, "I recognized the black-and-blue marks of the *bac'si.* We in the West don't know all the answers in medicine. You still need a few days off that leg of yours."

"Not yet, Doc."

"I could put you on permanent medical profile and ship you out of Vietnam."

"Doc, I still have things to do."

"Junk Base 33?"

"Soon. Doc, my leg . . . ?"

He sighed. "I'll put a light cast on it to see you through the jump."

Dawn arrives in the tropics as gorgeous as the short-lived sunsets. The C-130 Hercules' small portholes admitted little early light as the big troop plane lifted from the airfield outside Vung Tau with 32 of my little airborne troops and me aboard. Red night-vision lights illuminated my helmeted Frogs waiting in the web seating, weapons tied to their shoulders, rucks containing food, water, and extra ammo secured to the reserve parachute D-rings. We did not need reserve chutes anyhow since we were jumping from a mere 800 feet. Even if a main malfunctioned, there wouldn't be enough time to pop a reserve.

Khe gave me a thumbs-up. Of course, he was still senior Viet; his alleged commander, Captain Ninh the Butterfly, had taken another unexpected vacation. We would be tailgating the aircraft, parachuting off the lowered tail ramp in two simultaneous sticks, one from each side. Khe was pushing one stick. I was pushing the other. We had both studied aerial photos of the drop zone—a short series of rice paddies with water on either side.

"We must exit the aircraft *fast,*" I emphasized to Khe. "Every trooper who misses the DZ and lands in the drink is one less rifleman on the firing line."

"My stick out *di di,*" Khe replied. "I laugh at Boss Frog in air while he still in airplane."

"Numbah one, Khe-san."

Bode, wearing his chain of ears, sat next to me in the webbing, Nguyen next to him. They took bodyguarding seriously. Below, Ashcroft's junks were moving in to surround Duong Island; landing craft full of ARVN troops churned the sea toward their beachheads. My parachute force landing at a narrows in the center of the island would cut the AO in two and provide the anvil against which the ARVN would hammer the resident VC.

The red jump lights blinked on at 10 minutes out from the DZ. A U.S. Special Forces sergeant was jump-mastering. The odor of nervous tension mixed with man sweat filled the tube of the aircraft as the JM began the jump commands countdown. We expected a hot DZ—a combat jump with lead flying at us during that minute or two when we were most vulnerable hanging in the air underneath our parachutes.

"Get ready!" the JM shouted, exaggerating the hand signals and stomping for attention.

"Stand up!"

"Hook up!"

Snapping of static lines to the steel overhead cable. The sound of hydraulics as the tail ramp slowly opened wide to display a bright morning sky and an ocean painted with white mares' tails. I saw we were low over the water and apparently approaching the island and our DZ. The aircraft throttled back to jump speed. The deck thrummed beneath my feet at the slower speed.

"Equipment check! Sound off!"

"Stand in the door!"

With a last thumb-up, hawk-faced Khe drove his body against the jumpers in his starboard stick ahead of him, compressing it and forcing it toward the yawning morning of the open tailgate. I did the same thing with my port stick. The first two jumpers stood at the edge of the ramp as though frozen, waiting for the *"Go!"* Khe and I would be last jumpers out.

Suddenly, unexpectedly, the aircraft shivered violently. Four big engines kicked in full power. The Hercules surged forward.

There was no time for *"Go!"* The unforeseen advance in power literally threw every jumper out of the airplane. Tumbling out into the turbulent air on top of each other.

The low morning sky filled with popping parachutes. Chutes banging off each other like bumper cars. Little soldiers bicycling to unravel riser twists caused by the powerful blasts of air from the roaring engines. I couldn't lift my head to check my canopy; I had riser twists down to the back of my helmet.

Fortunately, the fucking pilots had thrown us out over the DZ. I pinpointed green rice fields below between my feet. I remembered thinking they were dry this time of year. Although last man out of the aircraft, I hit the ground first because of my weight. My parachute had not much more than opened before I struck with a jolting stab of pain that went like electricity through my encased right knee.

I lay in the dry rice for a minute waiting for the pain to subside. Watching the lightweight Viets as they seemed to hang in the air forever on parachutes made for much heavier westerners. Popping of rifles from the tree lines. VC welcoming party. My eyes darting, looking for hits.

Above, the C-130 climbed out steeply and away, engines roaring on full power. The sonofabitch. The pilots had panicked over a few rounds of ground fire and shoved the throttles to the wall. Fuck the jumpers. Every man for himself. I threw the pilots a bitter single-digit salute as the C-130 specked out on its fast retreat to the mainland.

Khe reported all up in a quick head count. Miraculously,

no one was injured on the jump or pinged by fire in the air. The VC welcoming party *di di*'d into the jungle.

I stood up and could barely walk wearing Doc Shultz's leg cast. Khe watched me, concerned. I pissed on the cast to soften the material, then cut if off with my K-bar. I could stand the pain. *Oooo-aaugh! First* SEAL and all that happy gung-ho horseshit.

Saigon hailed the Duong Island operation as a huge success. We suffered no friendly casualties, while toting up a small but significant body count of our own and capturing 40 or so prisoners. The ARVN seized a lot of war materiel. I limped along the shoreline with my .357 magnum putting the *coup de grâce* to "Hands Across the Sea" outboards on the VC sampans. Nguyen came along with an ax and chopped holes in the hulls.

Ashcroft and I stood together near the one village and watched the looting and prisoners being beaten and dragged away. A shot rang out now and then as a prisoner tried to "escape." To the victor belonged the spoils. It was a warrior's right. ARVN soldiers along with LDNN and *Biet Hai* went through the subdued hamlet like a Genghis Khan plague. It could not be stopped without igniting desertions and revolt in the troops. Pigs, ducks, geese, and chickens with their legs tied were hoisted aboard Ashcroft's junks.

Brutality came easy in Asia and particularly in such a war as this in Asia. You adjusted to it. But each day was another day of soul decay.

Doc Shultz was always asking, "Are we winning?"

Ashcroft, the Army first sergeant who kept my jeep while I was in the bush, the Special Forces jumpmaster from the Duong Island drop, and I scooted over to the Vung Tau hotel for a meal and a few drinks. I had given my men a 72-hour stand-down liberty following action. Several U.S. Air Force pilots were in the bar gathered around a table. One of them, a burly youngster, was laughing and telling the others about an operation that sounded strikingly familiar.

"We started taking fire on approach," he said. "I'm not

going for any of that shit. Fuck 'em. I hit the throttles and we *di di*'d, hauled ass out of *that* AO."

It was *him?* I stalked toward the Air Force table. Ashcroft sighed. "Here we go again."

"Who was in your airplane?" I asked the sky jockey.

"No big deal. We were only dropping a load of fucking gook paratroopers on Duong Island."

"Shame on you, my feathered friend. Look up here at me."

"What's your problem, buddy?"

"I was one of them fucking 'gooks.' You could have killed our asses. The next time you tell this story, it's going to be with a great deal of pain."

I hooked him to the jaw with a right cross, then followed that up with a couple of lefts for good measure. His flyboy buddies had to evacuate him to Saigon for medical treatment. Shortly thereafter, I received formal notification that I would be court-martialed. The fucking guy *deserved* a broken jaw, but *I* was being court-martialed for it.

FIFTY-SIX

★ ★ ★ ★ ★

Saboteurs who blew a hole in the hull of the USS *Card,* a jeep aircraft carrier tied up to Pier 13 in Saigon, proved again that in *this* war *no one* could be trusted. Onboard the *Card* was a cargo of aircraft for the Vietnamese air force. MAAG sent me to dive for evidence and assess the damage. I took Chanh with me.

Diving into the murky harbor water, we soon recovered unexploded particles of C-3 and C-4 explosives. But my most significant finding included scraps of a U.S. flotation bladder used for packing 20-pound increments of plastic explosives. It was called a Hagerson Demolition Pack.

"Where in hell did the VC get a Hagerson Pack?" mused the American salvage diver from the *Card.*

Khe drove up to the piers in a truck to deliver extra air bottles and lungs.

"Need talk to you alone, Boss-san," he said, frowning.

We walked along the pier. "You know anything about this, Khe?"

He drew a deep breath. "You not like it," he said. "Six of our *Nguoi Nhai* gone."

"Gone?"

"They go. Take eight Hagerson Packs when they go. Also take volt tester, explosive machine, roll of det cord, electric wire, many caps. These same-same men Cham Boot punish in barbed-wire cage."

Cham Boot translated as *Butterfly.* Prior to the Duong Island jump, Nguyen had come running to me.

"Come quick, Boss-san. Butterfly have Frogs."

Captain Ninh, the sonofabitch, had six of my Frogs confined for punishment at Cat Low on the hot sand in a four-square-foot two-foot-high cage of razor wire. They were begging for water.

I found Butterfly vacationing in a cottage on the beach. He had other "commitments" when I told him I needed every available man for a combat jump.

"I want those men out of that cage by this afternoon," I said, adding, "Ninh, I'm coming after your worthless ass if I don't get them."

I got my six men back. Now, they were deserters and had apparently blown up the *Card.*

"Them hate Butterfly who flit from here to there all day," Khe said. "Nguyen say them go with People's Liberation Army."

Yeoman Porter typed up my report to Captain Hardcastle, along with my sardonic postscript that the defecting LDNN had done a good job on the *Card,* exactly as I taught them. I hoped Charlie gave them a "You Did Good" medal. Nguyen and the others giggled with nervous glee, like mischievous children. I shared their delight. After all, what was I but also a simple child?

"We will take advantage of every opportunity," Commander Minh said, smiling, when he learned of the defections. "My friend, it may take years, but you are fighting a losing cause."

"*I'm* fighting to win. The politicians are losing."

"What difference, ultimately, does it make if the war is lost anyhow?"

Minh was an educated man. I was simply a rough sea dog. Having dinner with him was a bit like spending time with a Harvard political science professor or the curator of the Smithsonian. Of all the topics broached between us, only current military subjects were taboo. Between us lurked the awareness that we were, after all, fighting on different sides.

Minh seemed in deep thought before letting me out of his cab in front of the Tax Building. Finally, he got it off his mind. "Old friend, you need to know. You have a traitor."

"It looks like we had six of them."

"This one is still with you. He has been ordered—not by me—to kill you."

"Can you tell me more? *Will* you tell me more?"

"That is all I can say."

He looked at me like he thought he might never see me again.

A few days later, Khe said, "Boss-san, we have identified the traitor. Tranh Sao is the double agent. Bode has seen him in the villages with VC."

Tranh was one of Ashcroft's *Biet Hai,* not a Frog. A skinny agreeable kid who admired the way I braised three 30-round carbine magazines together to allow a feed of 90 rounds of fire with a simple twist of the wrist. I liked the kid, but if Bode said Tranh was a double agent, then Tranh was a double agent. The information confirmed the warning I received from Minh.

Either Nguyen or Bode, or even Chanh or Khe, would

have taken care of the problem at a single word from me. I thought it more poetic, however, for Tranh to take care of himself.

One of the *Biet Hai* on leave visiting his family's village returned with news that a VC tax collector confiscating one-third of the village's rice crop had ordered the hamlet to prepare to feed seven or eight travelers on a specific date. Undoubtedly, they were high-ranking NLF members. I couldn't let a target like that pass.

Ashcroft and his patrol junks dropped off my raiding party in three sampans at the mouth of the canal that flowed past our *Biet Hai*'s father's village. I had selected Tranh as a member of the ambush team. We paddled the dugouts through the inky night to where the canal narrowed at a bend near the ville.

I assigned Tranh the honor of initiating the ambush. I handed him one set of my braised 90-round magazines. Earlier, I had let Bode see me load the magazine with nothing but tracers. A burst from the clip on full automatic would blaze a pathway back to the firer that a blind man could have followed.

Bode understood. I appointed him to watch over Tranh somewhat forward of the main ambush. I wanted Tranh isolated. Bode separated himself from the double agent, to prevent taking any of the inevitable return VC fire, but remained close enough to make sure Tranh didn't slip his comrades a warning.

Tranh seemed exceptionally nervous as the ambush set itself in thick grass alongside the canal. For several hours there was nothing but the swarming buzz of mosquitoes and an occasional animal call or cry. Then, just before dawn, I heard the soft dip of paddles in black water.

Shortly, two sampans loaded with men shadowed into view.

Tranh had no idea that he was firing solid tracers. He had no choice, with Bode watching him, but to open up as planned. He confirmed his loyalties by aiming high, pumping a near-solid stream of red tracers *over* the boaters' heads. He at least wasn't going to be the one to kill his VC friends.

Separately, I had ordered my men not to open fire except on my command. I delayed that order a crucial moment. The VC sampans winked and flared with return fire. Their bullets walked down Tranh's red stream, cutting him almost in half.

Then I gave the order.

A withering hail of fire chewed the canal surface into a froth stained pink by the blood of the dead and the dying. The night's take included five enemy KIA, two WIA prisoners, two sampans, and two AK-47 rifles that were dropped inside the sampans rather than into the canal. I let Nguyen and Khe keep the AKs; they would be fighting this war long after I had gone.

An eerie silence hung in the dawn after the brief fury of the action. The victorious Viets giggled with childish glee amidst life destroyed. They pulled the dead bodies up onto the muddy bank in a row and plundered for cash and valuables. Better my Frogs take the spoils than noncombatants. Seemingly coldhearted and unemotional except for their laughter, they rifled pockets and bloodstained rucks, sticking their fingers into bullet holes and opening mouths to check for gold teeth. How fleetingly fragile, I thought, this veneer called civilization.

Bode returned with Tranh's carbine and the magazine that had caused his death.

"Tranh Sao honorably made suicide," he said solemnly.

FIFTY-SEVEN

★ ★ ★ ★ ★

The Vietcong never *occupied* anything in a true military sense; they were content to *control*. By day they were indistinguishable from other rice farmers and small tradesmen. But when the sun faded, they dug up their weapons and assembled into squads and platoons to carry out the evening's work. So it was that Commander Minh's VC never really occupied former Junk Base 33. They turned it into a bustling trading post for the surrounding countryside, which they controlled and taxed heavily. From the ashes of the old base had risen a new Phoenix hugged against the strong moving waters of the brown Mekong.

Both for Jerry Ashcroft and me, reprisal for the night Minh drove us from the junk base like curs had become a matter of pride and honor. Redemption lay only in returning in force to retake it. We had plotted ever since that humiliating night on the best way and the best time to hit it. We knew finally that the time had come when *Biet Hai* spies reported that a big VC summit meeting was going to take place at the former junk base. Important NLF leaders from all over the Delta would attend. Including Minh, no doubt.

Ashcroft grinned. "Payback," he said.

We pored over maps and recent aerial photos. Grass that I set afire with gasoline during the attack had grown back. Rice now sprouted over cleared fields of fire in diked paddies. The old bunkers and fighting trenches had disappeared, replaced by 100 or so hootches and long tin-roofed merchant buildings. A road, a widened trail actually, connected Vam

Lang to the new hamlet. VC always designed escape routes when they dominated a village.

"They won't use that road," Jerry concluded. "It's too obvious, too exposed, and too near the river."

One of the new dikes was two or three feet wider than the others. A perfect roadway, it led from the hamlet, across the little plain, over a bridged stream and into the forest near where Minh had sprayed us with his 50-caliber machine gun. *Biet Hai* spies confirmed that it was indeed a VC road.

We began serious planning. The final scenario called for a three-pronged attack. My *Nguoi Nhai* and I accepted the most hazardous prong. We would slip ashore at night to establish an ambush site where the wide dike funneled across the bridge. Ashcroft's junks would attack the village just before dawn with machine guns and mortars in conjunction with a helicopter rocket assault to drive the enemy to their escape route across the bridge. The simplest plans were almost always the best plans.

"All we have to do now is find out when the meeting is taking place," I said.

"My men are in the village now pretending to be fish peddlers."

Ashcroft looked at me. "And if Minh is there?" he questioned. He and I were finishing off a bottle of bourbon in my room at Madam Vinh's.

I had finally told him about Minh and about the relationship between Minh and Co-Van. For his own protection.

"Jesus Christ!" he had exploded. "Don't tell Arnie Levine at MAAG. He has ulcers already trying to protect us from Progress Is Our Most Important Product."

"In the bush," I replied, "Minh is VC and the enemy."

I always knew there would come a day when Minh and I would have to meet in battle.

"Would you kill him?" Jerry persisted.

"He understands. He would kill me."

"That's not what I asked, Boy-san. Would you kill *him?*"

"It is war," I said.

FIFTY-EIGHT

★ ★ ★ ★ ★

As Commander Ashcroft's junks burbled up the darkened river beneath the canopy of a moonless night, finally returning to Junk Base 33, I experienced an elevation of spirit, a kind of full-circle feeling of closure. I hated like hell to leave anything undone; Doc Schultz was still making sounds about sending me back to the States because of my knee.

Ashcroft had armed five of his boats with 30-cal machine guns and 3.5 rocket launchers. In the darkness of the overhanging jungle he leaned an elbow on the machine gun mounted forward of the open flying bridge and clasped my shoulder with one thick hand.

"If anything goes bad," he said, clearly uneasy, "send up two red flares and I'll meet you here mosh-skosh."

"You worry too much, River Rat. This ain't going to be like last time."

I jerked my Marine patrol cap low over my eyes as the boats nosed into the bank. I had already paint-camouflaged my face green and black. I checked my carbine function and made sure the ammo pouches on my LBE were filled. Bode, lugging a machine gun was already going over the side ahead of his squad. I heard the slight riffling of water as he eased ashore.

My force consisted of 16 fighters, about half what I expected. Sometimes with the Vietnamese, even with the disciplined *Nguoi Nhai,* you never knew how many would actually show up for a mission. They had all been a bit nervous about returning to the site of their first major battle—and their only defeat.

"River Rat," I said to Ashcroft, using his radio call sign, before I slipped overboard. "Frogfoot One is out of here."

We shook hands.

"When it's over, Boy-san," Ashcroft said.

The distance from the drop-off to the village was about three klicks. Bode and Chanh had scouted out a route the previous night. Chanh took point. Six Viets in the center of the formation carried the heavy prima cord net consisting of 30 grenades taped in sequence to a long length of detonating cord. All the grenades would explode almost simultaneously when I detonated the net.

The caterpillar of little amphibians wended its way through thick jungle. There were normal jungle sounds—sleepy birds, monkeys interrupted in their dreams. We moved cautiously, halting every few minutes for a listening break. I checked my watch to make sure we were on schedule.

We kept to the forest and silently skirted the plain by the village. My men were all veterans by this time and good in the field. Not even a dog barked. We encountered no sentries, only some night bird that exploded ahead of our approach and damned near gave me a coronary.

When we came to the small bridge, I crouched behind the dike and glassed the settlement with binocs while Khe sent out security to either side. Darkness shrouded the hamlet. Nothing extraordinary seemed to be happening until someone in the village pushed aside a blanket covering a door and released a pale flash of light. Then I detected other dark figures moving around outside the hootch. The summit was in progress. I smiled grimly in anticipation.

The smile faded when I thought of Minh.

I couldn't dwell on the thought. This was war. It was not a time or place for friendships and sentimentality.

Working quickly, the *Nguoi Nhai* laid out the grenade prima cord net on either side of the dike road and concealed it with soil and vegetation. I attached one end of an electrical wire to the det cord and, running stooped over along the dike, attached the other end to a "hell box" concealed in a thicket of woods safely off the road. I kept the detonator handle in my pocket until after I checked the placement of the ambush.

I rigged a final explosive charge to the bridge and wired it into the hell box. Khe nested a machine gun beyond the bridge. It commanded a clear field of fire across the bridge and straight down the road. Automatic riflemen were placed out of the explosive radius of the prima cord net but with a crossfire capability on the road. The object was to kill as many VC as possible with gunfire once the escape stampede began, driving the survivors off to either side where the grenade net would finish the job. Nothing could survive such a kill zone once I activated it. It was devious, hellish, and I was pleased. This was war.

The men settled in place to wait once we completed preparations. I used a hooded red-lensed flashlight to click the all-ready code to Ashcroft's force across the river. Three dots—S; four dots—H; two dots—I; dash—T. *SHIT*. Short for *Shit Hits Fan.*

Boy, were we having fun.

I lay prone with Bode next to a tree, the hell box detonator between us, handle in place. I lay silently without moving and watched the hootches in the settlement gradually take dim outline with the expanding band of gray-pink across the horizon. For me, waiting was always the hardest part. When the imagination had time to work. When the mind automatically started cataloging your life for you, picking out the highlights both honorable and less than honorable, pointing out what might have been or could have been or might not be if you failed to survive today's action.

I had come a long way since reporting aboard my first ship, the USS *Griffin,* when I was 17 years old and Pearl Harbor had not yet happened. I figured, in those days, that I was cut out for something *special.* And maybe I had been.

That was over 20 years ago.

I thought of the shark that got Dubiel; I hadn't thought of it in a long time. Why had it taken him and not me? I thought of the 27 months of sea warfare in the South Pacific, of the first Frogmen I had ever seen with their striped, blue-green bodies. Of the fantasy I had entertained all these years—undersea warrior commandos—and then, step by step, through diving and UDT, turned into reality with the birth of the U.S. Navy SEALs. The Cuban missions, the assassination in the Dominican Republic. . . . Gradually it had all led to *this*—guerrilla warfare at its rawest with a band of half-wild Frogmen/SEAL types on foreign soil and on terrain half-water and half-mud and all hostile.

I was something *special* all right.

I thought of Tawny, my first love whom I would always love in a way, and of ex-wife Ellie and of the children. And, now, tonight, hobbling around from old injuries acquired along the way, I thought of Minh my friend whom I might kill within the next several minutes.

This was what it had been like. Roy Henry Boehm—undersea commando warrior. I wouldn't have had it any other way. But sometimes . . .

Machine gun fire, harsh, rhythmic, stuttering, slapping and echoing off the river in the predawn jarred me out of melancholy and abruptly back to the present. Ashcroft's junks as planned had opened up the attack first from the waterfront. I reached out and felt the rough bark on the tree. Rubbed it. It was real. Then I was ready. My mind focused on combat and the necessity of the mission.

Engines roared as Ashcroft's junks sortied on the village. Popping of lead ripping and tearing through the grass hootches. Vermilion tracers penetrating the huts and streaking on through, soaring in arcs, like colored horizontal rain.

Throaty *whooshes* of rockets, followed by blinding flash-bangs. Flowers blossoming with the rains. Ashcroft delivering his hell storm with thunder, lightning, and deadly rain.

Then it was helicopter time. Two Huey gunships bounced high into view from the jungle line across the river. They charged on-line across the brown water, low, and sprinted above the hamlet like winged shadows of death. Stinging the village with unleashed rockets and machine gun fire. Igniting fires. Igniting panic. Using their weapons to close off all avenues of escape. Except one.

Green tracers answered the assault fire here and there. VC trying to get lucky, trying to organize a defense. But return fire was sporadic at best.

I heard them coming before I saw them in the darkness that remained next to earth. A shouting, screaming mob vomiting out of the village and stampeding along the wide dike toward the bridge and the perceived safety of the forest.

A moving black protoplasm of life. Strung out now in the panic of flight. Bode lying next to me tensed like a bird dog on point.

Bare feet pounding on the bridge.

The dying time began. Khe's machine gun suddenly rapping out in a clear distinct voice its awful musical destruction. A choir of automatic rifles harmonizing with the lead voice. An orchestra of death.

A scythe of lead harvested the villagers, mowing them down like a crop of ripe rice.

Survivors bailed off the side of the dike. I twisted hard the handle of the hell box. The grand finale.

The dike, the bridge, everything disappeared in a volcanic explosion of flames, smoke, misted blood, and flying body parts. White phosphorus from the grenades ignited one or two walking wounded who danced in and through and around the smoke like fiery puppets manipulated by a Satanic hand. Dante could never have imagined anything like this.

I picked off the flaming puppets with my carbine, to end their misery. *Nguoi Nhai* pumped lead into the maelstrom until most of the moaning and weeping subsided. I called *cease fire.* Startling silence over the kill zone. Only a shot or two from the hamlet as Ashcroft dumped his *Biet Hai* ashore to round up prisoners. The two Hueys hovered watchfully overhead.

I had vowed to return to Junk Base 33. And I had. With bloody goddamned vengeance.

I steeled myself to join my men in venturing onto the killing field. I walked silently among the piles of mangled corpses, some of which still moved feebly and which were dispatched mercifully by a single shot here and there. I estimated 35 to 40 dead. Some of the dead men carried sidearms, marking them as high-ranking VC cadre. There were many weapons among the carnage.

N-2, Naval Intelligence, was going to love us. Scattered in the blood along with weapons were maps, orders, war plans, and other documents. We had hit the jackpot.

Smoke wisped from the ground, oozing and entwining itself in rivulets around corpses and the largely silent men who searched the corpses. I stood in the aftermath and simply stared at the waste I had initiated. A beautiful red ball of a sun surveyed the scene with us, but kept its distance.

I walked through the gore then, looking for a familiar face. Expecting to find it. Hoping I wouldn't. A tiny body caught my eye. Mangled, head twisted completely backward, glassy eyes staring sightlessly up at me accusingly. A little girl of eight or nine, lying twisted like a broken doll.

There were a couple of other, older children among the dead, along with four or five women. VC sometimes brought their families with them.

Khe accompanied me in respectful silence. Then Bode joined us, and finally Nguyen.

"Boss-san, what you look for?" Khe asked.

A familiar form facedown on top of the dike. Heart pounding, I turned it faceup. Let out a sigh of relief. It wasn't *him*. It was one of the six deserters who had stolen Hagerson Packs and blown a hole in the USS *Card*.

I examined all the bodies twice before I felt satisfied. My friend, Commander Minh of the 514th VC Battalion, was not among the corpses. I walked away from the scene and stood there in the morning light with my back to it.

One of the Huey choppers landed in the rice field nearby. Three Americans jumped out and walked over to me. One was a stocky block of a man wearing U.S. Navy bos'n insignia on his fatigue collar. He stuck out his hand.

"My name's Bill. I'm with the Seabees. What's your moniker, Lieutenant?"

"Roy Boehm."

He took a deep swig of the morning and gazed toward the village, as into a great distance. Fires still smoldered.

"What do you see over there, Roy?"

I looked at him. "One hell of a mess. What do *you* see?"

"I see a Phoenix rising out of VC-free ashes. I see a marketplace with electric lights. It's filled with fish for sale and lots of vegetables grown in night soil. I see the beginning of a new democracy."

I looked at the village. I must have lost my vision for what *might* be. I saw poor grass huts on fire with a pathway of bloody corpses leading to them.

FIFTY-NINE

★ ★ ★ ★ ★

I grabbed my well-worn submarine bag off the deck of the command junk as Ashcroft and I clambered ashore at the Saigon piers. We were both too exhausted and filthy to bother to exchange more than those words necessary to convey rudimentary information. The war had continued to escalate since our return victory at former Junk Base 33. Where previously our "advised" troops made contact on perhaps every fifth or sixth mission into the bush, now they were fighting almost every time out. The VC we encountered were better armed, better trained, more disciplined. Intelligence informed us VC cadres were being trained in Hanoi as well as in Moscow and Peking and then infiltrated back into South Vietnam to recruit and lead guerrillas.

The war was escalating rapidly. Washington made noise

about sending conventional troops to Saigon, not only Special Forces and SEAL "advisers." If one-upmanship continued at this rate—you slap me, I'll slap you *harder*—this little war in Vietnam was going to become this big war in Vietnam.

"I understand you returned to the junk base, as you said you would," Commander Minh said in Cholon a week or so after that massacre.

I wasn't too proud of the fact that women and a few children had died in the ambush.

"It had to be done," I said.

"Yes, Roy. We each must do what must be done. I think we were fortunate, both of us, that we were not destined to meet again in battle. I have been transferred to a new assignment."

Naturally, he couldn't and wouldn't tell me what it was. Whatever his new assignment, I hoped it meant we would never have to fight each other again. Enemies made better friends that way.

Now, limping alongside Ashcroft's stocky form past the statue of the Trung sisters, I looked forward to a shower, a bourbon, a steak, and a few days' escape from the war. Ashcroft lifted a weary hand in farewell as he turned off for the Majestic Hotel.

"Give Co-Van my love," I said.

"The lady likes you. I can tell because she hasn't stabbed either one of us yet."

The narrow street leading to my apartment at the Tax Building was starting to come awake with the Saturday morning. I intended to freshen up, then head to Khuyen My's place for a haircut and more intimate ministrations in her upstairs room. As I limped slowly along, head up my ass in anticipation, I hardly noticed the crowd of U.S. enlisted soldiers and sailors in civvies breakfasting at a popular sidewalk café ahead.

I also failed to notice the kid watching me. The city was filled with 10- and 11-year-old street urchins like him, orphans of the war or merely young hustlers corrupted by the war and turned into pickpockets and common thieves.

It was too late by the time I *did* notice. He nimbly relieved me of my submarine bag and streaked off down the street, looking back at me and laughing over his shoulder.

"Fucking little bastard!"

I instinctively gave chase, although the bag contained little other than toilet articles and a change of uniforms. Probably I wouldn't have, except for his laughing at me.

My knee was swollen from last night's jungle ambush and patrol and ached like hell. The little sonofabitch could have easily outdistanced me and disappeared into the Saturday throngs. Except he didn't. He skipped along ahead of me far enough to stay out of danger of being caught but near enough to keep me interested. He looked vaguely familiar.

Then, very uncharacteristically of a thief, he dropped my bag and vanished down an alley. Puzzled, I hobbled up to retrieve it. From the corner of my eye I thought I glimpsed a man watching me from across the street. Minh! When I turned to look, he was gone.

Suddenly, a clap of reverberating thunder filled the street with the fury of a dozen typhoons released. The blast pounded the air from my lungs and slammed me to the sidewalk in a tangle of arms and legs with other pedestrians.

The sidewalk café had disappeared in a boiling cloud of black and gray smoke. I watched on my hands and knees, too stunned to move, as injured people started reeling bleeding and blackened out of the smoke. A passing pedicab and its operator had been blown across the street and deposited in the back of a French minitruck hauling melons. Mangled bodies sprawled motionless in the street, most of them the U.S. servicemen who had been eating at the sidewalk tables.

Apparently, coincidence brought me blundering onto the scene moments before the bomb went off. Probably it had been built into a bicycle or pedicab parked near the café. If not for the young thief's intercession—and possibly Minh's—the sappers might have reaped an additional bonus, the VC bounty on my head.

"I owe you," I thanked Minh the next time I saw him.

"You owe the young lad who snatched your bag, Roy. You should have recognized him," he scolded. "He's shined your boots. You must be getting tired. You can see what you're up against, my friend. All of you must be eliminated. It is the end result that is significant."

SIXTY

★ ★ ★ ★ ★

I owed Minh my life. Perhaps I owed him for it more than once. I had to keep reminding myself that he *was* the enemy. The next time I saw him, it was under circumstances where I knew I had to take action. I couldn't let *this* pass, not even for Minh.

I had hopped a C-129 from Tan Son Nhut to the military airfield at Vung Tau where the Army first sergeant met me with our commandeered jeep. As we had coffee together in the canteen, a C-130 glided out of the sky and off-loaded a platoon of South Vietnamese Rangers. I watched the procedure idly through the window.

My coffee cup froze halfway to my lips. I stared in open astonishment.

Commander Minh, Vietcong warlord and high-ranking NLF cadre member, got off the airplane with the other soldiers. He wore the uniform and insignia of a major in the ARVN Rangers.

I ducked out of sight, confused, and watched as a six-by truck picked up Minh and the platoon and roared off. Minh continued to amaze. Where did he find the time and ingenuity? Taxi driver by day, VC chief by night. Apparently, he squeezed double agent in there somewhere. But a *major* in the ARVN!

The discovery placed me in a moral quandary. He was a dead man if I exposed him. The ARVN would execute him on the spot. I had to stop him. Yet, I also owed him at least a warning.

For the first time I went directly to Co-Van and told her I needed to see her brother urgently. She studied me for a long minute. The bitterness and hate in her eyes and expression dissipated.

"Where?" she asked.

"There's a French restaurant on the outskirts of Vung Tau."

"The food is very good there."

"At 1400 hours tomorrow afternoon."

"He will receive the message."

Minh already had a table for us in the restaurant when I arrived. He was dressed Western in a white, open-necked shirt, gray slacks, and black loafers. I ordered a beer to match his, then requested a steak smothered in hot peppers and *nhuoc mam.*

"You're going to tell me how you're sitting on the fence, playing both sides," I began without formalities.

"Oh. Whatever happened to *savoir-faire?"*

"It left with the French." I paused. "I saw you with the Rangers."

He gave an involuntary start. A cagey look flitted across his face, then vanished.

"That's enough to get me beheaded at dawn."

"Sooner. So far, it's my secret."

"But not for long?"

"That depends upon you. Minh, you're a major in the ARVN. What made you turn to the NLF?"

Emotion warred through his expressions, transforming his face into something hard and unrelenting and unforgiving. Then he began talking, and as he spoke I saw a side of my friend that had been concealed until now.

"Ngo Dinh Nhu caused the death of my father during his

brother's regime as president," he said. "I was an officer in the army. I saw the corruption and the brutality in the government. Did you know that the slaughter of the temple Buddhists was deliberately engineered by General Dinh in an effort to blame the communists and maintain Ngo Dinh Diem in power?"

"That regime is gone now," I argued, "replaced by the Generals' Revolt."

"But nothing has changed in the government. There is still the corruption."

He withdrew into deep thought.

"My friend, I could never ask you to keep a secret like you now possess and remain honorable to your cause. I've told you I have a new assignment. It requires my withdrawal from the Army of the Republic of Vietnam. You will not see me again in uniform or out. Roy, this must be our farewell dinner. Our friendship has become too dangerous for both of us.

"Before we part," he said, passion rising, "I must tell you this. You cannot win this war. Your nation is great and strong in material and technology. But the people will prevail against you because your country is morally weak and stupidly self-righteous. With rare exceptions such as you, few among you care enough about us to learn our culture, our language, our ethics. Your people will die on our soil, but you will not take the time to learn about us.

"Your Ambassador Lodge is a political appointee who surrounds himself with lackeys who know little more about what is needed in Vietnam than he does. The money and aid your country sends to this government finds its way to the pockets of greedy and crafty officials rather than to the people for whom it is intended. In the south of Vietnam, there is filth, profiteering, corruption, and the only loyalty is to deceitful political schemes."

"North Vietnam is better?"

"No. But north and south must be reunited to make it better for all," he continued. "We will take advantage of every opportunity to win. We will vanish before your eyes, only to reappear in a different form to blend with our surroundings like a many-fanged reptile waiting to strike again. You see, for my country, for my destiny, we *have to win.*"

The discussion continued for another hour. Finally, we stood and faced each other. He was tall enough that our eyes met on nearly the same plane. He reached for my shoulders with both hands.

"I wish we could have been comrades," he said in a low emotional tone. "What a brother. . . . But, no, it can never be. Destiny has made us enemies. Good-bye, *my friend.*"

He embraced me hard, once. And then he was gone into Vietnam.

SIXTY-ONE

★ ★ ★ ★ ★

At times my knee swelled to such elephantine proportions that all I could do was hobble stiff-legged to bed either at Madam Vinh's in Vung Tau or to the apartment I shared with Doc Shultz and Ted Reilman at the Tax Building in Saigon. Ashcroft fussed over me, telling Doc he should ship my stubborn ass to the hospital. Doc threatened to redline me and send me back to the States. I argued I still had work to do; my Viet tadpoles were not yet ready to swim on their own as full Frogs.

"Besides," I added with a wry grin, "they're probably going to court-martial me as soon as I get out of a combat zone."

"If you live," Doc said.

Gen. Jumping Joe Stillwell, who had helped me obtain Army Special Forces training for my SEALs during our fledgling days, had heard about my spat with the pilot who dumped us at Duong Island and personally sent an Army captain from the Judge Advocate General's office as my representative. The captain said, "Don't say anything, don't sign anything. The bastard deserved every punch you administered."

I had dinner and a few bourbons at the Majestic with Ashcroft. When Jerry left the room, Co-Van surprised me by dropping a tiny hand briefly on my shoulder.

"You very ill," she said gently. "Go home, Roy-san. Please go home. Minh sends the same message."

"See?" Ashcroft gloated. "I told you she likes you. She actually *talked* to you."

"It's my charming personality."

Khe first noticed the yellowish tint to the whites of my eyes. Within the span of a few days my skin darkened underneath the deep tropical tan. I could have served my urine for coffee. It took such great effort to get out of bed that some nights Khe had to take the *Nguoi Nhai* out on his own. Captain Ninh, of course, was still *indisposed.* Bode and Nguyen hovered over me, looking worried and nervous. One or the other of them always hung around outside my door.

Nguyen the evil child produced another *bac'si,* but I chased him off. I feared I might not have any spirit left if he chased off the evil spirits.

I knew Vietnam had worn me down, that my time in-country was about up. Yet, I fought against that reality. So many people, it seemed, depended on me. My *Nguoi Nhai,* my Asian LDNN whom I had turned into miniature replicas of my SEALs. I couldn't leave them yet. I couldn't leave Ashcroft and Doc to fight this war without me.

I slipped into Saigon, so weak I could hardly walk, and took to my bed at the Tax Building. Reilman and Doc Shultz were both away on missions. I had the apartment to myself. I slept for two days.

Doc returned to find me passed out from weakness and fever. "This is it, Boehm," I recall his saying. "It's over for you. You're on your way to the hospital, you stubborn bastard."

I had viral hepatitis and a badly mangled knee joint. Fever came and went for days, keeping me bedridden. Somewhere along the way I was informed that as soon as I regained strength I would be transferred to the military hospital at Clark Air Force Base, Philippines, and then stateside. One day burned into the next.

I had visitors regularly as I improved. Ashcroft, Reilman, and Doc. Khe, Bode, and Nguyen. Ed Porter, my yeoman. Khuyen My came nearly every day. I figured Captain Hardcastle was probably celebrating my pending departure from his AO.

Raymond Burr of TV's *Perry Mason* stopped by on a visitation to American troops in Vietnam. He lumbered into my room and glanced at my elevated leg.

I grinned at him. "Who needs you?" I quipped, always the wiseass. "Where's Della Street?"

He rumbled his deep laughter with great good humor. "She couldn't make it, so she sent me."

We shook hands. "Care for a daiquiri?" I asked.

"Where in the world are you going to get a daiquiri in this place?"

I winked and produced a bottle of smuggled vodka. I mixed in some lime sherbert left over from lunch.

"How do you like it?"

Burr coughed. "Never had anything quite like it," he confessed.

"It only costs a little more to go first class."

Idleness forced me to come to terms with what I had experienced in Vietnam. The First SEAL leaving Vietnam was not the same man who arrived in Vietnam. This war had changed me in ways other wars and the Cold War had not. World War II had purpose and direction and meaning. Good guys against the bad guys. It was the world's last noble war.

All that followed—Korea, the Cold War, now Vietnam—had eroded meaning and sanity and was beginning to cast much of my nation bitter and afloat. Even then, in 1964, before LBJ sent over ground troops, the war was becoming FUBAR—*Fucked Up Beyond All Recognition.* There were no clearly discernible goals or objectives in fighting the war. Captain Drachnik's administrative nonwarrior "Progress Is Our Most Important Product" symbolized for me the flawed philosophy that was guiding the war into lingering disaster. He and others like him set the pace. Captain Hardcastle merely became part of the legions who went with the flow and became the wallpaper that let the war go on and on without a mandate to win or the courage to give it up.

Warriors like the U.S. Army Special Forces and the U.S. Navy SEALs, whom I had helped create for the new kind of warfare after WWII, along with fighters like Reilman and Doc and Ashcroft, all thought they were in Vietnam to *win.* It took all of us awhile to realize that politicians were casting us into the arena with one arm tied behind our backs. Vietnam was beginning to fracture national thought and purpose.

I stared blackly out the hospital window.

But the people in the war. The people you never forgot. Not only war brothers and fellow Americans like Jerry Ashcroft and Doc Shultz. So many other people had provided me insight into the country and its people. I lay in my hospital bed and thought of them.

Minh, first of all an enemy but also a friend, who gave heart and soul to the Vietcong cause and made me aware that, for all the war's brutality and conflicting ideologies, we were common men with common threads.

Nguyen the happy child and stern, silent Bode with the string of human ears around his neck. Savages both, but loyal savages willing to give their lives if need be for the *Old Frog.*

Khe, who was in many ways like Minh. A man with a cause dedicated to duty and honor.

Madam Vinh and Father Dupree, whose own cause was the little nation's children and orphans.

Co-Van, Minh's sullen but gorgeous sister who, although she had finally spoken, remained an enigma.

Khuyen My, the Eurasian beauty whose lovely room, bed, and body had provided refuge from the horrors of war.

The diminutive monk Thay Wu whose long afternoons shared with me in the mission's garden provided a calm port for the soul to regenerate.

I could not leave Vietnam without another of those spirited afternoons with him in the little garden. That, most of all, was what I wanted to carry home with me in my memories about this country.

I called the Army first sergeant at Caribou Airlines and asked him to pick me up in our commandeered jeep. He drove me to the Catholic mission in Vung Tau. Father Dupree looked as thin as ever, even thinner. Constant warfare was also wearing him down. Thay Wu, he told me with a sad look, was no longer in Vung Tau.

"Our friend's travels take him from us," he said. "He divested himself of all worldly possessions when he donned the saffron robe of the monk. However, he left something behind."

It was a delicately touched painting of the Buddhist Marble Temple on a leaf.

"The pigments for the paints," Father Dupree went on, "were made by Thay Wu from what the earth has produced. The canvas is the membrane of the Bo tree leaf. The Bo tree is the tree under which Gautama sat for 49 days while he resisted the temptations and threats of Mara, evil tempter of the world. When the battle was over, Gautama had prevailed and achieved the enlightenment he sought. Thereafter, he became known as Buddha, the Enlightened One."

He paused. "We all fight such battles in the wilderness," he said. He handed the beautiful painting to me. "Thay Wu wanted you to have it," he said.

I was deeply touched. Choked up. I murmured, "I have never been so honored."

AFTERWORD

First SEAL: More Muddy Rivers (1964–1971)

"With the ancient is wisdom; and in length of days understanding."
—Job 12

The Navy began talking medical discharge after my evacuation from Vietnam. I thought my career was finished. The Navy would *have* to throw me out; Roy Henry Boehm, the *First* SEAL, *would not* quit. *Could not* quit. Not while my shipmates were still doing battle.

I contacted my old mentor, sea daddy, and friend, Adm. Whitey Taylor, as I had done before over the years during crucial times. I told him what was happening. I would not beg. Not even if I were going before a firing squad.

"You did a good job with the SEALs," he said simply.

Commander Arnie Levine from MAAG in Vietnam was now executive officer of the Naval Amphibious School at Coronado, California. He requested my assignment to him while I was still in the hospital; Admiral Taylor arranged the transfer. I was assigned to be an instructor at the school in a new curriculum for counterinsurgency training. To my surprise and delight, Commander Jerry Ashcroft had left his junks behind in Vietnam to head up the curriculum. The stocky bulldog himself greeted me with a pleased growl and engulfed both my hands in his.

I wasn't crazy about becoming a *schoolteacher,* but it beat hell out of getting tossed out of the Navy. Although I had earned a college equivalency over the years, largely through Whitey Taylor's urging and blackmailing, I remained self-conscious about my lack of formal education. Underneath the bars of a naval lieutenant, an officer, and a gentleman, I remained Bos'n Mate Boehm, rough around the edges, more proficient with my fists than with gentlemanly etiquette, more at home in a seafront bar with men like Lump-Lump Williams than at the Officers' Club.

I felt the clausty walls of academia closing in on me as I stood looking out the windows in the Special Operations Department while Ashcroft busied himself with some message traffic. Those who can, *do;* those who can't, *teach.* I watched a class of Basic Underwater Demolition trainees jog by in their helmets and wet fatigues covered with sand. UDT had not yet merged with SEALs.

How I envied those young men their adventures of becoming a part of the SEAL/UDT brotherhood. I longed to experience it myself, all over again—the excitement, the adrenaline flow, even the frustrations and the heartaches. How I longed to be back with the special sea warriors my dreams had helped create.

Instead, at 41 years old, I was a *teacher.*

I turned slowly from the window and collapsed onto an office sofa. "Jerry," I said, "let me off the hook. I don't belong here."

Ashcroft straddled a straight-backed chair and faced me. "Boy-san, haven't you always said someone needed to educate these troops before they were sent off to become cannon fodder? You said they needed to know *why* they were going, *where* they were going, *who* was sending them, *what* to expect when they got there, and *how* to fight."

"I still feel that way. It's just that you need a *teacher* to teach them."

"What the hell do you think you were doing when you were bos'n mate on a five-inch gun in the South Pacific? How about all the years you were diving, experimenting with it, and passing that knowledge on? How about when you trained UDT Frogs? How about the SEALs? The SEALs were *your* creation, more than any other man's. You *trained* them. You *taught* them. How about the *Nguoi Nhai* in Vietnam? Who *taught* them? *You* did.

"You're a *teacher,* Boy-san. One of the best. Teaching is more than being able to spell 'unconventional warfare.' Hell, you don't need to spell it. You *lived* it; you can *do* it. Boy-san, you're here. There ain't gonna be no walking."

As teachers, Lt. (jg) Gary Brewer and I received the Secretary of the Navy Commendation for Achievement for establishing and implementing the first U.S. Navy Counterinsurgency Functional Training Program. Not bad for a guy who spent two of the happiest years of his life in the seventh grade.

On the morning of 21 August 1966, Jerry Ashcroft had sausage and eggs with my wife, Polly, and me. I had married Polly shortly after Ellie finally divorced me. Jerry was thrilled that his daughter was moving to California to be with him. He had bought her a used Jaguar convertible and was tuning it for her.

After breakfast, he left for his office to catch up on some weekend paperwork. I received notification about an hour later that he had been involved in an auto accident. The Jaguar had swerved onto a sand dune and rolled over. Jerry was dead by the time I reached the hospital.

A U.S. Marine lieutenant colonel replaced Commander Ashcroft at the counterinsurgency school. He announced plans to eliminate all practical field training and replace it with academic classroom subjects.

"Why don't you observe the field training before you strike it out?" I requested. "Hands-on indoctrination for Vietnam-bound servicemen may well mean the difference between their buying the farm and plowing the farm."

"Interesting homily," the Marine sniffed. "Lieutenant, your problem is, you're trying to make half-assed Marines out of these sailors."

That pissed me off. "Sir, we swab jockeys have been in Vietnam since the beginning in 1962. It's now 1966 and the Marines have just been introduced in-country. As for making half-assed Marines out of sailors . . . Sir, a half-assed Marine around here would be an improvement."

I received transfer orders shortly afterwards.

Back at the beginning of the SEALs in 1961, Vice CNO Adm. Horatio Rivera remarked that, "We [the Navy] have no business fighting a war in muddy rivers."

Apparently, he wasn't much for American history. The U.S. Navy had fought for control of the Mississippi River and other streams during the Civil War.

"Nor must Uncle Sam's web feet be forgotten," Abraham Lincoln said in 1863. "At all the watery margins they have been present. Not all on the deep sea, the braced bay, and the rapid rivers, but also up the narrow muddy lagoon and wherever the ground was a little damp, they have been and made their tracks."

After requalifying as a UDT/SEAL in a roundabout way as officer-in-charge of UDTR-37, becoming the *oldest* SEAL as well as the *first,* I found myself assigned as an instructor to the Naval In-Shore Operations Center at Mare Island, Vallejo, California. Cpt. Phil Bucklew, Commander Special Warfare Pacific, had thought to move me to Siberia, out of the way.

Bucklew had appointed himself my personal nemesis. Although he was never qualified in UDT or in SEALs, he had kissed ass to command them on the West Coast. I saw through his braggadocio and never missed an opportunity to point it out.

"Your war stories," I told him, "are two tons of bullshit built on a half-ounce of fact."

No one had even heard of Naval In-Shore Operations at the time I reported to Mare Island. Cpt. Charles R. Johnson was the commanding officer.

"Captain, I *know* what I did to get exiled here," I greeted. "What I can't help wondering is what *you* did to get sent here."

"Mr. Boehm, this might be viewed as a shitcan job—but

that it isn't. We will be training men for Navy riverine warfare in South Vietnam. We will have river assault capabilities as well as patrolling the rivers and canals of South Vietnam to deny enemy access and transportation of materiel, supplies, and troops."

Something like Jerry Ashcroft and his *Biet Hai* had done with his junk force. He would have relished this assignment. I felt almost like I had at the beginning of the SEALs. Again, I was ordered to accomplish a job while thwarted by every bean counter up the line. What the hell. I was accustomed to being threatened with court-martial.

Operation *Game Warden* began. Admiral Rivera and Captain Bucklew would have heart attacks when they found the First SEAL loose again and still capable of more firsts.

Special boats had been designed to operate in Vietnam's brown waters. The first PBRs—River Patrol Boats—were armored fiberglass boats 31 feet in length, 9½ feet across the beams, and heavily armed with twin 50-caliber machine guns, M-60 machine guns, and an assortment of small arms. The improved Mark II version increased the beam to 10½ feet.

The boats with their twin 220 hp engines were capable of traveling at 25 to 30 knots, depending upon weight of cargo, and were each crewed by four sailors. Hydrojet propulsion controlled the boats rather than rudders or propellers.

"We are going to throw rocks at the Vietcong from *glass boats!*" I marveled. "How many boats are we putting in-country?"

"As many as we can send in to do the job," Captain Johnson said. "Roy, this is going to be a big effort."

"Let the training begin."

For a training area, the Navy acquired a 15-square-mile tract of land in the Suisan Slough near the mouths of the Sacramento/San Joaquin rivers. Part of the area was game preserve, the other private property. The sloughs, swamps, canals, and streams cutting through marshes and thickets approximated the terrain of the Mekong Delta. Reeds, rodents, and mosquitoes. Everything except Vietcong.

The river rats of the Civil War were about to be resurrected.

I teamed with Navy Lt. Joe Luallen, another mustang officer, to build and develop a training program for Vietnam's first riverine operations. The course unfolded into 16 weeks of what one volunteer called "pure-dee unadulterated hell." Training was designed solely toward preparing sailors for the brand of warfare unique to the inland waterways of South Vietnam. It started with a four-week introductory course at the Counterinsurgency School in Coronado, then progressed into eight more weeks at the naval In-Shore Operations Center. Here, prospective river rats learned boat handling; inspecting, searching, and controlling boat traffic; waterborne troop assaults and combat tactics; navigation and piloting; communications, weapons, and first aid; radar, engine, and electronic repairs; water survival, boat abandonment, and boat salvage; downed pilot rescue and evacuation of wounded. The last four weeks prior to a trainee's going to Vietnam were spent in the Philippines learning escape and evasion, guerrilla warfare, and resistance to interrogation.

Each training evolution was a teach and do, again and again, until reaction to problems became automatic, instinctive. I had trained my SEALs the same way in preparation for their coming under fire.

"You fight the way you train," I lectured. "No matter what you become in life, you are always a part of your past, a part of those who have touched your lives before."

I wanted one tough, badass, unrelenting sonofabitch of a First SEAL to have touched their young lives. It was the last chance I had to give trainees the benefit of the experience my instructors and I had obtained in actual combat. The last chance where a mistake did not lead to a fatality. Problems required *immediate* solutions.

"Where are you?" I would suddenly radio a PBR on patrol.

"Wait one."

"Wait, hell. You should know where you are at all times. Where are you *now?"*

One man fell asleep at his gun position on base defense. I had him "captured" and staked out "Indian-style" on the tidal flat with the tide creeping in. I hid nearby and watched him struggle desperately against the leather thongs that bound him as the water eased over his body and fiddler crabs scurried. When everything except his face was submerged, I released him. I doubt he ever slept on watch again.

Another cocky young officer trainee made the mistake of leading his men into an "ambush."

"You are the only survivor," I told him, then ordered him to file an After Action report listing the casualties' names and service numbers.

"I don't know all their names," he protested.

I handed him the "dead men's" service records. "I want you to write a letter to each man's family explaining how their son died gallantly in combat."

The student's face turned ashen.

"In Vietnam," I said, "your inattention to detail would have had you doing just that. It might be better to be dead yourself."

Graduates of the riverine school began feeding into the growing war machine in Southeast Asia. Not since the American Civil War had an American river force sustained river combat operations. Eventually, Operation *Game Warden* included two elements—a Riverine Patrol section known as Task Force 116, and a Riverine Assault element, Task Force 117. Later, Task Force 115, code-named *Market Time,* joined *Game Warden* in operating a net of more than 100 fast patrol boats, 30 U.S. Coast Guard cutters, and hundreds of South Vietnamese junks against enemy smuggling in the South China Sea. American river rat forces made more regular contact with the enemy than any other U.S. outfit in the war while suffering fewer casualties per capita.

I liked to think it had something to do with their training.

I needed a haircut one morning and stopped by the barber shop at the naval base at Mare Island.

"Sir, would you mind waiting?" the barber asked. "I have an eight-thirty appointment to cut Admiral Rickover's hair."

"What time is it now?" I asked.

"Eight-thirty-four."

"He's late. Cut away, Jose."

Admiral Rickover walked in. He picked up a magazine and sat down to wait. The barber looked nervous.

"Commander," he pleaded, "would you mind if I go ahead and cut the admiral's hair?"

"I sure as hell would. Admiral Rickover makes his own schedule and answers to nobody. Now you take me. I work for Wade Cantrell Wells. That nasty bastard keeps us as busy as a one-armed paper hanger with the hives. Keep cutting. I'm in a hurry."

A year or so later while working with Wells on sensor doctrine, the so-called McNamara Fence in Vietnam, I attended a briefing at which Admiral Rickover was present. I was the last to be introduced.

"Admiral, I would like you to meet—"

The admiral cut in. "Commander Boehm and I have already met. He is a man who will give up his seat in a barber chair to no mortal."

A man could die with less reputation than that.

I requested a second tour in Southeast Asia as a UDT/SEAL adviser with MAAG. Instead, in 1968, the Vice CNO, Admiral Clary, sent me on a fact-finding trip to Vietnam to report on the SEALs and the Riverine Force. The war had escalated on a scale larger than I had ever imagined.

I hardly recognized former Junk Base 33 at Vam Lang. What the Seabee warrant officer from the helicopter had envisioned had come to pass. U.S. Seabees had flown in an electric generator and constructed a huge corrugated metal building for an open market. Riverine PBRs had replaced the faithful junks Jerry Ashcroft had used so effectively with his *Biet Hai.*

During my "fact-finding" excursions, I accompanied riverine patrols. I also observed some pretty shabby operations run by one SEAL platoon wearing mohawk haircuts. I placed Warrant Officer Gene Tinnin, one of my original SEALs, in charge of the platoon to whip it back into shape.

The Vietnam War was fought by junior officers and enlisted men. Two of my original SEAL enlisted, Rudy Boesch and Jim Finley, headed a SEAL platoon harassing and interdicting the VC and NVA, the North Vietnamese Army, which had been establishing a greater presence in South Vietnam since 1965. Boesch and Finley ran *strak* missions, the best I had ever seen. I accompanied Boesch's team and 80 Viet PRU, Provincial Reconnaissance Units, on a raid against a VC officers' academy in Vinh Long province. The enemy body count tabbed over 60 KIA.

I hopped a chopper and flew to Cho Loch to meet Khe, my LDNN senior sergeant. He was still fighting the war. The reunion left me saddened, for I learned that Nguyen, the evil happy child, had been killed in a firefight two years earlier. Bode had been captured on one of his ear-gathering expeditions. VC tortured him, skinning him alive. His mutilated body was recovered hanging upside down from a tree limb. His ears had been cut off and his penis stuffed down his throat.

Khe said he was working to get his family out of Vietnam. He thought we were losing the war.

"Everything falling apart," he said.

The Vietnamese saw it, even then. The myopic U.S. military didn't want to see it. The military continued to hang on to its failures while men died and millions of dollars poured down a bottomless pit.

Father Dupree had followed Thay Wu and disappeared somewhere in Vietnam. I hoped to see Minh again, but had no idea how to find him. I was having a bourbon in the bar of the Tax Building where I once shared a room with Doc Shultz and Ted Reilman when I looked up and there stood Co-Van. As beautiful and sulky as ever with almond eyes somewhat rounded by her French ancestry. I grinned, pleased to see my old friend's sister.

"Hello, you round-eye-hating bitch."

Co-Van laughed. I had never seen her laugh before.

"How's your brother?"

She glanced around. "We can't talk here."

"Do you have a place we can go?"

"No place that's safe for you."

There was always one safe place. Co-Van giggled with delight when I escorted her to a Vietnamese government-run whorehouse. "You are taking a sandwich to a banquet," she joked.

I ordered room service. As we ate, I said, "Tell me about Minh. How is he?"

Her smiled vanished. "I am sorry. Someone shot him from a long way off."

"Not him too. A sniper? When?"

"Last year. I am the only one left in our family."

We talked for a long time through the sadness of deaths. Co-Van told me she no longer hired out as a housekeeper to spy on Americans. She was now an active VC who felt South Vietnam would fall easily once the Americans left.

"You and Doc and Jerry-san were different than the others," she said. "You fought and you killed—but you were different. You went out every week to also help Vietnamese people."

She touched the gold leaf on my collar. "Now, you are big shot," she said.

"No, Co-Van. I'm still the man you and your brother knew, nothing else."

Co-Van stood up slowly, thoughtfully. After a moment during which our eyes held, she dropped her *ao dai* to the floor at her feet. The woman was *gorgeous.* I was always attracted by her sultry beauty but put off by her seeming inaccessibility.

"I have always wanted you," I admitted, taking her small firm body into my arms.

"You have me now," she whispered.

The next morning we made love again. Then she said, "I must go now. We will say good-bye here and I shall vanish. Be careful, *Ohmja Nguoi Nhai,* Old Frog. Vietnam is not the same."

I never saw her again.

I watched Vietnam fade behind and below the silver wing of the C-141. Vietnam always looked better from the air. Then Vietnam was gone. Gone the filth and stench of the war to which I had once adjusted so easily. I thought of Co-Van and of Khe, survivors so far on different sides in a world made worse for them by U.S. intervention. Who in the fuck were we to impose our way of life upon people we did not understand and whom we really didn't give a damn about?

The flight back to "The World" offered hours of reflection and reverie. I looked back upon the 27 years of my naval career. Perhaps all lives are destined at birth. My destination to the sea and, perhaps, to Special Operations and unconventional warfare began the day my father and Big Mike Sullivan took me to the Brooklyn Naval Shipyard to watch the launching of the USS *North Carolina.*

"You're just like your dad," Mom had said. "You'll either grow up to be a hero—or you'll end up dead or in prison. There is no middle way for the Boehm men."

That I lacked a middle way had been the source of much of my problems in the Navy. The shark knew only one way—*straight ahead*—when it locked its sight on a goal. That was the only way I knew—*straight ahead*—and to hell with everyone who got in my way. The mission came first.

The world was changing. Maybe I wasn't. World War II had had its mottos: "Do or die." "My God, my country." "Death before dishonor." WWII had had a noble aim.

The wars since then had not. Korea was the yo-yo war. Take that hill today, give it back tomorrow. But the lives lost today could not be retaken tomorrow.

The Cold War had bred the new era of unconventional warfare. It was the father of the U.S. Army Special Forces and my SEALs. But noble goals—to make the world free from tyranny—had gradually faded or been twisted by the politicians and the bean counters. What was left noble in Vietnam when the war was being run by CEOs who looked only at the bottom line for the body count instead of by warriors who wanted to *win* because winning meant fulfilling the ideals of God and country and liberty?

What was happening to my world? *Moral decay* came to mind. It was like nobody was out there anymore who cared about honor, duty, character, and love for country, who did things not because they were politically expedient or because they gratified today's whims and desires but instead because they were the *right* thing to do. Our elected officials were misconstruing *elected* as meaning *anointed.* Our people were starting to value security and self-indulgence over freedom.

Minh had told me once that I was an idealist, a romantic. He might be right. No realist believed in honor and duty anymore. These were becoming qualities of a romantic historical past, of an era of warrior honor codes. Warriors were a dying breed. The *First* SEAL was becoming a troglodyte, a relic of the past.

"Roy, it's time to get the hell out of the Navy before you go crazy," my friend and fellow SEAL Dick Marcinko counseled.

In Marcinko I saw the young Roy Boehm. I liked his brashness, his in-your-face leadership and his devotion to his men. I liked him because, although he would never admit it, he was also a romantic who saw the way of the warrior as a sacred calling, not merely a profession. Marcinko had the balls to get a job done—officer warriors of his caliber were fast becoming an endangered species. We were being denied promotion, court-martialed, or kicked out of the service. Replaced by a new breed: the office manager to whom *progress,* not winning or duty, was the all-important product.

Maybe Marcinko was right. Perhaps it was time I stepped ashore.

Fuck it. Dad had been right all along. Somebody *had* put the ocean too near the goddamned shore.

I was completing a briefing on Vietnam at the Naval In-Shore Training Center at Mare Island, California, when Commander Dusty Rhoades came in and stood at the door. He looked grimmer than usual. He silently handed me a message.

Gene Tinnin, one of my original SEALs, the man I placed in charge of the fucked-up SEAL platoon in Vietnam, had been killed in action. Another brother lost.

I stormed out of the office and headed for the Suisan Swamps where I had trained river rats for the Riverine Force. The look on my face warned everyone to stay out of the way and not try to stop me. Frogs and SEALs always sought solace in water. I had no team now with which to share my grief of a lost brother, so I would grieve it alone in a place Gene would understand and appreciate. The *First* SEAL seeking equilibrium. Even the deadly shark sometimes lost equilibrium.

I mourned Gene alone along the shallow brown waters of the San Joaquin River. Perhaps I mourned for myself too, mourned the loss of what had been for me and for the U.S. Navy.

The dead are free, I told myself. *It is the living who have yet to die.*

Note: Lt. Comdr. Roy Henry Boehm, the U.S. Navy's *First* SEAL, retired from active duty service in 1971. He now lives in Punta Gorda, Florida, with his new wife, Susan.